The Westfalians

The Westfalians
From Germany to Missouri

by Walter D. Kamphoefner

PRINCETON UNIVERSITY PRESS

Copyright © 1987 by Princeton University Press

Published by Princeton University Press, 41 William Street,
Princeton, New Jersey 08540
In the United Kingdom: Princeton University Press, Guildford, Surrey

All Rights Reserved

Library of Congress Cataloging in Publication Data will be found
on the last printed page of this book

ISBN 0-691-04746-4

Publication of this book has been aided by a grant from the
Whitney Darrow Fund of Princeton University Press

This book has been composed in Linotron Sabon

Clothbound editions of Princeton University Press books are printed on
acid-free paper, and binding materials are chosen for strength and
durability. Paperbacks, although satisfactory for personal collections,
are not usually suitable for library rebinding

Printed in the United States of America by Princeton University Press
Princeton, New Jersey

For My Parents

CONTENTS

LIST OF FIGURES	ix
LIST OF TABLES	xi
PREFACE	xiii
INTRODUCTION. Not Uprooting But Reunion: The Significance of Chain Migration in the Immigrant Experience	3
CHAPTER I. At the Crossroads of Economic Development: Background Factors Affecting Emigration from Northwest Germany	12
CHAPTER II. Poor But Not Destitute: Personal Characteristics and Motivating Factors	40
CHAPTER III. Transplanted Villages: The Effects of Chain Migration on Regional Distribution and Settlement Patterns of German-Americans	70
CHAPTER IV. Native and Adoptive Americans: The Extent of Acculturation in Social Patterns and Agricultural Practices	106
CHAPTER V. Detours and Shortcuts on the Way to a Farm: Occupational and Geographical Mobility from Westfalia to Missouri	135
CHAPTER VI. Westfalians and Other Immigrants: Chain Migration and Acculturation in Comparative Perspective	170
APPENDIX A. Sources and Coding Procedures for Emigrant List Data	201
APPENDIX B. Use of Census Data and Procedures of Matching with Emigrant Lists	204
APPENDIX C. Data and Calculation Procedures for Figure 1.1	207
INDEX	211

FIGURES

1.1	Index of Relative Intensity of Emigration by District	14
1.2	Detail Map of Northwest German Areas of Study	22
1.3	Sources of Heaviest Migration from Westfalia	34
2.1	Time Series Analysis	55
2.2	Yearly Emigration from the Kingdom of Hannover	57
3.1	Regional Origins of Germans by Township	88
3.2	Origins of Emigrants to Missouri	90
5.1	Age and Sex Profile, 1860	149

TABLES

1.1	Average Yearly Emigration from Selected Areas of Northwest Germany	15
1.2	Economic and Demographic Patterns in the Three Districts of Westfalia	20
1.3	Correlation between Emigration Rate and Protoindustry for Selected Areas of Westfalia	23
1.4	Multiple Regression of Economic and Demographic Variables with Emigration Rate, 1859–1861	25
1.5	Average Yearly Emigration from Selected German Cities and Their Hinterlands	33
2.1	Occupational Structure of Male Emigrants from Northwest Germany	42
2.2	Comparative Occupational Profiles of Emigrants from Brunswick and Their Fathers	44
2.3	Wealth of Emigrants by Occupation and Family Status	48
2.4	Wealth of Emigrants by Father's Occupation, Osnabrück District	49
2.5	Occupational Structure of Male Emigrants from Lippe-Detmold	51
2.6	Time Series Analysis	53
2.7	Destination of Emigrants from Brunswick	56
2.8	Clandestine Emigrants from Bavaria and Tecklenburg	66
3.1	Relative Concentration of Natives of Various German States in the German Population of Selected American States	74
3.2	Relative Concentration of Natives of Various German Regions in the German Population of American Regions	76
3.3	Proportion of Germans from Various States Living in American Cities	82
3.4	Relative Concentration of Natives of Various German States in the German Population of Selected Cities and Rural Areas in America	84
3.5	Relative Concentration of Natives of Various German States in the German Population of Parts of Missouri	86
4.1	Propensity to Marry within Ethnic Group	112
4.2	Sex Ratio and Proportion Married by Ethnic Group	113

TABLES

4.3	Religious Affiliation of First- and Second-Generation Germans	114
4.4	Degree of Residential Clustering by Ethnic Group in the 1850 U.S. Census of St. Charles and Warren Counties	118
4.5	Relative Concentration of Various Ethnic Groups in Nonagricultural Occupations	119
4.6	Occupations in Which Old French Predominated	120
4.7	Occupations in Which Germans Predominated	121
4.8	Occupations with Approximately Equal Proportions of Germans and Americans	121
4.9	Occupations in Which Americans Predominated	122
4.10	Relative Concentration of Various Ethnic Groups in Agricultural Occupations	123
4.11	Real Estate Holdings of Males 18 and Older by Ethnic Group	124
4.12	Agricultural Production of Germans and Americans	127
4.13	Agricultural Production of Germans and Americans	130
5.1	Mean Value of Real Estate and Other Wealth of Adult Male Emigrants	138
5.2	Percentage of Adult Male Emigrants Owning Real Estate	142
5.3	Mean Value of Real Estate and Other Wealth of Adult Male Emigrants	143
5.4	Occupational Mobility of Adult Male Emigrants	153
5.5	Occupational Continuity of Male Artisans	156
6.1	Social Characteristics of Scandinavian Immigrants in America	193
6.2	Rate of Emigration from Selected German States and Degree of Concentration in America	196
C.1	Data for Figure 1.1	208

PREFACE

CARRYING this project with me over the course of a decade and several Atlantic crossings, I have incurred a number of debts along the way. At the outset, the German Academic Exchange Service (DAAD) provided for a year of essential study and research in Germany. The friendly, unbureaucratic personnel of the state archives in Osnabrück, Münster, and Detmold overturned some cultural stereotypes, but were not to be outdone by the forthcoming, efficient staff of the Missouri State Historical Society. The history department at the University of Missouri–Columbia helped fund data preparation and typing at the dissertation stage.

Both as a Research Associate in Münster on a project of the Deutsche Forschungsgemeinschaft and as a Mellon Postdoctoral Instructor at California Institute of Technology, I benefited from policies encouraging outside research. While in Germany, I published a lightly updated translation of my dissertation under the title *Westfalen in der Neuen Welt: Eine Sozialgeschichte der Auswanderung im 19. Jahrhundert* (Münster, 1982). Anyone interested in a more exhaustive documentation of local German sources in Chapters 1 and 2 should consult this volume. The present study also incorporates several primary sources that were subsequently discovered or obtained—in particular, newly published emigrant lists that made possible the tracing of a much larger group from Westfalia to Missouri.

At the dissertation stage, it was my good fortune to have in essence three coadvisors: Thomas B. Alexander was a *Doktorvater* in the truest sense of the word in his selfless devotion to his students, but not in a possessive sense, encouraging me to follow my own intellectual interests even when they developed away from his own. Konrad H. Jarausch was very helpful in developing the German side of my research proposal, and has continued to be a trusted sounding board for my ideas. For my grounding in European social history I am indebted to Richard Tilly, whose institute in Münster has become an intellectual home away from home for me. And James Jackson, Jr., whom I came to know when we were both DAAD fellows in Germany, has over the years generously shared ideas, insights, and source material.

Early on, Charles Tilly read the dissertation and provided some very helpful suggestions for revision. Fred Luebke commented on several chapters in conference panels, and in general provided much encour-

PREFACE

agement, as did Morgan Kousser. Lesley Kawaguchi generously shared her time and insights as well as her Philadelphia Social History Project files on Germans. I received helpful critiques of several chapters from colleagues Phil Hoffman, Lance Davis, and Rod Kiewiet at Caltech and Laura Becker at Miami, and from seminars at Bielefeld, Caltech, Harvard, and Minnesota. While much of this was taking place, Gail Ullman, Social Science Editor at Princeton University Press, continued to be patient and supportive.

Among the many features that were transplanted from Westfalia to the ethnic community that I grew up in and later studied were regional stereotypes. The *Westfälische Dickschädel* ("thick-skulled Westfalian") became the "hard-headed Dutchman" where I came from. If any errors or weaknesses still remain in this volume, it is not for lack of good advice, but simply because this hard-headed Dutchman insisted on going his own way.

The Westfalians

INTRODUCTION

Not Uprooting But Reunion: The Significance of Chain Migration in the Immigrant Experience

HUDDLED in the steerage of a three-masted immigrant ship, listening as the storm raged ever more violently and the waves broke repeatedly over the deck, Johann Heinrich Dothage was beginning to wonder whether he would even live to set foot in America. The day had begun so promisingly: after seven weeks of unrelieved blue the first glimpse of green, the verdant capes of Hispaniola. But a sudden Caribbean storm had turned the promise to a threat. The sailors, who had celebrated the first landfall with an ample portion of rum, were in no proper condition to handle the ship, now in danger of being driven aground on one of the capes. Johann thought of what friends had written from America: "The voyage is certainly strenuous, but not dangerous." Well, if he lived to tell the tale, he would set them straight on that. Suddenly the ship hit something, lurching to a sudden, groaning halt—run aground. Now there was nothing left to do but to abandon ship before it was broken apart in the pounding breakers. The crew managed to string a line to shore and began hauling the passengers to safety one by one in a large basket. Dothage, his wife, and their two children made it safely to shore, but as the grandmother, a stately woman approaching seventy, was being hauled in, a sudden wave overturned the basket, sweeping her under, never to be seen again.

That was 1840. It was six months or more before the Dothages got up the nerve to continue their journey to their intended destination, Warren County, Missouri. In the meantime, a son was born in Santo Domingo and shows up with this birthplace in the 1860 census, confirming a story that is otherwise based mostly on oral tradition.[1]

---

[1] Oral-history accounts of the shipwreck are presented by Frances B. Bonney, *The Hilgedick Family: The American Descendents of the Hilgedicks of Lienen, Germany* (St. Paul, Minn., 1973), pp. 238–239. Confirmation is provided by the local chronicle in Lienen, which recorded in 1840, "According to reports received, the majority have established themselves in the state of Missouri and settled there. The last emigrants, about 108 in number, were hindered in their journey and shipwrecked on Cape Haiti, and their fate is still unknown" (Friedrich E. Hunsche, *Auswanderung aus dem Kreis Steinfurt* [Steinfurt, 1983], pp. 36, 265). In the Münster emigrant lists, no. 791 (see Appendix A) includes with the family the grandmother, aged sixty-seven; she does not appear in any

INTRODUCTION

Johann Dothage's trial by water was not typical of most German immigrants in the mid-nineteenth century. The two-month passage in the steerage of a sailing vessel was not an experience that most of them would be eager to repeat, and occasionally an outbreak of cholera could decimate a ship's population. But despite the discomforts, it was not unusual for a ship to arrive in America with a net gain in passengers. Shipwrecks were relatively rare occurrences even in the days of sail. As many immigrant lives were probably lost on river steamboats as on the high seas.

In other respects as well, Dothage was not exactly typical of German emigrants from his native province of Westfalia. Judging from tax lists, he fell into the middling ranks among peasant proprietors, but he was in any case a landholder. Much more common among Westfalian emigrants were so-called *Heuerleute*, dependent tenants working tiny plots. These classes relied on supplementary income from such sources as linen weaving and migratory labor in Holland, which were slowly but surely drying up as the nineteenth century progressed. Of course, bad harvests affected peasant proprietors as well as their tenants, but for such a man as Dothage, the cheap farmland and better opportunities in America probably played a greater role than absolute material want in Europe.

But the decision to migrate was not based on economic factors alone; the social context also came into play. In this respect Dothage could hardly have been more typical. He knew where he was going and what awaited him there. A brother-in-law from the neighboring farm had emigrated to Missouri in 1837 and had been followed by his brother two years later. In fact, during the eight years prior to Dothage's departure in 1840, a large settlement from his home town and neighboring areas—practically a transplanted village—had sprung up fifty miles west of St. Louis along the Missouri River.

What Dothage's reception may have been like when he finally reached this area is illustrated by a letter from Wilhelm Brüggemann, who emigrated from the neighboring village of Lotte and settled just down the road from Dothage. Upon his arrival in 1860, he first stopped off in St. Louis. "That's where life started again. They all said, 'Brüggemann has arrived!' I went to see all the people from Lotte. The visiting lasted the whole night through." He went on to mention the names of eight different people or families from the home village whom he met there, and reported seeing many others, and many from the neighbor-

American records. For an account of a similar shipwreck in the same time period, see Johannes Meyer-Deepen, *Schiffstragodie vor Spiekeroog* (Jever, 1979).

ing town of Westerkappeln as well. As he put it, "It was as if the prodigal son had returned to his father, that's how we celebrated."²

Immigrants such as Dothage, Brüggemann, and other transplanted Westfalians have seldom found a place in the historical record. Neglect of this phenomenon of chain migration is perhaps the greatest weakness of Oscar Handlin's evocative and still influential interpretation of the immigrant experience. As his title, *The Uprooted*, suggests, the image conveyed by Handlin is one of extreme discontinuity and disorientation endured by the huddled masses of European peasants. Central to his thesis is the isolation of the individual or the nuclear family in the migration process. More important than the change in livelihood was the total break with the peasant community that had shaped so many aspects of village life. While not denying entirely the role of "village and regional affiliations," Handlin plays down their extent and significance. Moreover, he contends that rural immigrant settlements scarcely differed from urban areas in these respects. Handlin's immigrants appear, to borrow an image from physics, as isolated molecules bounced about at random by the Brownian movement of American society, their paths determined by little more than chance.³

But chance could not have produced the kind of homogeneous clusters my study discovered in rural Missouri. The trek to America was anything but a leap into the dark for chain migrants. Preparing to depart, Brüggemann had been reassured by his brother and sister-in-law, "Now that you've made up your mind, go forward calmly and with an optimistic spirit, and don't torment yourself with needless worries." Brüggemann had been well instructed for the way: where to find acquaintances in St. Louis, what route to take from there, what the exchange rates were for various currencies, and the risks of American paper money. The dangers that lay in wait for the supposedly ignorant and helpless peasant have clearly been exaggerated in many historical accounts. Nor can immigrant agents, propaganda, and promotional literature have exerted anywhere near the influence that is often attributed to them.

The area where the transplanted Westfalians settled was the subject of one of the most famous pieces of promotional literature, Gottfried

---

² Letters to and from Brüggemann are included in an appendix of Kamphoefner, *Westfalen in der Neuen Welt: Eine Sozialgeschichte der Auswanderung im 19. Jahrhundert* (Münster, 1982), pp. 195–199, an earlier German-language version of this book. My thanks to Stella Backhaus Nadler of New Melle, Missouri, Brüggemann's great-great-granddaughter, who furnished me with copies of the original letters.

³ Oscar Handlin, *The Uprooted*, 2d ed., rev. (Boston, 1973), pp. 55–56, 95–97, 130, 149, 166–167, 305–306, and passim.

INTRODUCTION

Duden's *Report*, which gained it more than its share of historical attention. However, the peasant immigrants who made up the bulk of the settlers have gone virtually unnoticed in these accounts. In part this is due to the bias of the sources, but the bias of historians comes into play as well. The attention of much of Germany had been focused on this area of Missouri in 1829 by Duden's glowingly optimistic letters. In reaction to his account, at least three emigration societies, largely bourgeois in makeup, attempted to colonize this area. Since their members were the only ones to leave extensive written records, they have come to dominate historical accounts almost to the exclusion of the peasantry. More serious a limitation than lack of sources, however, are the assumptions that only the bourgeois elite provided leadership in the community and that peasants were incapable of immigrating on their own initiative. Even the former assumption is questionable. In the "German caucus" of the Missouri legislature after the Civil War, university graduates mingled with the sons of peasants, tenant farmers, and shoemakers. And the latter is totally false. Peasants clearly could and did make their own migration decisions.[4]

As a matter of fact, and as will be shown in greater detail later, all the emigration societies were failures as communal ventures, their members scattering widely, their examples probably repelling rather than encouraging followers. The immigrant population in this area included only a scattering from the main recruitment districts of the emigration societies, but virtually transplanted villages of Westfalian peasants. In fact, peasant immigrants to this part of Missouri predated two of the emigration societies and were independent of the third, and it was the former and not the latter who were the effective recruiters. In October 1832, only a few months after the first emigrants had departed, a concerned local official from Dothage's home town wrote, "A few young people from the village of Cappeln [Westerkappeln] are said to be faring quite happily in America, and since their relatives have spread this around too much, many think it could not fail that they would make their fortune just as well." His concern was well founded. The next summer, within the short period of about a week, a dozen families in Westerkappeln registered their intent, as one of them put it, "to emi-

---

[4] This is not to disparage the pioneering work of collection and translation done by William G. Bek, "Followers of Duden," *Missouri Historical Review* 14 (1919) through 19 (1925). The problem is that most subsequent historians have been content simply to quote Bek. An example of the exaggerated importance given to emigration societies is the introduction to James Goodrich et al., eds. and trans., *Report on a Journey to the Western States of North America and a Stay of Several Years along the Missouri (During the Years 1824, '25, '26, and 1827)* (Columbia, Mo., 1980), p. xviii.

grate to North America, to the district of Missuri [sic], to seek his fortune there, since so many good reports have come in from there about *Fortkommen* [good living] there." While the Duden book may well have steered the first peasant immigrants to Missouri, there is no hard evidence that it did—no mention of it, for example, among the permits filed by the earliest emigrants from Westfalia. But whatever steered the pathfinders, it was their reports to relatives and friends that kept the chain going. Right up to the Civil War, groups of emigrants from this part of northwest Germany continued to flock to Missouri, sometimes by the shipload. Chain migration, then, provides the key to understanding much of the process of immigrant location and adjustment in America.[5]

This study took shape in the intellectual atmosphere of the New Social History and shares its concern for writing "history from the bottom up," reconstructing the experiences and life course of the mass of ordinary individuals who have generally remained silent in the historical record. It was inspired by Stephan Thernstrom's attempts to measure how well the opportunities of American society, particularly for impoverished newcomers, lived up to its egalitarian rhetoric. But above all, it is a response to Frank Thistlethwaite's challenge, issued in 1960 to historians of migration, to penetrate the "salt-water curtain inhibiting [American] understanding of European origins" of immigration and similarly obscuring for Europeans the fate of migrants once they left their native shores. Thistlethwaite urged scholars to adopt a new viewpoint, "from neither the continent of origin nor from the principal country of reception . . . neither of emigrants nor immigrants, but of migrants, and to treat the process of migration as a complete sequence of experiences." Moreover, at both ends of the trail, the investigation must be much more closely focused than the national or even provincial level; "mass-migration" was in fact the cumulative effect of the peculiar migratory traditions of thousands of villages and neighborhoods.[6]

On the European side, my study focuses on the Province of Westfalia

[5] Hunsche, *Kreis Steinfurt*, p. 30; Staatsarchiv Münster, Reg. Münster, Bd. 181, 1. An example of group migration was reported by the St. Louis *Mississippi Blätter*, 28 November 1858: "Yesterday evening 350 German immigrants arrived on the steamboat *Morrison* from New Orleans. They are almost all from the region of Osnabrück and Prussian Westphalia. They crossed the ocean in two Bremen ships, the *Ernestine* and the *New Orleans*. . . . Most of them expect to make their homes in Missouri, so far as we can discover" (Steven Rowan and James Neal Primm, eds. and trans., *Germans for a Free Missouri: Translation from the St. Louis Radical Press* [Columbia, Mo., 1983], p. 72).

[6] Frank Thistlethwaite, "Migration from Europe Overseas in the Nineteenth and Twentieth Centuries," *Rapports du XIe Congrès International des Sciences Historiques*, vol. 5, *Histoire Contemporaine* (Stockholm, 1960), pp. 32–60, esp. pp. 32, 34, 37.

INTRODUCTION

and adjacent regions of northwest Germany, one of the most emigration-prone areas of Germany in the first half of the nineteenth century. On the American side it focuses on two adjacent Missouri counties—St. Charles and Warren—where three-fourths of the German immigration came from the northwest, and much of that from within a thirty-mile radius. Providing continuity across the salt-water curtain was a group of 150 families totaling over 400 individuals who were traced from the Westfalian *Kreis* Tecklenburg to this part of Missouri, and a similar group traced from the Principality of Lippe-Detmold. Thus Dothage, Brüggemann, and their neighbors were studied in both their old and their new homelands.

This community of transplanted Westfalians would never have come to light had I relied on traditional literary sources. In order to unearth it, I had to develop new sources and methods, particularly individual-level linkage between emigrant lists and census data. As one German pioneer of transatlantic tracing realized in the 1930s, there was little more to be gained from further studies of "what was *said* about German emigration and plans of colonization by patriots, scholars, humanitarians, screwballs, and people out to make a buck." Instead, he wanted to put "the human beings who themselves emigrated . . . in the midpoint of such works." But in 1975 a copy of his book lay in the university library at Münster, its still-uncut pages testifying to the futility of his efforts. One intellectual historian of the emigration somewhat disparagingly characterized that study as the "genealogical method." In fact, this approach does draw on the same sources and methods as those used by genealogists; the difference lies in the questions asked of the material.[7] Historians on the German side have been particularly slow to take advantage of these new sources, even when emigrant lists had been transcribed and published by genealogists, but there are signs that this is now beginning to change.[8] Scholars of Scandinavian migration, aided by a remarkable system of parish registers, have led the way

---

[7] Joseph Scheben, *Untersuchung zur Methode und Technik der deutschamerikanischen Wanderungsforschung* (Bonn, 1939), p. 109; Mack Walker, *Germany and the Emigration, 1816–1885* (Cambridge, Mass., 1964), p. 269. For a general overview of useful genealogical sources on German immigrants, see Kamphoefner, "Problems and Possibilities of Individual-Level Tracing in German-American Migration Research," in *Generations and Change: Genealogical Perspectives in Social History*, ed. Ralph J. Crandall and Robert M. Taylor (Macon, Ga., 1986), pp. 311–323.

[8] Willi Paul Adams, *Die deutschsprachige Auswanderung in die Vereinigten Staaten: Berichte über Forschungsstand und Quellenbestände* (Berlin, 1980); for a recent work that utilizes emigrant lists and statistical material to good effect, see Wolfgang von Hippel, *Auswanderung aus Südwestdeutschland: Studien zur württembergischen Auswanderung und Auswanderungspolitik im 18. und 19. Jahrhundert* (Stuttgart, 1984).

in applying individual-level tracing and empirical approaches to migration studies. Though conceived independently of them, my study addresses many of the same questions, to the extent that materials are available on Germans.[9]

In examining regional population patterns, Scandinavian researchers have stressed that the early establishment of a migration tradition from a given area played an important role in the development of heavy emigration rates in subsequent decades.[10] While it is true that chain migration and heavy out-migration rates are to some extent mutually reinforcing phenomenon, my research suggests that heavy population pressure was often a factor in the establishment of migration chains in the first place. As is shown in Chapter 1, the mass exodus from Westfalia to Missouri was clearly related to the socioeconomic structure of the region of origin. The rural linen industry had created a large rural lower class of dependent tenant farmers who had no place to go but overseas when their sources of supplementary income began to dry up in the 1830s and 1840s.

In Chapter 2, the focus shifts from the regions to the individuals who predominated in the emigration. Here it becomes clear that the rural lower class—tenant farmers and agricultural laborers—predominated in the chain migration. It was above all those who were dependent on supplementary income from rural industry who were pushed out. While this migration was conservative in the sense that regional ties and cultural institutions were maintained, there was little to evoke nostalgia for the rural social order back home. Economic and political discontents were closely intertwined as motives for emigration.

Chapter 3 examines the makeup of the German-American population, bringing extensive evidence at both the macro- and the microlevel of chain migration. The mix of immigrants from various regions of Germany differed widely from state to state and from city to city. This in turn was the result, especially in rural areas, of even more intense local concentrations, as the example of the transplanted Westfalians in eastern Missouri demonstrates.

The social and economic structure of this Missouri settlement is examined in Chapter 4. The picture of cultural continuity that emerges is somewhat mixed. On the one hand, immigrants appear to have adjusted rapidly in the economic realm, showing only subtle differences

---

[9] Harald Runblom and Hans Norman, eds., *From Sweden to America: A History of the Migration* (Minneapolis, 1976), provides a convenient summary of the Uppsala University research project "Sweden and America after 1860," which involved over thirty researchers during the course of more than a decade.

[10] Ibid., pp. 138–140.

INTRODUCTION

from the native population in occupational structure, and adopting with little alteration Anglo-American farming practices and cropping systems. But in the social sphere, the transplanted Westfalians preferred to keep to themselves, residing, worshiping, and marrying mostly among their own kind. Immigrants of bourgeois origins were much more prone to assimilation in these respects than peasant chain migrants.

The issue of transatlantic social mobility is taken up in Chapter 5 on the basis of two homogeneous groups that were traced from Westfalia and nearby Lippe-Detmold to Missouri. In general, the opportunities offered on the American frontier were impressive. The great majority of immigrants, including those who had been landless in the old country, succeeded in becoming independent farmers. The security of landownership also proved attractive to former artisans, many of whom forsook their trades for agriculture. Urban residence was as much related to life-cycle stage as to occupational background, and it was often a temporary stop for those bound for homogeneous rural settlements.

This project began to take shape when I looked at a map of Germany and discovered, hardly twenty miles apart, the namesakes of two hamlets in my home county. Not local patriotism, but the confidence that I would find the German roots of a large number of immigrants led me to choose this site of investigation. There are some practical advantages, not the least that I can often reconstruct a German family name despite a severe mangling by a Yankee census taker. My community has been so stable well into the twentieth century that I have a much better perspective on the agricultural, ethnic, and religious geography of the area than one could obtain from literary sources alone. A number of family histories, including my own, helped me to flesh out the bare bones of census information. But most important, aided in part by oral history and personal observation, I can follow the trajectory of cultural preservation and ultimate assimilation beyond the point where my data stops. As this is sketched out in the concluding chapter, it becomes clear that this chain-migration community showed a remarkable degree of cohesiveness and cultural continuity.

At the time I set out for Germany in 1975 to begin research on this project, I might have regarded the transplanted Westfalians as simply an interesting anomaly. But by the next year this was no longer the case: Two studies appeared examining Scandinavians in a transatlantic perspective, and documenting similar instances of local homogeneity among Swedish immigrants.[11] Since that time, the evidence has been

---

[11] Ibid.; Robert C. Ostergren, "Rättvik to Isanti: A Community Transplanted" (Ph.D.

mounting that such ethnic enclaves were rather widespread, particularly in the rural heartland. As is demonstrated in Chapter 6, the similarities do not stop with just the existence of such communities. Their social makeup shows a number of points of correspondence as well.[12]

Still, the transplanted Westfalians do not represent *the* immigrant experience any more than do Handlin's *Uprooted*. As Jon Gjerde points out in his study of a Norwegian enclave, *the* typical immigrant experience does not exist. My concluding chapter poses a typology contrasting chain and individual migrants, and demonstrating that homogeneous settlement patterns exerted an influence in numerous aspects of immigrant life. The transplanted Westfalians thus represent not just one piece in a mosaic, but one end of a continuum that helps us understand the whole spectrum of the immigrant experience.

diss., University of Minnesota, 1976). Some preliminary findings were published earlier by Ostergren, "Cultural Homogeneity and Population Stability among Swedish Immigrants in Chisago County," *Minnesota History* 45 (1973): 255–269. The work of Kristian Hvidt, *Flight to America: The Social Background of 300,000 Danish Emigrants* (New York, 1975), which had appeared in Danish in 1971, pioneered in the quantification of emigrant-lists data, though it does not include much of a transatlantic perspective.

[12] Jon Gjerde, *From Peasants to Farmers: The Migration from Balestrand, Norway, to the Upper Middle West* (Cambridge, 1985); Yda Saueressig, "Emigration, Settlement, and Assimilation of Dutch Catholic Immigrants in Wisconsin, 1850–1905" (Ph.D. diss., University of Wisconsin, 1982); Ostergren, "Rättvik to Isanti." There are some interesting parallels not only in the findings, but in the origins of these studies and the present study as well. All began as dissertations at Midwestern state universities. Each author was of the same ethnicity as the group studied and in most cases also had some ties to the local area of study, on one or both sides of the Atlantic. All prominently acknowledged Frank Thistlethwaite's challenge as a source of inspiration.

CHAPTER I

At the Crossroads of Economic Development: Background Factors Affecting Emigration from Northwest Germany

The dividing of lands and fields undoubtedly increases the population . . . but it increases only the number of consumers, not, to the same extent, the producers . . . and then what is left over for times of need or for the state? . . .

. . . The division even of individual fields should be allowed near towns and in factory and artisan districts; let it run its course undisturbed, for example, in Ravensberg, Mark, Tecklenburg, and Berg; but take care to prevent it in the rural areas around Paderborn, Münster, Julich, and Cologne. These lands are the granaries when those of the factory districts give out.[1]

THOUGH apparently unrelated to emigration, these recommendations by an early-nineteenth-century German agronomy expert illustrate one of the most important factors of European population dynamics on the eve of industrialization. Local economic conditions, not the mechanistic operation of inheritance customs, were the main determinants of whether peasant holdings would be subdivided. The needs of the state for a prosperous peasantry that would yield large surpluses of grain and taxes, and the desire of local communities to keep their poor-relief rolls unburdened, militated against partition in regions of full-scale peasant agriculture. Where the land was in any case too poor to provide much more than subsistence, and much of the surplus income was generated by artisan production for distant markets, attitudes toward partition and population growth were much more favorable. But even such an acute observer as Schwerz failed to realize that such "factory and artisan districts" were approaching a crossroads of economic development in the early nineteenth century. Some made the transition to modern machine industry, as did Berg and Mark and neighboring areas along the Ruhr. Those which did not, such as Tecklenburg and Ravensberg, saw a large proportion of their artisan population made redundant by the competition of industrializing regions. Where such displaced groups—rural but only marginally agricultural—made up a large share of the population, heavy overseas emigra-

[1] Johann Nepomuk von Schwerz, *Beschreibung der Landwirtschaft in Westfalen* (1836; facsimile reprint, Münster, 1979), pp. 12–13, 21.

CROSSROADS OF ECONOMIC DEVELOPMENT

tion was usually the result. In such purely agricultural regions as the Münsterland or Paderborn, population pressure seldom reached such extremes.

Accounts of German emigration as far back as Friedrich List have ascribed to inheritance systems the primary role in influencing regional variations in emigration. While in the greater part of Germany impartible inheritance (*Anerbenrecht*) prevailed, in southwest Germany, and in Rhineland Prussia and most of Hesse after the Napoleonic occupation, partible inheritance, equal division among heirs (*Realteilung*) was the rule. The latter system, it is argued, encouraged population growth and led to progressive splintering of peasant holdings, a "dwarf economy" in which many marginal operators were driven to emigration.[2]

This view is not entirely wrong, but it is misleading unless further qualified. Although eighteenth-century emigration was largely restricted to areas of southwest Germany such as the Palatinate, Baden, and Württemberg, pietism and the depredations of French invaders probably rivaled partible inheritance and fragmented landholdings as precipitating factors. This region was the source of the earliest and heaviest exodus in the nineteenth century, but partible inheritance was neither a necessary nor a sufficient condition for heavy emigration (see Figure 1.1). Rates from the industrial areas of the Rhineland were among the lowest in Germany despite partible inheritance. Moreover, there were Districts in northwest Germany such as Osnabrück and Minden (areas of impartible inheritance) with emigration rates comparable to those of Baden and Württemberg in the southwest.[3]

Because of the emphasis on southwest Germany, these heavy rates of emigration from parts of the northwest have been largely ignored. The

---

[2] The best source on German emigration is Mack Walker, *Germany and the Emigration, 1816–1885* (Cambridge, Mass., 1964), esp. pp. 1–69, 153–194. On distribution of emigration within Prussia, see also T. Bödicker, "Die Einwanderund und Auswanderung des preussischen Staates," *Preussische Statistik* 26 (1874): i–viii. On inheritance systems, see Walker, *Germany and Emigration*, pp. 47–49; Wolfang Köllmann and Peter Marschalck, "German Emigration to the United States," *Perspectives in American History* 7 (1973): 513, 524–528; Marcus Lee Hansen, *The Atlantic Migration, 1607–1860* (Cambridge, Mass., 1940), pp. 211–214.

[3] When capitalized, the word *District* will be used here to refer to Prussian *Regierungsbezirke* and their equivalents in other states, administrative areas averaging about 300,000 in population. Since the definition of emigration and the thoroughness with which it was recorded varied widely from state to state in Germany before national unification, I used the United States Census of 1870 to determine the cumulative amount of emigration from the various German states: Prussia, Baden, Bavaria, etc. Then I used German state statistics to "allocate" this emigration, so to speak, to the various Districts within each state and calculate the per capita emigration rates. For information on sources and the exact values of index figures for each District, see Appendix C.

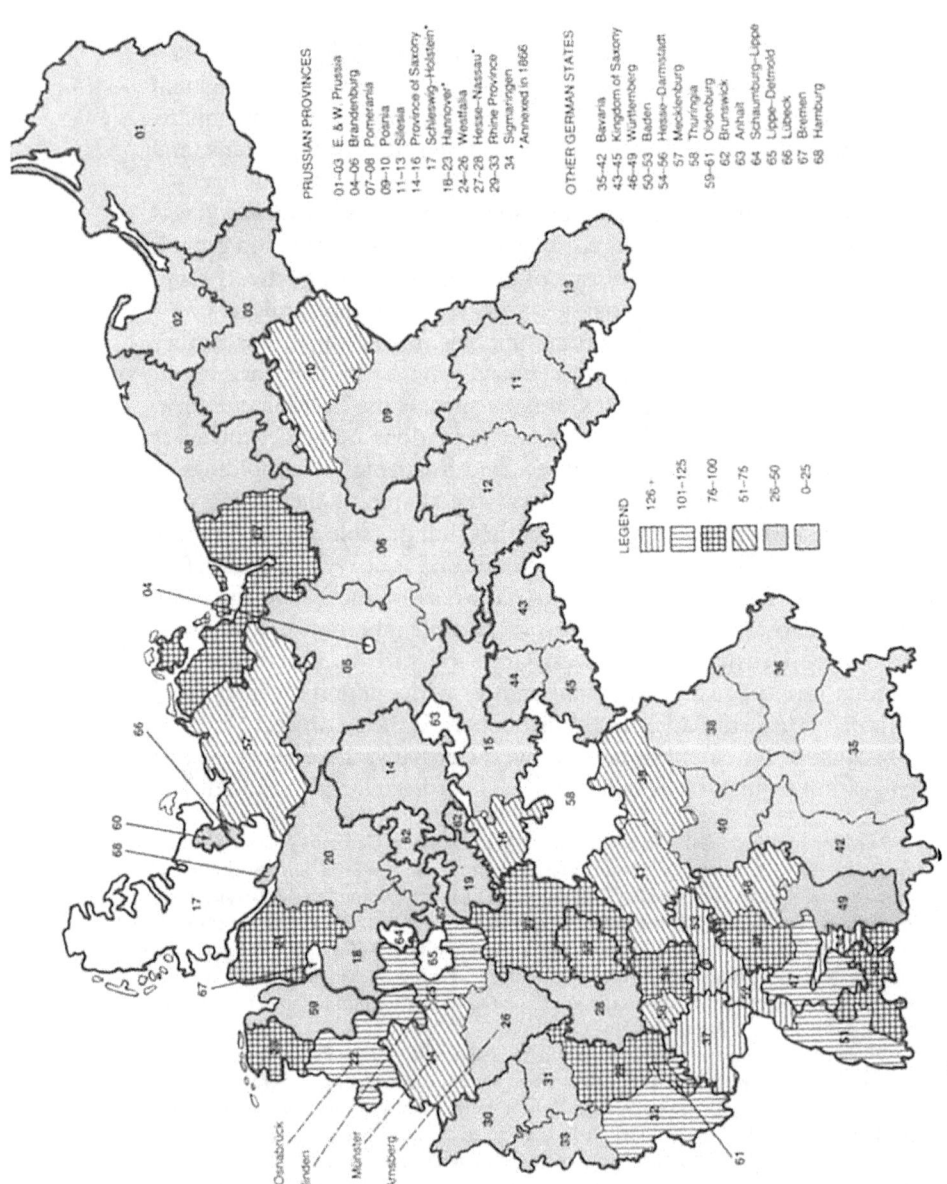

FIGURE 1.1
Index of Relative Intensity of Emigration by District (Immigrants in the United States per 1,000 Inhabitants of District of Origin, 1870/1871)

Source: See Appendix C, which includes methods of calculation and exact figures by District.

TABLE 1.1. AVERAGE YEARLY EMIGRATION FROM SELECTED AREAS
OF NORTHWEST GERMANY
(per 10,000 inhabitants)

	1836–1845	1846–1850	1851–1855	1860–1866	1844–1859
Osnabrück District	78	81	79	55	—
Fürstentum Osnabrück	105	104	110	—	—
Amt Bersenbruck	135	152	96	—	—
Amt Damme, Oldenburg	177	154	120	—	—
Münster District	15	26	—	20	18
Kreis Tecklenburg	41	57	—	—	—
Minden District	—	—	—	27	33
Lippe-Detmold	—	42	48	—	—

SOURCE: See Kamphoefner, "Transplanted Westfalians," p. 31.

District of Osnabrück, with less than 1 percent of Germany's inhabitants, was responsible for more than 7 percent of all German immigration to the United States during the 1830s. Bordering portions of Oldenburg were even harder hit, and the neighboring Prussian *Kreis* Tecklenburg experienced similarly heavy emigration (see Table 1.1). Statistics at the District level mask considerable local variation, though Bersenbrück and Tecklenburg represent the extremes in their respective Districts. High rates of emigration from this region persisted over several decades. In the thirty years before the American Civil War, the population of the *Fürstentum* Osnabrück continued to flow overseas at an average annual rate exceeding 1 percent. In the years from 1860 to 1866 (assuming equal accuracy of record keeping in Hannover and Prussia), Osnabrück had a higher rate of emigration than any Prussian District. Minden, the Prussian District adjoining Osnabrück, also ranked consistently near the top among Prussian Districts in intensity of emigration, rivaling even Sigmaringen in the heart of Baden-Württemberg.[4]

[4] The *Fürstentum* Osnabrück, the historic lands of the bishopric, constituted about three-fifths of the District; the latter encompassed on the west the secular territories of Lingen, Bentheim, and Arenberg-Meppen, annexed after the Napoleonic Wars. On emigration from northwest Germany, see Karl Kiel, "Gründe und Folgen der Auswanderung aus dem Osnabrücker Regierungsbezirk (1823–1866)," *Mitteilungen des Vereins für Geschichte und Landeskunde von Osnabrück* 61 (1941): 85–176; Adolf Wrasmann, "Das Heuerlingswesen im Fürstentum Osnabrück," *Mitteilungen des Vereins für Geschichte und Landeskunde von Osnabrück* 42 (1919): 52–171, and 44 (1921): 1–154;

CHAPTER I

A feature common to all these areas of heavy emigration was a well-developed cottage linen industry carried on by the rural lower class on a part-time basis but rapidly succumbing to machine competition in the nineteenth century. This downfall of cottage industry is the predominant factor that must be superimposed upon inheritance systems to understand patterns of emigration. Though its effects were perhaps most dramatic in the northwest, it was also important in central and southwest Germany. What is significant for America is that, at least until the Civil War, expulsive forces in Europe were the main factors behind emigration, and the displaced rural lower class constituted the majority of emigrants. Thus any success that German immigrants achieved in America requires a better explanation than that they were middle class before they left.

Flight to America was not necessarily the only alternative. A second, related factor affecting emigration was the development of—or failure to develop—centers of modern machine industry that could absorb surplus population. Both of these factors will be examined with special reference to the region of northwest Germany: the states of Hannover, Oldenburg, Brunswick, and Lippe, and the Districts of Minden and Münster in Prussian Westfalia. Despite this lack of political unity, and confessional differences and a somewhat varied geography as well, this region nevertheless is unified linguistically by its Low German dialect and culturally by traditions of independent peasantry (*Grundherrschaft*) and impartible inheritance. These characteristics set the northwest apart from the districts of great estates (*Gutsherrschaft*) east of the Elbe, and on the south from Hesse and the Rhineland, the approximate northern extent of High German dialects and customs of partible inheritance. Within the northwest, special attention will be focused on the Minden, Münster, and Osnabrück Districts, centers of the handloom linen industry and sources of particularly heavy emigration.[5]

Albin Gladen, *Der Kreis Tecklenburg an der Schwelle des Zeitalters der Industrialisierung* (Münster, 1970); Johannes Ostendorf, "Zur Geschichte der Auswanderung aus dem alten Amt Damme (Oldenburg)," *Oldenburger Jahrbuch* 46/47 (1942–1943): 164–297; Herbert Hitzemann, "Die Auswanderung aus dem Fürstentum Lippe" (doctoral diss., University of Münster, 1953). For figures on emigration from Prussia, see Bödicker, "Einwanderung und Auswanderung," pp. i–viii. On Osnabrück, see Kiel, "Gründe und Folgen," pp. 165–176; Wrasmann, "Das Heuerlingswesen," 44: 85.

[5] Those who would object to my dividing of the Province of Westfalia should note that "northwest Germany" as I have defined it corresponds exactly to the adjacent regions "Lower Saxony" and "Northern Westphalia" as defined by Frank B. Tipton, Jr., *Regional Variation in the Economic Development of Germany during the Nineteenth Century* (Middletown, Conn., 1976), pp. 8–9. As late as 1880, the northwest remained disproportionately rural (pp. 61, 182–183, 189). Treating Westfalia as a unit masks

The influence of rural industry on population growth, though already noted by contemporary observers, first gained scholarly attention in Rudolf Braun's study of the Zurich highlands. Franklin Mendels then provided a more rigorous economic formulation and testing of this thesis for the area of Flanders and also coined the term *protoindustry*. As it will be used here, *protoindustry* refers to the decentralized, rural, labor-intensive production of goods for a distant market, usually supplemented by marginal agriculture.[6]

Although Mendels made an important contribution by illuminating the interrelationship between economic and demographic processes, other aspects of his model are less convincing. Quoting the subtitle of his dissertation, he calls protoindustrialization "the first phase of industrialization," but subsequent studies suggest that he was overly optimistic. One might argue that it was a necessary precondition for industrialization, but by no means a sufficient one. Examples of "deindustrialization"—regions that failed to make the transition to modern, mechanized industry—were every bit as common as success stories. It is precisely these regions where modern industrialization took place belatedly or not at all that will constitute the chief focus of this study.

The handloom linen industry prevalent in northwest Germany differed in minor details from that in other regions, but protoindustry everywhere brought with it similar demographic consequences. It contrasted sharply with a system of full-scale peasant agriculture that contained built-in demographic safeguards. Since an heir had to wait until his father's death or retirement before he could marry and take over the farm, late marriages and small families were the rule. These restrictions on population growth were eliminated almost completely in a system

---

important differences between the industrializing Ruhr and the rest of the province. Tipton combines the Districts of Arnsberg and Düsseldorf as an economic unit spanning province boundaries.

[6] Rudolf Braun, *Industrialisierung und Volksleben: Die Veränderung der Lebensformen in einem ländlichen Industriegebiet vor 1800 (Zürcher Oberland)* (Zurich, 1960); Franklin F. Mendels, "Industrialization and Population Pressure in Eighteenth-Century Flanders" (Ph.D. diss., University of Wisconsin, 1970). Mendels (p. 7) defines *protoindustry* as "any type of market activity involved in the transformation of natural raw materials into commodities of a higher type of elaboration, as long as the overwhelming majority of the labor force involved in that activity is doing it at home and/or on a part-time basis." See also Charles Tilly and Richard Tilly, "Agenda for European Economic History in the 1970s," *Journal of Economic History* 31 (1971): 184–198. The discussion on protoindustry was greatly stimulated by Peter Kriedte, Hans Medick, and Jürgen Schlumbohm, *Industrialization before Industrialization: Rural Industry in the Genesis of Capitalism* (Cambridge, 1981), originally published as *Industrialisierung vor der Industrialisierung* (Göttingen, 1977).

CHAPTER I

of rural industry. A loom and a rented cottage were the only prerequisites for marriage and the establishment of an independent existence. With early marriage came large families, especially since children were now an economic asset, ready to be put to work spinning at the age of five. This process created an expanding rural lower class, which could find employment only through the expansion of rural industry. The end result was concentrations of population too large even to be fed, much less adequately employed, by local agriculture alone.[7]

In northwest Germany, protoindustry was always closely associated with the *Heuerling* system. Which came first is difficult to determine, though in most cases rural industry developed where a rural proletariat was already present. In any case, the growth of the two was clearly mutually reinforcing. The word *Heuerling* has no real equivalent in English, though perhaps "tenant farmer" or "sharecropper" comes closest both as an occupational description and in class connotation. A *Heuerling* normally owned neither house nor land, but rented, usually for a brief tenure of four years, a cottage that was often a converted outbuilding or even a barn, and a plot of land no larger than two to three acres. For this, in addition to a small cash rent, he was usually subject to service for the landowner (a *Kolon*, or landowning peasant). A *Heuerling* either worked a fixed number of days, usually without pay, or more commonly whenever called upon, for a substandard wage. Under these conditions, subsistence without the income from the spinning and weaving of home-grown flax was hardly possible. Even in the late eighteenth century when the linen trade was flourishing, this was often supplemented by seasonal labor in Holland.[8]

During the first half of the nineteenth century, the handloom linen industry in Germany suffered a series of shocks that reduced it from a major supplier for export to economic insignificance. First, the Napo-

[7] I have been better able to document the end result of protoindustry (i.e. population pressure) than the process by which it occurred. Census data for the area of study are not available until the mid-nineteenth century, when protoindustry was already in decline, emigration was heavy, and fertility patterns could be expected to change. Nevertheless, the early marriage and large families of protoindustrial workers were the subject of frequent comment in the literature. Furthermore, a growing body of literature, based primarily on parish-record reconstruction, attests to the differential fertility of protoindustrial and agricultural populations. An exhaustive review of this literature, including an extensive theoretical discussion on protoindustry in general and its impact on family structures and strategies in particular, is provided by Kriedte et al., *Industrialization*, esp. pp. 82–86.

[8] A contemporary account of the *Heuerling* system is provided by Wilhelm von Laer, "Bericht über die Lage der arbeitenden Klassen des Kreises Herford" (1851), in *Die Eigentumslosen*, ed. Carl Jantke and Dietrich Hilger (Munich, 1965), pp. 93–100. For a more detailed characterization, see also the studies of northwest Germany by Wrasmann, Kiel, Gladen, Ostendorf, and Hitzemann cited in n. 4 above.

leonic Wars and the Continental blockade denied Germany access to its main markets in the Western Hemisphere, especially Latin America. The exclusion of British competition from the Continent temporarily compensated for this loss, but the end of the war found the South American colonies on the road to independence and their markets firmly in the hands of the British, accompanied by an enormous expansion of handloom weaving in Ireland. Second, linen production was being mechanized—first the spinning and then the weaving—with Ulster taking the lead and German production centers making the transition only belatedly and incompletely. Third, linen itself was increasingly being replaced on the market by cotton, which was better adapted to mechanized production. Thus a once-booming rural industry faded into insignificance, and many of the areas where it had flourished reverted to simple agriculture.[9]

For the landless or land-poor classes dependent on linen weaving for supplementary or even primary income, the decline of the industry had serious consequences that reached catastrophic proportions in such times of agricultural crisis as the mid-1840s. These crises produced waves of emigration, which appear upon cursory observation to have been especially heavy in areas with a concentration of rural industry.

The three Districts of Westfalia present in microcosm three contrasting patterns of economic and demographic development (see Table 1.2). In the east, Minden-Ravensberg, a center of protoindustry in the form of linen weaving and spinning, was the most densely populated area in all Prussia at the beginning of the nineteenth century. But its

[9] For accounts of the linen industry in northwest Germany and its decline, see Karl Biller, *Der Rückgang der Handleinwandindustrie des Münsterlandes* (Leipzig, 1906); Edith Schmitz, *Leinengewerbe und Leinenhandel in Nordwestdeutschland (1650–1850)* (Cologne, 1967); Wolfgang Mager, "Protoindustrialisierung und agrarisch-heimgewerbliche Verflechtung in Ravensberg während der Frühen Neuzeit," *Geschichte und Gesellschaft* 8 (1982): 435–474; Gerhard Adelmann, "Strukturelle Krisen im ländlichen Textilgewerbe Nordwestdeutschlands zu Beginn der Industrialisierung," in *Wirtschaftspolitik und Arbeitsmarkt*, ed. Hermann Kellenbenz (Munich, 1974), pp. 110–128. An excellent source that includes far more than the title implies is a series of articles by Stephanie Reekers, "Beiträge zur statistischen Darstellung der gewerblichen Wirtschaft Westfalens um 1800," in *Westfälische Forschungen*: "Teil 1: Paderborn und Münster," 17 (1964): 83–176; "Teil 2: Minden-Ravensberg," 18 (1965): 75–130; "Teil 3: Tecklenburg-Lingen, Reckenberg, Reitberg und Rheda," 19 (1966): 28–78; "Teil 9: Lippe und Stadt Lippstadt," 29 (1978/1979): 24–116. The literature on northwest Germany cited in n. 4 above also includes considerable information on the linen industry. Of all the areas considered here, only in and around Bielefeld did a successful if "difficult transformation to industrialization . . . with a temporary and partial de-industrialization" take place (Kriedte et al., *Industrialization*, pp. 152–153). Tecklenburg, Osnabrück, Lippe, and much of the Minden District can be classified without qualification as areas of de-industrialization.

CHAPTER I

TABLE 1.2. ECONOMIC AND DEMOGRAPHIC PATTERNS IN THE THREE DISTRICTS OF WESTFALIA

	Münster	Minden	Arnsberg
Economic Type	Agricultural	Protoindustry	Modern Industry
Birthrate to 1850	low	high	high
Crude Rate 1841–1855[a]	123	164	160
Tendency Thereafter	steady	lower	higher
Crude Rate 1862–1867[a]	127	156	181
Emigration Rate	moderate	high	low
Recorded Yearly Rate 1844–1859[b]	17.8	32.8	6.7
Net Migration Loss, 1843–1852[c]	26.0	56.3	0.5
Population Trend	slow, stable growth	fast growth then stagnation	continued fast growth
Annual Growth Rate 1818–1843	.70%	1.24%	1.77%
Annual Growth Rate 1843–1858	.27%	.12%	1.46%

SOURCE: See note 10.
[a] Live births and stillbirths per 1,000 women aged 14–44.
[b] Officially recorded emigration per 10,000 population.
[c] Difference in population gain between censuses and surplus of births over deaths during the same time span: annual net migration loss per 10,000 population.

patterns of high birthrates and rapid population growth were reversed before midcentury by the collapse of the linen industry, leaving in its wake widespread misery and massive emigration that subsided only when parts of the region made a successful, if belated, transition to modern textile and other industries.[10]

The rugged District of Arnsberg in the south, traditionally a center of small-scale charcoal-iron industry, witnessed during the nineteenth century the booming growth of Germany's largest concentration of heavy industry, the Ruhr valley. Here emigration was the lowest, and birthrates and population growth the highest, in Westfalia, although

[10] Sources of Table 1.2: John Knodel, *The Decline of Fertility in Germany, 1871–1939* (Princeton, 1974), p. 43; Bödicker, "Einwanderung und Auswanderung," p. iv; Alexis Markow, *Entwicklung der Aus- und Einwanderung, Ab- und Zuzüge in Preussen* (Tübingen, 1889), pp. 174–175, 189–191, 214–217; Stephanie Reekers and Johanna Schulz, *Die Bevolkerung in den Gemeinden Westfalens* (Dortmund, 1952). From the figures on emigration in Bödicker, p. iv, it appears that the District of Minden had a lower emigration rate than Münster in the 1840s. However, this is purely the result of underenumeration, as shown by Markow's statistics on net migration balance. Minden-Ravensberg consists of the old Prussian parts of the Minden District: *Kreise* Lübbecke, Herford, Minden, Halle in Westfalia, and Bielefeld. The more recently Prussianized southern half of the District was not nearly so heavily protoindustrial.

CROSSROADS OF ECONOMIC DEVELOPMENT

the shifting economic center of gravity from southeast to northwest did require some internal migration.

To the west, the sandy plain of the Münsterland, level and easily worked if not especially fertile, had traditionally been the home of a prosperous, independent peasantry engaged in comparatively large-scale agriculture. Patterns of late marriage and low birthrates brought only a low rate of emigration and slow growth of population into the period of industrialization.

These characteristics are clearly reflected in District statistics even though the economic regions do not correspond exactly with administrative boundaries. Not all of the Minden District was protoindustrialized. *Kreis* Recklinghausen in the southeast of the Münster District is really a part of the industrial Ruhr valley, while *Kreis* Tecklenburg in the north is a western extension of the hilly, protoindustrialized region of Minden-Ravensberg. In general, the economic regions conform more to geography than to political boundaries. Protoindustry was largely restricted to the area between the Teutoburger Wald and the Wiehengebirge, stretching from Tecklenburg across the intervening tongue of Hannoverian territory around Osnabrück and the northern half of the Minden District to the dwarf state of Lippe-Detmold (see Figure 1.2).

While the broad regional outlines of the extent of protoindustry are easily sketched, a more differentiated measure of its intensity at the local level is not so easily obtained. Where weaving was the primary activity, as in the Münster and Osnabrück Districts, the number of looms is a good indicator; but where large proportions of the population were engaged in spinning, as in Minden, statistical information is harder to find. For *Kreis* Tecklenburg and most of the *Fürstentum* Osnabrück, the number of looms per 1,000 inhabitants exceeded 120 in the early nineteenth century; for Minden-Ravensberg the index figure was only 36 in 1796. But an 1838 figure shows 22,594 spinner families in Minden-Ravensberg, or nearly 1 for every 10 inhabitants. Assuming 5 persons per family, 60 percent of Tecklenburg's population would have been directly dependent on protoindustry; with the combination of spinning and weaving, the proportion in Minden-Ravensberg would have been even higher. Another indication of the importance of rural industry is the volume of linen sales, which amounted to nearly 10 taler per capita annually in some areas.[11]

These areas were no longer agriculturally self-sufficient, another reflection of the dependence on protoindustry. By the end of the eight-

[11] Reekers, "Statistische Darstellung, Teil 3," pp. 34–50; idem, "Statistische Darstellung, Teil 1," p. 128; Adelmann, "Strukturelle Krisen," p. 118.

CHAPTER I

FIGURE 1.2
Detail Map of Northwest German Areas of Study

eenth century, Tecklenburg grew enough grain for its own use only in the best of years; with bad and even average harvests, imports were necessary. If this was the case in Tecklenburg, with a population density of 155 persons per square mile in 1843, the dependence on imports must have been much more severe in Minden-Ravensberg, where only one *Kreis* in five had a density below 250, with two of them exceeding 330 persons per square mile. So for a considerable proportion of the population, agriculture no longer provided an alternative when protoindustry failed them.[12]

[12] Biller, *Rückgang der Handleinwandindustrie*, p. 2; Hans Uekötter, *Die Bevolke-*

TABLE 1.3. CORRELATION BETWEEN EMIGRATION RATE AND PROTOINDUSTRY FOR SELECTED AREAS OF WESTFALIA

	Independent Variable	Dependent Variable	Correlation Coefficient	N of Cases
Münster District by *Kreis*	Looms per capita, 1816	Emigration rate, 1832–1850	.87	10
Münster District by *Kreis*	Looms per capita, 1831	Emigration rate, 1832–1850	.88	10
Münster District by *Kreis*	Looms per capita, 1849	Emigration rate, 1832–1850	.86	10
Minden District by *Kreis*	Spinner families plus looms per capita, 1838–49	Emigration rate, 1851–1860	.63	10
Kreis Tecklenburg by *Gemeinde*	Looms per capita, 1827	Emigration rate, 1832–1850	.59	17

SOURCE: See note 13.

The widely varying intensity of rural industry in the early nineteenth century is reflected in several inventories of linen looms at the local level in the Münster and Minden Districts. The number of looms per capita in 1816, 1831, and 1849 were correlated with the per capita rates of emigration for the years 1832 through 1850 from each rural *Kreis* of the Münster District (see Table 1.3). The results in all cases are very similar: an r value approaching .90 for the association between rural industry and emigration. Expressed in terms of the R^2 value, knowing the number of looms in each *Kreis*, one could have predicted approximately three-fourths of the variation in the level of emigration. For the Minden District, credible emigration statistics are not available until the 1850s, and spinners as well as weavers have to be taken into account to approximate the importance of rural industry. Here, too, the correlation with emigration rates is rather close, though not so high as in Münster. In Minden, the proportion of *Heuerleute* in the population prove to be an even better predictor of emigration, but this only shows how interdependent all three phenomena were.[13]

---

rungsbewegung in Westfalen und Lippe, 1818–1933 (Münster, 1941), pp. 80–82. Some of the difference in population density between Tecklenburg and Minden-Ravensberg resulted from the greater soil fertility of the latter.

[13] Even higher correlations would have resulted had *Stadtkreis* Münster been included, but the low emigration there probably resulted from factors other than the low number of weavers. Figures on looms for the District of Münster were obtained from Biller,

CHAPTER I

It should be noted that the distribution of emigration over the twenty-year period differed somewhat from *Kreis* to *Kreis* in Münster. This is not entirely unexpected, for emigration was not an economically mechanistic process; such factors as individual decisions, the spread of information, and mass psychology affected especially the timing of emigration. But even at the village (*Gemeinde*) level, where sociopsychological factors would have had the greatest impact, rural industry proved to be a good predictor of emigration rate in *Kreis* Tecklenburg. Another economic factor also may have played a role: Handloom linen was not a uniform product, and different local specialties did not all succumb to mechanical competition at the same time.

For these areas of Westfalia at least, the association between rural industry and emigration is very strong. To learn more about patterns of regional variation in intensity of emigration, a more diverse area—the Kingdom of Hannover—was subjected to a statistical analysis of the relationship between rates of emigration and various measures of population density and economic specialization. In a way, this investigation resembles a drama in which the two leading characters never actually appear on stage. No suitable figures exist on handloom weaving in Hannover, and statewide emigration figures are available only from 1859 on, after the peak years of emigration. Nonetheless, areas with high emigration rates in earlier years generally continued these patterns throughout the period studied, and protoindustry shows itself clearly if indirectly through its effects on other "characters."[14]

Despite these limitations, a multiple regression with six variables explained over one-third of the variation in emigration rates at the *Kreis*

Rückgang der Handleinwandindustrie, pp. 61, 75, 147; emigration figures from emigrant lists (see Appendix A). The figures on looms by *Gemeinde* were taken from Gladen, *Kreis Tecklenburg*, p. 197, and Reekers, "Statistische Darstellung, Teil 1," p. 174. Emigration figures for Minden in Staatsarchiv Detmold, M1 IA, pp. 95, 101, 111; weavers and spinners in 1838 from Staatsarchiv Münster, Oberpräsidium 1042, 1: 161ff.; weavers in 1849 from *Tabellen und amtliche Nachrichten über den Preussischen Staat für das Jahr 1849* 4 (1855): 678ff.

[14] None of the independent variables used in the multiple regression was intercorrelated so highly as .64. Raw data for this section were obtained from *Zur Statistik des Königreichs Hannover* (Hannover, 1850–1865), vols. 2, 6, 9, 11. Population figures were derived from the 1864 census; occupational figures and livestock from 1861. Various types of livestock were combined into cattle equivalents according to the formula of the Prussian census: 1 cow = 2/3 horse = 10 sheep. For more information on variables and for bivariate correlations with emigration rates, see Walter D. Kamphoefner, "Transplanted Westfalians: Persistence and Transformation of Socioeconomic and Cultural Patterns in the Northwest German Migration to Missouri" (Ph.D. diss., University of Missouri, 1978), pp. 40–43.

CROSSROADS OF ECONOMIC DEVELOPMENT

TABLE 1.4. MULTIPLE REGRESSION OF ECONOMIC AND DEMOGRAPHIC VARIABLES WITH EMIGRATION RATE, 1859–1861
(Kingdom of Hannover by Kreis)

	Simple r	Beta
Persons/Dwelling	−.39	−.32
Persons/Unit Land Area	−.15	.35
% Pop. Agricultural Dependents	.50	.55
Children < Age 1/Women Aged 20–45	.02	.04
Livestock/Person in Agriculture	−.18	−.02
Livestock/Unit Land Area	.004	−.32
R^2 for all variables = .35		
N of Cases = 101		

SOURCE: See note 14.

level and over 80 percent at a higher level of aggregation. The variables in Table 1.4 were selected from a larger list for the most combined explanatory power, with one exception. Fertility rates, included for illustrative purposes, were apparently inconsequential as a factor in emigration. But just because this was true in 1860 does not mean that it was so thirty years earlier. By midcentury, emigration had begun to affect population structure and birthrates. In fact, another variable—the crude birthrate uncontrolled for age and sex—showed greater explanatory power, but in the "wrong" direction: high birthrates corresponding with low emigration. This merely reflects the fact that, because of the selectivity of migration, there were fewer women of childbearing age in areas of heavy emigration, and a skewed sex ratio besides. Also, to the extent that the healthy and able-bodied were overrepresented in the exodus, those left behind were probably less likely to marry or to bear children if they did.

The negative bivariate correlations with residential and population density convincingly refute any crude *Lebensraum* interpretations and suggest that urban industry presented an alternative to emigration. But once urbanization is controlled for, the beta coefficient shows that emigration increased with population density. In fact, the relationship when plotted appears slightly curvilinear. The purely agricultural regions, with the lowest population densities, fall in the middle range of emigration rates. At one pole stand the industrializing areas, with the highest density and the lowest emigration; at the other, the protoindustrial regions, with statistically moderate levels of crowding (in reality more severe because of their rural character), the sources of heaviest emigration.

Further confirmation of these patterns is provided by occupational statistics. The strongest predictor of emigration proved to be the proportion of the population who were dependents of the agriculturally employed. The number of agricultural dependents was of course closely correlated with the total agricultural population, and the latter variable was nearly as good a predictor, but the difference suggests that emigration was heaviest where families of *Heuerleute* rather than unmarried farmhands constituted the main source of agricultural labor. Since rural industry was practiced almost entirely on a part-time basis, most linen weavers also fell under the agricultural rubric in the occupational census.

This is supported by the fact that emigration was highest where there were many agriculturists but little agriculture. The more livestock per farmer or unit of land area, the less emigration. The precarious economic situation of the rural lower classes is reflected in these figures. Few *Heuerleute* had enough land to require or support a draft animal. For example, an 1849 survey revealed that the 12,692 *Heuerleute* in the Osnabrück region owned a total of only 436 horses.[15] Over the whole of Hannover, there was little association between cattle holdings and patterns of emigration, but in the Osnabrück District (where emigration was highest), there is a considerable negative association with the number of cattle per capita or unit of farmland. The agricultural lower class was apparently finding it difficult to keep cattle since the division of common lands in many communities deprived them of the free grazing rights that they had previously enjoyed by custom if not by law. The negative correlation between sheep holdings and emigration was especially strong. This had to do mostly with the type of area in which sheep raising prevailed: sandy, infertile, sparsely populated regions such as the Lüneburger Heide. Intensification of agriculture with the spread of root crops brought a 30 percent increase of land in cultivation from 1833 to 1853 in the District of Lüneburg, allowing excess rural population to be absorbed.[16] Statistical information from Hannover shows that the expansion of land in cultivation tended to retard emigration. Taken together, these patterns of association further un-

---

[15] Figures on *Heuerleute* are from *Zur Statistik des Königreiches Hannover*, 2: 66. Statistics from the 1855 census in the district of Minden show a similar relationship between livestock holdings and emigration.

[16] Hans Linde, "Das Königreich Hannover an der Schwelle des Industriezeitalters," *Neues Archiv für Niedersachsen* 5, no. 24 (1951): 431.

derscore the tripartite division into regions of protoindustry, modern industry, and agriculture.

To guard against the ecological fallacy, the occupational structure of the emigration was investigated at the individual level. This provided additional evidence that the rural lower classes were indeed being displaced by the decline of protoindustry. Although several scholars have argued that much of the German emigration was middle class in character through 1860, this generalization is not borne out by empirical evidence from Northwest Germany. Instead, in all areas with substantial protoindustry, two-thirds or more of the emigrants were landless tenants or agricultural laborers, the classes most dependent on supplementary income from rural industry. This evidence will be discussed in more detail in the next chapter.

The preceding evidence has established the importance of protoindustry in influencing levels of emigration in northwest Germany. What remains to be examined is how far this thesis can be extended to other areas of Germany. Its impact was mainly limited to the first two-thirds of the nineteenth century. In the new waves of emigration after the American Civil War and the founding of the German Empire, protoindustrial decline no longer played the predominant role. From that point on, East Elbian Prussia became increasingly prominent as a source of emigration, and factors other than rural industry come into play. Also, the flood tides of emigration peaking in 1846 and 1853 marked the last agricultural crises of the preindustrial type. Thereafter, the problems of food production and distribution no longer plagued Germany, and the fluctuations of emigration rates correspond ever less with those of grain prices.[17]

For the earlier part of the nineteenth century, nevertheless, it is important to evaluate the role of protoindustry in other areas of heavy emigration, particularly those with inheritance systems of equal division of land among heirs. Two extreme hypotheses have been posed: 1) Inheritance systems made little difference. If there is no significant population growth, any system will work; if there is considerable growth, any system will run into trouble. 2) While impartible inheritance is basically a self-regulating demographic system, except when subverted by protoindustry, partible inheritance is an inherently unstable system

---

[17] Friedhelm Gehrmann, "Regionale Wachstumsdifferenzierung in Deutschland, 1850–1961," *Forschungsbericht*, Project Ho 81/42 of the Deutsche Forschungsgemeinschaft (Bonn, n.d.), pp. 25–39. Gehrmann shows that before 1860 the fluctuations of emigration rates were higher in agricultural than in industrial states, but thereafter industrialized states showed greater extremes. Moreover, the correlation between wheat prices and emigration rates became progressively weaker after 1855.

CHAPTER I

that encourages overpopulation and splintering of agricultural holdings. But the truth probably lies somewhere between the two extremes. While partibility had a greater latent tendency toward excessive population growth, this tendency could be realized under either inheritance system when it was encouraged by opportunities for part-time employment outside agriculture.[18] It is important to remember that inheritance systems do not originate in an economic vacuum, nor is their operation in practice always what one might expect from the legal provisions. Local inheritance customs often continued unabated after inheritance laws were altered with the rise of modern German states.

Having seen the importance of the rural textile industry in northwest Germany, it would appear profitable to reexamine southwest Germany and explore the relationship between protoindustry and emigration. Württemberg, Baden, and Hesse all had a considerable amount of handloom weaving, suffered varying degrees of de-industrialization, and were states with some of the earliest and heaviest emigration in nineteenth-century Germany.[19] The exact dimensions of the textile industry in southwest Germany are difficult to determine from existing statistics, for there as in Westfalia protoindustry was intertwined so closely with agriculture that it was often hard to distinguish the main occupation from the sideline. Several estimates from the mid-nineteenth century, including one by Gustav Schmoller, place the number of people engaged in manufacturing and commerce in Württemberg at nearly equal to the agricultural population. But an occupational census in 1852, which found 44 percent of all enumerated artisans also engaged in agriculture, illustrates the impossibility of any precise delineation of the occupational structure. With reference specifically to textile workers, an 1861 statistic placed Baden second in the whole

---

[18] See the discussion of inheritance systems by Lutz K. Berkner, "Peasant Household Organization and Demographic Change in Lower Saxony (1689–1766)," in *Population Patterns in the Past*, ed. Ronald Demos Lee (New York, 1977), pp. 53–57, which compares peasant holdings in areas of partible and impartible inheritance in southeastern Hannover. Of the two subdistricts compared in the study, Calenberg, with impartible inheritance, had an emigration rate only half that of Göttingen, with partible, according to Hannoverian statistics from 1859 to 1864. But as Berkner points out, the main question is whether there were such intervening variables as protoindustry involved.

Statistics on the *Kreis* or equivalent level for the whole of the German Empire showed that among those areas with the largest proportion of extremely small landholdings (under two hectars), three of the first five and six of the first twenty were in Württemberg. But those in first and third place, Zellerfeld in the Harz and Siegen in southern Westfalia, both traditionally centers of mining and metalworking, had rather low emigration rates, again showing the importance of local economic factors (Hans Lang, *Die Entwicklung der Bevölkerung in Württemberg* [Tübingen, 1903], p. 19).

[19] Kriedte et al., *Industrialization*, pp. 146, 152.

Zollverein in number of master linen weavers, with 54 per 10,000 inhabitants. When part-time weavers are taken into consideration, the figure is 110 for Württemberg, compared to roughly 170 for Westfalia. In Baden, part-time weavers were apparently not enumerated. Besides linen weavers, there were a considerable number of workers in protoindustrial woolen production. Though the figures on textile workers appear low in relation to total population, it must be remembered that since most flax was locally grown and most wool locally spun, each weaver was backed up by several spinners.[20]

One important contrast between the northwest and the southwest was the wine industry of the latter. Winegrowers, like linen weavers, were not always self-sufficient in foodstuffs, and were dependent on a distant, uncertain market. Moreover, their product was very sensitive to weather. The fluctuating conditions in the wine industry explain much of the differences in the emigration curve between the two regions of Germany. The great drop in linen prices came in the early 1840s; in the Osnabrück District in the northwest, emigration reached its peak in the 1840s rather than in the 1850s. In the southwest, the collapse of the linen industry was cushioned by bountiful wine harvests; the 1846 vintage was the most profitable within the preceding or subsequent decade. However, 1850, 1851, and 1854 were among the four worst years in the century, and the intervening two years were also below average. This combined with high grain prices to drive the emigration curve to record heights.[21]

Württemberg's early statistics and stable administrative boundaries provide an ideal set of cross-sectional data with which to test the factors influencing emigration. The association patterns of the winegrowing variable are most striking: very influential in the 1850s, but negligible in the 1840s and even slightly negative in the 1860s, as

[20] Figures on Baden from Georg von Viehbahn, *Statistik des zollvereinten und nördlichen Deutschlands*, pt. 3 (Berlin, 1868), pp. 902–910. Lippe-Detmold, a dwarf principality bordering Westfalia, was in first place. When part-time weavers are taken into consideration, the index for Lippe is nearly 220 looms per 1,000 inhabitants, for Westfalia roughly 170, for Württemberg 110. In Baden, part-time weavers were apparently not enumerated. See also Wolfgang von Hippel, *Auswanderung aus Südwestdeutschland: Studien zur württembergischen Auswanderung und Auswanderungspolitik im 18. und 19. Jahrhundert* (Stuttgart, 1984), pp. 181, 229–233; Peter Borscheid, *Textilarbeiterschaft in der Industrialisierung: Soziale Lage und Mobilität in Württemberg (19. Jahrhundert)* (Stuttgart, 1978), pp. 51–136, 467–484.

[21] Data on wine vintages from 1827 to 1890 are contained in *Württembergisches Jahrbuch* (1890), pt. 1, pp. 55–57. Data on grain yields and population were obtained from the 1900 volume of the same source. Data for Hannover were taken from *Zur Statistik des Königreiches Hannover*, vols. 6, 9, 12.

CHAPTER I

industrialization in the Neckar region began to gain momentum. But protoindustry was also important; the proportion of weavers in the population was the second best predictor of migration in both the 1840s and the 1850s. Livestock holdings exercised a similar influence in southwest as in northwest Germany. The more livestock per person, and to a lesser extent the more per unit of land, the lower the emigration rate. There was a mild degree of association between emigration and population density, but viniculture was more important than inheritance patterns in producing heavy population concentrations and fragmented holdings. Outside the wine region of the Neckar, even where partible inheritance prevailed, there were few areas with a population density exceeding 250 per square mile. This further underscores the point that inheritance systems grew out of local economic conditions, and were not applied mechanistically or contrary to good economic sense by irrational peasants.[22]

To take yet another example, the District of Trier in the Eifel region of Rhineland Prussia might appear to be a classic illustration of the ills of partible inheritance. It had the highest emigration rate in all of Prussia from 1844 to 1859. But here, too, the decline of a traditional industry, if not strictly protoindustry, played a decisive role. The charcoal-iron industry in nineteenth-century Germany suffered a fate similar to that of handloom weaving, with similar results in terms of emigration, as the case of the Eifel demonstrates. While iron manufacturing could scarcely be called a cottage industry even though it was located in rural areas, it nevertheless shared with the linen industry the characteristics of seasonality of labor and dependence on nonlocal markets. Though the persons at the furnace may have worked full time, the numerically much larger contingent of woodcutters, charcoal burners, teamsters, and ore loaders consisted almost exclusively of peasants working part time. Ore digging was almost entirely seasonal labor confined to the winter. Like the linen industry, the iron industry was a prime factor in producing heavy concentrations of rural population. As a German scholar who conducted a thorough case study of migration patterns from the Eifel concluded, "There is little doubt that the relatively high population density of the greatest part of the Eifel at the beginning of the nineteenth century was to a considerable degree influenced by the iron industry."[23]

[22] For a more detailed comparison, including multiple regressions with Württemberg data, see Kamphoefner, "At the Crossroads of Economic Development: Background Factors Affecting Emigration from Nineteenth Century Germany," in *Migration across Time and Nations*, ed. Ira Glazier and Luigi De Rosa (New York, 1986), pp. 174–201.

[23] Richard Graafen, *Die Aus- und Abwanderung aus der Eifel in den Jahren 1815 bis*

CROSSROADS OF ECONOMIC DEVELOPMENT

With the development of modern iron-making processes using coke from coal and relying on steam instead of water power to run hammers and rolling mills, a modern iron industry sprang up near the coal fields, and the charcoal-iron industry could no longer compete. As with textiles, the changes took place first in England and were then imitated in Germany. The Eifel iron industry received a staggering blow in 1839, when English and Belgian iron began flooding the German market. Compounded by several years of bad harvests, the crisis lasted well into the 1840s and set off a wave of emigration that brought population growth in the District of Trier almost to a standstill. Nearly half of the emigration during the decade came from two *Kreise*, Adenau and Daun, areas of "restricted agricultural opportunities and strong dependence of a large proportion of the population on industry."[24] But *Kreis* Schleiden, the center of the iron industry, was the source of relatively few overseas emigrants despite an absolute decline in population after 1840. Instead, Schleiden's proximity to Aachen allowed most of its surplus population to find employment in the rapidly developing modern industries there. For most of the Trier region, however, German industrialization did not offer this alternative and the consequence of de-industrialization was, as a German scholar points out, an exodus overseas:

> Even examples of well-to-do persons emigrating cannot negate the *bitter necessity* of the Eifeler migration in general. . . . Much more decisive than the only modest development of agriculture in this context is the absolute decline of industry in the Eifel. . . . The industrial regions of the Rhineland on the Inde, Ruhr, and Saar were strong enough from 1840 to 1870 slowly to eliminate the industry of the Eifel, but not yet strong enough to hold the majority of those Eifelers lacking bread and to prevent them from leaving the Fatherland.[25]

A related issue needing consideration is the influence of urbanization and industrialization and the extent to which internal migration posed an alternative to overseas emigration. Some of the most extensive work in this area has been done by Scandanavian scholars, thanks to the detailed system of parish registry in Sweden. An important outgrowth of this research is the concept of "urban influence fields," the observation

---

1955 (Bonn, 1961), pp. 22–27. It is true, however, that *Kreis* Prüm, which until the nineteenth century had a form of indivisible inheritance (p. 34), had the lowest population density in the Eifel and a low emigration rate, but industry was also not so heavy there.

[24] Ibid., p. 45.

[25] Ibid., p. 52. On the decline of the Eifel, see also Tipton, *Regional Variations*, pp. 79–80, 131–132.

CHAPTER I

that "expanding larger towns and cities attracted the population in the surrounding rural areas and thereby curbed the amount of emigration to America." This effect was naturally most widespread from a large city such as Stockholm but often extended as far as twenty kilometers from a town as small as 20,000. The same phenomenon is observable in other countries as well, for instance, in the Netherlands. The three most urban provinces—North and South Holland and Utrecht—together constituted about one-third of the Dutch population but were responsible for less than one-fourth of the mid-nineteenth-century emigration. Likewise in Denmark, the city of Copenhagen was surrounded by a zone of extremely low emigration, and the same is true to some extent for Danish provincial towns.[26]

Emigration from nineteenth-century Germany shows evidence of urban influence fields similar to other areas of Europe. The influence of urbanization and, perhaps more important, industrialization has already been seen in the low rates of emigration from the Ruhr valley, Silesia, the Kingdom of Saxony, and Berlin. Further evidence is presented in Table 1.5, which compares emigration rates from a number of cities with those from the surrounding and administratively separate rural *Landkreis* and then with the whole District in which both were located.[27] Münster, Trier, Freiburg, and Karlsruhe fit the model especially well, showing a regular upward progression in emigration rates as one moves away from the city. Osnabrück and Stuttgart both had relatively low emigration rates, but apparently were not growing fast enough to absorb much population from the surrounding countryside. With Brunswick, too, the contrast with the rural surroundings is less than spectacular. But emigration rates from Berlin regularly ranged from one-third to less than one-half that of its hinderland, the District of Potsdam. All these figures underscore further the point that German emigration was disproportionately rural in origin.

[26] Harald Runblom and Hans Norman, eds., *From Sweden to America: A History of the Migration* (Minneapolis, 1976), pp. 134-136, 158-159; Robert P. Swierenga and Harry S. Stout, "Dutch Immigration in the Nineteenth Century, 1820-1877: A Quantitative Overview," *Indiana Social Studies Quarterly* 28 (1975): 17-23; Kristian Hvidt, *Flight to America: The Social Background of 300,000 Danish Emigrants* (New York, 1975), pp. 40-63.

[27] Sources of Table 1.5: Munster emigrant lists, see Appendix A; Kiel, "Gründe and Folgen," p. 176; *Beitrage zur Statistik des Herzogthums Braunschweig* 1 (Brunswick, 1874); Josef Mergen, *Die Amerika-Auswanderung aus dem Stadtkreis Trier im 19. Jahrhundert* (Trier, 1962), p. 74; *Zur Statistik des Königreichs Hannover* 9: 2-12, 134-159; Bödicker, "Einwanderung und Auswanderung," p. vii; *Beiträge zur Statistik der inneren Verwaltung des Grossherzogtums Baden* 5 (1857): 1-35; Hauptstaatsarchiv Stuttgart, Innenministerium, E 143, Bü. 491; E 146, Bü. 1793.

TABLE 1.5. AVERAGE YEARLY EMIGRATION FROM SELECTED GERMAN
CITIES AND THEIR HINTERLANDS
(per 10,000 Inhabitants)

	City	*Landkreis*	District
Münster, 1832–1850	4	8	16
Osnabrück, 1832–1866	25	95	92
Hannover, 1859-1861	6	1	14
Brunswick, 1853–1860	17	17	24
Trier, 1855–1863	14	21	27
Stuttgart, 1854–1855	17	92	101
Karlsruhe, 1850–1855	10	53	91
Freiburg i.B., 1850–1855	17	27	64
Berlin, 1844–1859	3	—	7
Berlin, 1860–1866	5	—	13
Berlin, 1867–1871	3	—	12

SOURCE: See note 27.

The choice between the alternatives of internal versus overseas migration was not, however, governed entirely by proximity to urban areas, as Figure 1.3 indicates. The predominance of protoindustrial regions in overseas migration from Westfalia continued at least until the time of German unification. The five *Kreise* of Minden-Ravensberg alone were responsible for nearly 44 percent of all emigration from the province, and Tecklenburg and Ahaus also experienced a heavy exodus. But the most striking feature of the map is the negative correlation between emigration overseas and internal migration to the city of Bochum in the booming coal fields of the Ruhr. Though much of the city's population was recruited from the neighboring countryside, there was also a considerable longer-distance migration, nearly 12 percent from *Kreis* Höxter alone, and sizable amounts from Paderborn, Büren, Warburg, and Brilon as well. Distance alone or difficulties of transportation hardly differentiate these areas from Minden-Ravensberg, especially after 1850 when the Cologne-Minden Railroad Company gave the latter direct connections to the heart of the Ruhr. Most internal migration from protoindustrial areas probably flowed toward Bielefeld, for the city appears to have absorbed much of the potential emigration from its immediate hinterland.

It would, of course, be dangerous to draw sweeping conclusions from the experience of Bochum alone; migration to the textile centers on the Wupper may have followed different patterns. But it does ap-

CHAPTER I

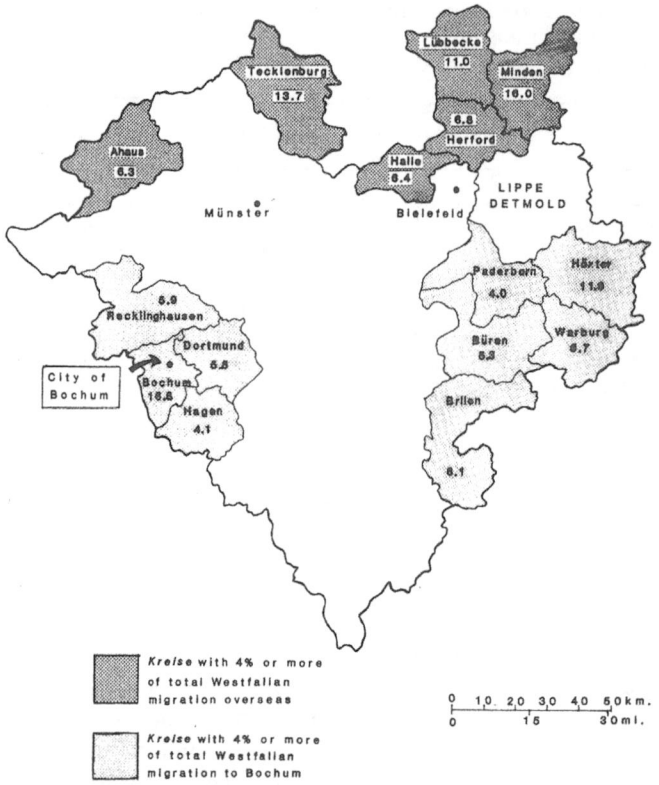

FIGURE 1.3
Sources of Heaviest Migration from Westfalia to the
City of Bochum and Overseas, Respectively
Source: See note 28.

pear that protoindustrial workers largely rejected the alternative of internal migration to centers of heavy industry in favor of overseas migration. Perhaps coal mining was simply too foreign to their work experiences, though many agricultural laborers made this transition. But Scandinavian research suggests that the most important factor was probably the preexisting tradition of emigration to America. Inhabitants of two Swedish towns reacted very differently to economic crises at the turn of the century, depending on their previous migratory traditions. In both cases, the response was a surge of out-migration, from one town directed overseas, from the other to other parts of Sweden, each following the path of earlier migrants. In the protoindustrial regions of Westfalia, emigration overseas had set in well before the Ruhr began its great expansion in the 1850s and was able to offer an alternative. Later migrants continued to follow these accustomed paths, while people from other rural areas without this migratory tradition were more likely to move to the Ruhr.[28]

Although it has been argued that protoindustry was the predominant factor in producing heavy rates of emigration from parts of northwest Germany, this is not to say that other factors were entirely without influence. Perhaps the most important of these was the *Hollandgängerei*, seasonal labor in the fields, dikes, and peat bogs of Holland. Like the linen industry, this practice was an important source of income for the rural lower class and also experienced its downfall in the early nineteenth century, so that the influences of the two are difficult to separate.

At first glance there appears to be a rough correlation between heavy emigration and large numbers of *Hollandgängers*. *Graftschaft* Diepholz, northeast of Osnabrück, had far and above the most migratory laborers in all of old Hannover and one of the highest emigration rates. Southern Oldenburg, including *Amt* Damme, was also home to a large number. *Amt* Bersenbrück, with the highest emigration rate in the Osnabrück District, also had by far the greatest number of *Hollandgängers*: over 3,000 according to an 1811 statistic. But four other *Ämter* in the District had emigration rates nearly as high despite numbers of migratory laborers ranging from 200 downward. *Amt* Lingen, with far greater numbers of *Hollandgängers* but little protoindustry, had an emigration rate lower than any protoindustrialized *Amt* but higher than those areas which had neither. The District of Minden experienced one of the heaviest emigrations in all of Prussia, despite the fact that out of a population of over 300,000 only around 1,000 laborers trekked to Holland yearly during the 1820s. In fact, at the *Kreis* level there is practically no correlation between emigration rate and participation in migratory labor. Though Tecklenburg accounted for over 40 percent of the *Hollandgängers* from the Münster District, the villages with the most migratory laborers generally had the fewest emigrants. The balance of trade in the tiny Principality of Lippe-Detmold also illustrates the relative economic importance of the two income sources. During the first five years of the nineteenth century, migratory labor brought only 6 percent as much money into the land as linen exports

[28] Runblom and Norman, *From Sweden to America*, pp. 161–163. Sources of Figure 1.2: internal migration from David Crew, "Industry and Community: The Social History of a German Town, 1860–1914" (Ph.D. diss., Cornell University, 1975), p. 50; emigration from *Preussische Statistik* 26 (1874): 304–318. There was, of course, some migration from Minden-Ravensberg to the Ruhr; the point is that it was small in comparison with overseas migration or with internal migration from other areas.

CHAPTER I

did, the latter accounting for over three-fourths of the total foreign exchange. The implication is that *Hollandgängerei* was considerably less important than protoindustry in inducing population pressure and emigration. Migratory labor was a less convenient side occupation than linen weaving and had a built-in safety factor that usually prevented such heavy concentrations of rural population as produced by protoindustry; seasonal migration was often the first stage of permanent emigration. According to an estimate from the late eighteenth century, one *Hollandgänger* in ten from the Osnabrück region failed to return each year.[29]

Another factor that is often cited as a cause of emigration is the *Markenteilung*, the division of common lands that took place in many communities around the beginning of the nineteenth century. There is no doubt that this worked to the disadvantage of the *Heuerling*, who was not consulted in the process and who usually lost the privilege of grazing his cows on the common pasture without gaining anything in return. Moreover, the division often created small parcels of infertile land that were of little use to large landowners, and so were sold or rented, thus allowing yet another family a precarious existence from protoindustry. Common lands were divided all over Germany but not always with the consequence of heavy emigration as happened in areas with concentrations of rural industry.

In fact, one of the forces behind the decision to divide the commons was that population growth often led to overuse and deterioration of the community pasture and forests, which could only be halted by turning them into private property. Thus, areas with heavy rural industry were frequently among the first to begin to divide their common lands. In Minden-Ravensberg, this had already begun by 1770; in Lippe, the first law passed in 1777; in Osnabrück after the year 1785, only a simple majority was necessary in a village to bring about division. In Tecklenburg, some communities had divided their commons before 1800. However, the proportion of common lands divided by 1853 in the Osnabrück District was near the average for the whole Kingdom of Hannover, and there is little correlation between the progress of division and the rate of emigration.[30]

---

[29] Statistics on *Wanderarbeiter* from Wilhelm Kleeberg, "Hollandgänger und Herringsfänger," *Neues Archiv für Landes- und Volkskunde von Niedersachsen* 2, no. 5 (1948): 200–201; Reekers, "Statistische Darstellung, Teil 3," p. 37; idem, "Statistische Darstellung, Teil 9," pp. 79–80. Emigration rates for Osnabruck from Kiel, "Gründe und Folgen," p. 176.

[30] Mager, "Protoindustrialisierung in Ravensberg," pp. 468–472; Hitzemann, "Auswanderung aus Lippe," pp. 25–26; Christa von Graf, "Johann Bertram Stüve und die

At first glance there appears to have been a close association between protoindustry and Protestantism, suggesting that a propensity toward either cottage industry or migration might simply be manifestations of greater enterprise in a Weberian sense. Indeed, the migration intensity in Protestant Minden-Ravensberg does stand in stark contrast to that in Catholic Paderborn. Likewise, Tecklenburg was one of the few Protestant areas in the Münsterland. But upon closer examination, one sees that Catholic weavers in *Kreis* Ahaus showed emigration rates rivaling those of the Tecklenburgers. If there were any nascent capitalists in the area, it was the *Tödden*, peddlers who carried their packs of linen goods all over northwest Germany and beyond—but they were predominantly Catholic. Other examples can be found in the Osnabrück region, where the arch-Calvinistic county of Bentheim had the lowest migration rates in the entire District. The protoindustrial areas of the former bishopric, a mixture of Catholics and Lutherans, showed consistently heavy emigration rates that had no correspondence to confession. If any more proof is needed, it is provided by *Amt* Damme, heavily Catholic, but with probably the highest emigration rates in the whole region.[31]

Though specific economic forces played a predominant role in influencing rates of emigration from the areas considered, the general economic health of different German states was probably not entirely inconsequential. Only part of the differences in emigration rates from Oldenburg and Osnabrück on the one hand and Tecklenburg and Minden on the other can be explained in terms of thoroughness of record keeping. The level of population decline in Oldenburg suggests that emigration was in fact highest there, and the difference in rates between Osnabrück and Minden continued even after 1866 when both were under Prussian administration. A certain hierarchy suggests itself here. Oldenburg was a small state in a backwater region with little potential for industrialization, its economic backwardness persisting in the postwar Federal Republic. Hannover was a medium-sized state with some beginnings of industry but was cut off from the potential markets of the *Zollverein* until 1854. Restrictions on internal migration and obstacles in the way of factory production further hindered the mobilization of an industrial labor force. More important than any direct inducements that Prussia offered the machine textile industry, or any obstacles that it placed in the way of overseas emigration, was the general economic

Befreiung des hannoverschen Bauerntums," *Mitteilungen des Vereins für Geschichte und Landeskunde von Osnabruck* 79 (1972): 33; Gladen, *Kreis Tecklenburg*, pp. 29–31; Linde, "Das Königreich Hannover," p. 443.

[31] Reekers, "Statistische Darstellung, Teil 3," p. 40.

CHAPTER I

climate within the state. Internal migration was completely unrestricted in an area comprising over half of Germany, and the already large potential market was further extended by the *Zollverein*. Thus within Prussia the alternatives to emigration were much more numerous and attractive than in smaller states, but the liberal Prussian freedom of trade and domicile applied only to its own citizens. In Hannover, and likewise in southwest Germany, restrictions on the rights of marriage and domicile greatly hindered population mobility and probably retarded industrialization, but succeeded less in lowering birthrates than in raising illegitimacy rates. Here was yet another factor in emigrant motivation, one in which social, economic, and political grievances were tightly intertwined.[32]

Although emigration from eastern Germany resulted primarily from the crass inequalities of land distribution in this region of Junkers and great estates, there were a few areas east of the Elbe where rural industry also played an important role. In Prussian Saxony, for instance, protoindustry was widespread, particularly in the Eichsfeld area, and the District of Erfurt to which it belonged ranked fifth in all of Prussia, right between Minden and Münster, in rate of emigration for the years 1844 through 1859. Silesia presents an exception to the general association between protoindustrial decline and emigration. Although many of the Old Lutheran emigrants from Silesia in the 1840s had been weavers, the emigration rate for the Liegnitz District was less than half that of Saxony. Several factors may account for this. Whereas the Elbe provided Saxons with a natural highway to the emigrant harbor of Hamburg, migration from Silesia was channeled down the Oder in the direction of Berlin. Silesians constituted that city's largest group of distant migrants in 1871. Because of the language barrier, potential emigrants were generally restricted to the German half of the population. The development of heavy industry within Silesia may have taken up some of the slack left by declining protoindustry, for the province generally showed a positive balance of internal migration during the 1850s.[33]

The present study also has important implications for students of American immigration and ethnicity. It is apparent that expulsive forces in Europe were the predominating factors in emigration before

[32] Linde, "Das Königreich Hannover," p. 434; Walker, *Germany and Emigration*, pp. 54–56; Adelmann, "Strukturelle Krisen," pp. 126–128; Klaus-Jürgen Matz, *Pauperismus und Bevölkerung: Die gesetzliche Ehebeschränkungen in den suddeutschen Staaten während des 19. Jahrhunderts* (Stuttgart, 1980).

[33] Bödicker, "Einwanderung und Auswanderung," p. vii; Hansen, *Atlantic Migration*, p. 139; Tipton, *Regional Variations*, p. 103.

1860 and that the people departing Germany were considerably less prosperous than has previously been assumed. This becomes even more evident when the occupational structure and personal characteristics of emigrants are examined in the next chapter. Thus the degree of socio-economic mobility that German immigrants achieved in America can only be understood adequately if one begins in Europe and investigates the occupational and social composition of the emigrating group.

CHAPTER II

Poor But Not Destitute: Personal Characteristics and Motivating Factors

The prosperity is ever more in decline. A considerable emigration to America has taken place. This was not rooted in any political motives, but simply the increasingly obvious realization that spinning and weaving are heading inevitably toward ruin. . . . So far this massive emigration has brought no appreciable relief to those remaining behind, all the less so . . . since only the more well-to-do Heuerlinge *emigrate, while the totally improverished families have to stay here for lack of means. Of course, the latter often help themselves in that the father of the family first goes alone, and then sends for the rest of the members later. Otherwise the emigration has not had any effect on the mood and conditions here, although it cannot be denied that the contentment of the* Heuerlinge *with their situation, has not been improved thereby.*[1]

THESE observations from the year 1852 by a local official in the Westfalian village of Heepen near Bielefeld address many of the issues that have concerned historians studying the social composition and motivation of the emigration. At first glance they seem to support the conventional view that political motivations hardly played a role, and that, because of the cost of passage, German emigration was largely middle class in character. But a closer look reveals a more complicated situation. First of all, the term *well-to-do* is greatly relativized when applied to *Heuerlinge*, but the account goes even further, conceding that the "totally impoverished" often found a way to America by sending one family member ahead to earn passage for the rest. Though denying any political motivation for emigrants, even this local official, who might have tended to whitewash the situation, does not equate this with civic contentment. A more objective viewer might conclude that economic and political motives were often so closely intertwined as to be nearly inseparable.

Because of the difficulty of obtaining any direct evidence about the motives of the mass of German emigrants and the problems with eyewitness accounts such as that cited above, this chapter approaches the question empirically but indirectly from three different angles: the occupational structure and wealth of the emigrating group; factors, eco-

---

[1] "Statistisch-topographische Beschreibung des Amtes Heepen, 1800–1959," manuscript, Stadtarchiv Bielefeld, Hgb. 7, pp. 81ff.

nomic and otherwise, which were associated with the fluctuations of emigration rates over time; and the way in which political developments were related to social and economic motivation.

Previous scholarship has tended to view German emigration as largely apolitical and with a strong middle-class character. A typology of emigration offered by Peter Marschalck, classifying emigrants according to motivation, distinguishes among "religious," "political," "business-speculative," and "socioeconomic" reasons for emigration. Of the four motives, he argues, the first three played only a very minor role in nineteenth-century Germany. But when Marschalck breaks the category of the socioeconomically motivated down further by time period, he presents a relatively optimistic picture of the status of those who emigrated during the first half of the century. He characterizes the *Auswanderung* before 1865 as consisting "primarily of families of independent small peasants and artisans," with only a minority of the rural lower class.[2]

Similarly, Mack Walker sees rural proletarianization as a factor that affected emigration only indirectly, by heightening middle-class anxiety and inducing more prosperous individuals to emigrate while they still had the means. Though admitting in a footnote that "the *Heuerleute* [of Hannover and Oldenburg] were of a lower social and economic class than the usual Auswanderer" during the years from 1830 to 1845, Walker nevertheless argues that they "were not proletarians; they were rather *becoming* rural proletarians." Also referring to Hannover, Hans Linde insists, "It was not the rural proletariat who made up the main contingent of emigrants."[3] If we mean by *proletariat* those not owning the primary means of agricultural production—land—then the majority of emigrants certainly fall into this category. In fact, the rural lower classes often identified themselves as the proletariat in their protests and petitions in 1848.

However, instead of becoming bogged down in a problem of definition, a more fruitful route of inquiry is to examine the empirical evidence on the occupational structure of emigrants. For the District of Münster, a complete set of emigrant lists from 1832 to 1850 has sur-

[2] Peter Marschalck, *Deutsche Überseewanderung im 19. Jahrhundert* (Stuttgart, 1973), pp. 52–71; for a revised and edited English version, see Wolfgang Köllmann and Peter Marschalck, "German Emigration to the United States," *Perspectives in American History* 7 (1973): 499–541, esp. 503, 522.

[3] Marschalck, *Deutsche Überseewanderung*, pp. 82–84; Mack Walker, *Germany and the Emigration, 1816–1885* (Cambridge, Mass., 1964), p. 51; Hans Linde, "Das Königreich Hannover an der Schwelle des Industriezeitalters," *Neues Archiv für Niedersachsen* 5, no. 24 (1951): 431.

CHAPTER II

Table 2.1. Occupational Structure of Male Emigrants from Northwest Germany (1830–1860)

	Münster District 1832–1850	Kreis Tecklenburg 1832–1850	Munster District, Clandestine 1832–1850	Minden District[a] 1830–1860	Osnabrück District[a] 1830–1860
Agricultural Laborers and Tenant Farmers	45.3%	65.4%	67.8%	61.6%	68.0%
Cottagers and Smallholders	7.0	5.2	1.0	7.7	7.1
Middle and Large Peasants	6.9	6.0	0.6	6.7	4.4
Apprentices and Journeymen	7.0	3.3	6.0	6.3	3.6
Independent Artisans	28.3	16.2	20.4	13.0	13.3
Master Artisans	0.7	0.6	0.1	0.2	0.0
Industry, Commerce Government, and Service	4.8	3.2	4.1	4.5	3.4
Number of Cases	3,925	1,423	828	794	639

Source: Emigrant lists; see Appendix A.
[a] Includes emigrant lists from only a small part of the total District.

vived (see Table 2.1). Even though this region includes areas with little or no protoindustry, the rural lower class of *Heuerleute*, day laborers, and farmhands made up over 45 percent of emigrants indicating occupations; including cottagers and smallholders, many of whom were also dependent on rural industry, more than one-half of the emigrants are already accounted for. The next largest category is that of independent artisans: those who identified themselves neither as masters nor as apprentices. Weavers alone constituted nearly one-fourth of this group, and many engaged in agriculture alongside their crafts, suggesting the closeness of many of these individuals to the rural lower class. Emigrants who identified themselves as master artisans were extremely rare, and the combined categories of industrial, commerce, government, and service workers accounted for less than 5 percent of the emigrants listing an occupation.

Though constituting only about one-tenth of the Münster District, *Kreis* Tecklenburg, with its extensive rural industry, accounted for nearly one-third of the total emigration. Here the concentration at the lower end of the economic scale is even more pronounced—the rural lower class made up nearly two-thirds of the emigration; the addition of smallholders pushes the figure over 70 percent. The smaller proportion of artisans is due largely to the fact that in this area weaving was almost without exception a seasonal occupation combined with agriculture, thus falling under the rubric of *Heuerling*. Though the proportion of peasants with substantial holdings appears small, even this figure may be misleadingly optimistic. The next column shows the occupational profile of clandestine emigrants, mostly draft dodgers, who came to the attention of Prussian officials in the District of Münster. With over two-thirds of this group in the rural lower class, it becomes evident how lists enumerating only legally registered emigrants could give an exaggerated view of the prosperity of those departing Germany.[4]

Evidence from the Districts of Minden and Osnabrück is more fragmentary. The emigrant lists that have survived, however, confirm the general picture conveyed by the Münster lists. Indeed, with heavier rates of emigration than Münster, these areas also had a greater representation of the rural lower class. The Osnabrück source also included some rare information on the occupations of single women who emigrated. They were recruited from the same classes as their male counterparts and traveling companions. Four-fifths identified themselves as maids or servant girls (the German word implies as much agricultural labor as domestic service). Other occupations, such as seamstress or midwife, appeared only rarely. Emigrant lists from Brunswick seldom list female occupations, but do commonly give the occupations of parents of emigrants regardless of sex. Here, too, it is evident that unmarried female and male emigrants were of very similar social origins. Married emigrants generally were of slightly higher standing, but there was little tendency for emigrating men to have married up, except that apprentices showed an understandable fondness for masters' daughters.

The Duchy of Brunswick was included in this study partly because of

[4] In the emigrant lists collected by Müller (see Appendix A), about fifty emigrants from *Kreis* Tecklenburg listed *Kolon* as their occupation, but only eight were substantial landholders, the rest were *Kotter*, etc., according to Albin Gladen, *Der Kreis Tecklenburg an der Schwelle des Zeitalters der Industrialisierung* (Munster, 1970), p. 211. The term *Kolon* is troublesome; it can either denote a substantial peasant or be used as a collective term for any landowner. Missing data probably also bias the figures upward on the occupational scale.

CHAPTER II

TABLE 2.2. COMPARATIVE OCCUPATIONAL PROFILES OF EMIGRANTS FROM BRUNSWICK AND THEIR FATHERS (1846–1875)

	Emigrants		Fathers of Emigrants	
	N	%	N	%
Agricultural Laborers and Tenant Farmers	432	31.4	296	21.5
Cottagers and Smallholders	111	8.1	379	27.5
Middle and Large Peasants	27	2.0	149	10.8
Apprentices and Journeymen	447	32.5	46	3.3
Independent Artisans	203	14.7	205	14.9
Master Artisans	157	11.4	302	21.9
Total Agricultural	570	41.5	824	59.8
Total Artisan	807	58.5	553	40.1
TOTAL	1,377	100	1,377	100

SOURCE: Emigrant lists; see Appendix A.

an excellent run of emigrant lists; it belongs to the fringes rather than the heartland of protoindustry. The proportion of agricultural land devoted to flax culture was less than 7 percent, compared to about 20 percent in Minden-Ravensburg and 28 percent in Tecklenburg, and spinning rather than weaving was the main side occupation of the rural lower class. Not surprisingly, the rate of emigration was not so high for Brunswick as for other areas under consideration, nor was the emigrating group so concentrated at the bottom of the occupational scale, in part because the time span covered was somewhat later and the area somewhat more urban.

More important, the Brunswick lists provide a rare opportunity to examine the patterns of intergenerational mobility between emigrants and their fathers. For simplicity's sake, Table 2.2 is restricted to the six agricultural and artisan groups, and to the cases where data on both father's and son's occupation was available.[5] The emigrants had made a pronounced shift from agriculture to artisanship compared with the

[5] Walter Achilles, "Die Bedeutung des Flachsanbaus im südlichen Niedersachsen für Bauern und Angehörige der unterbäuerlichen Schicht im 18. und 19. Jahrhundert," in *Agrarisches Nebengewerbe und Formen der Reagrarisierung im Spätmittelalter und 19./20. Jahrhundert*, ed. Hermann Kellenbenz (Stuttgart, 1975), pp. 110–111; Ernst Wolfgang Buchholz, *Ländliche Bevölkerung an der Schwelle des Industriezeitalters: Der Raum Braunschweig als Beispiel* (Stuttgart, 1966), pp. 39–44. Of the Brunswick emigrants in the published lists (Appendix A), the approximately 13 percent who were not

previous generation. Whereas the fathers were divided almost 60/40 between agriculture and artisan trades, with their emigrating sons these proportions were more than reversed. Although the concentration of emigrants in the rural lower class was somewhat greater than with the fathers, the number of smallholders and especially substantial peasants was decisively smaller than in the previous generation. Among artisans the decline in number of masters was more than compensated for by huge increases in numbers of apprentices. A cross-tabulation showed that over 45 percent of the emigrating sons of smallholders, tenants, and agricultural laborers followed artisan vocations.[6]

The decline in protoindustry must have produced ripples throughout the local economy and contributed to the emigration of artisans producing for local trades as well. Many of the young men who in past generations would have found employment in linen production now crowded into other occupations. Among the artisan groups most heavily represented in the emigration were tailors and shoemakers, both trades requiring a minimum of capital and easily combined with small-scale agriculture. But without the income formerly generated by protoindustry, the local demand for artisan products declined just at the time these occupations were expanding, thus driving many marginal artisans to emigrate.[7]

The typical artisan, then, had little in common with the proud guild master of Mack Walker's German home towns—no craft tradition extending back over generations, no shop full of apprentices. In fact, textile workers and particularly linen weavers are groups that Walker specifically excludes from his generalizations about home-town guilds and artisans. Absolutely and proportionally, emigration was lighter from home towns than from small villages where artisanship and agriculture were still very much entwined. Many emigrating artisans were acquainted with farming from their youth, and it was not uncommon for them to till a small plot on the side. In terms of skill and training, they might still have been at an advantage over their jack-of-all-trades

---

peasants or artisans are excluded, as are those peasants and artisans whose fathers did not fall into these categories or listed no occupation at all. Thus the number of cases was reduced by almost half.

[6] In part this shift from agriculture to artisanship may have been temporary, conditioned by the life-cycle stage, but even among emigrants aged thirty and older, the same tendencies were present, though not so pronounced. Of emigrants in this age category, 43.6 percent were engaged in agriculture, compared to 60.9 percent of their fathers.

[7] Precisely this interpretation is also advanced for Oldenburg by Johannes Ostendorf, "Zur Geschichte der Auswanderung aus dem alten Amt Damme (Oldenburg)," *Oldenburger Jahrbuch* 46/47 (1942–1943): 189–190. See also Walker, *Germany and Emigration*, pp. 49–50.

CHAPTER II

American counterparts, but the motive of German artisans in emigrating was less to protect a trade than to gain security and independence. In this they differed little from the rural lower classes. Thus it should not be surprising that artisans often returned to agriculture in the New World, where land was available so cheaply by European standards.[8]

A further indicator of social standing is the amount of money emigrants took along with them. The Osnabrück lists for the whole period include such information, as do the Münster lists for the period from 1846 to 1850. A number of scholars have argued on the basis of the mean amount of money possessed by emigrants that they were relatively prosperous, forgetting that a few extreme cases can heavily inflate an arithmetic mean. A good illustration is the published statistics from *Amt* Osnabrück and Melle, both showing the average per capita wealth of emigrants to be slightly over 80 taler. Nearly identical mean values were calculated from individual information in emigrant lists for parts of these areas. But the median value—the wealth of the person at the fiftieth percentile—was much lower. Over half of the emigrants had to get by on 50 taler per person or less, and the bottom third had to do with 40 taler or less. Emigrants from the Münster District were slightly better off, not surprisingly since emigration was not so heavy there.

If the amounts cited above appear fairly generous, it should be remembered that ship's passage and travel expenses had to be covered with these sums. The Münster lists clearly stated this on their printed emigration forms, and similar instructions were given to officials in Osnabrück. In fact, this seems to have been the general practice in nineteenth-century Germany, holding true in Hesse and Württemberg as well. One exception was Oldenburg, where only amounts in excess of travel costs, 30 taler per capita, were recorded. During the period from 1852 to 1864, only one-third of all single emigrants and three-fifths of the families had additional resources, and with the peak emigration from 1852 to 1854, the proportion fell below half of all families and one-fourth of all single emigrants.[9]

---

[8] Mack Walker, *German Home Towns: Community, State, and General Estates, 1648–1871* (Ithaca, N.Y., 1971), pp. 22–26, 73–107, esp. 99.

[9] Published figures on money per emigrant calculated from Karl Kiel, "Gründe und Folgen der Auswanderung aus dem Osnabrucker Regierungsbezirk (1823–1866)," *Mitteilungen des Vereins fur Geschichte und Landeskunde von Osnabruck* 61 (1941): 176. For information on emigrant lists, see Appendix A. The published Münster emigrant lists did not include the amount of money taken along, but this was added to the data set from the original archival sources for the years from 1846 to 1850. The preprinted forms normally used by Prussian officials explicitly stated "inclusive of travel costs."

Regarding the wealth data in emigrant lists from other areas, a decree from 7 March

A breakdown by occupational categories shows a striking consistency between the Münster and Osnabrück data (see Table 2.3). If *well-to-do* and *Heuerling* were not contradictions in terms, they were nearly so. Subsumed under this occupational rubric were a few *Neubauer*, technically recent purchasers of small plots of land, but usually of *Heuerling* origins and so badly indebted that they were no better off than the latter. The favorable position of peasant propietors among the emigrants is very apparent. Their median wealth was more than double that of a *Heuerling*; with mean wealth the discrepancy was even greater. Single men were somewhat better off in per capita terms than those with families, but single women seldom had more than the bare minimum. Another striking feature is the fact that wealth in rural areas was almost entirely based on landownership. Village artisans who emigrated, especially if they had families, were hardly better off than the rural lower class. The wealth advantage of propertied peasants appears even larger when measured per family rather than per capita. Per capita, a *Heuerling* was worth about one-third as much as a landowning *Kolon*; per family, barely one-fourth as much. This does not necessarily mean that landowners had higher fertility rates. It probably reflects the fact that they usually had the means to travel in one party, rather than having to send someone ahead to earn money or leave someone behind.

It should be noted that clandestine emigrants, usually the poorest of the lot, are not included in these wealth breakdowns. This doubtlessly biases wealth upward, as is evident when one compares wealth figures

---

1845, bearing the signature of the Royal Hannoverian *Landdrostei*, Osnabrück, reads as follows: "In compliance with Our proclamations of 7 February 1834 and 18 December 1837, We herewith instruct all authorities of Our Administrative-District . . . 5. With the statistics on the amount of money taken along, in those cases where there is presumably no money on hand, in any case to report the amount of the cost of the voyage." The report of the *Amtsvogt* of Laer, an annual overview of emigration filed 1 January 1846, includes the following comment: "In handing in the . . . overview I remark obediently that in the sums of money the travel costs are included" (Staatsarchiv Osnabruck, Rep. 350 Iburg, Nr. 5030, pp. 396–397, 475). The same instructions applied in the areas from which the Osnabrück emigration lists used here were taken.

Similarly, at the end of a yearly report on emigration, an official in Württemberg commented that "under the information on money holdings, the shipping costs are also included, as far as they can be determined, so that the figure given in the summary represents the approximate sum that the emigrants to North America expended overall" (Hauptstaatsarchiv Stuttgart, Innenministerium, E 143, Bü. 489, Oberamt Besigheim, p. 23). Kurt Gunther, "Beiträge zum Problem der kurhessischen Auswanderung," *Zeitschrift des Vereins für hessische Geschichte und Landeskunde* 75–76 (1964–1965): 500–506. *Statistische Nachrichten über das Grossherzogtum Oldenburg* 9 (1867): 163–177. For information on the cost of passage, see Rolf Engelsing, *Bremen als Auswanderungshafen, 1638–1880* (Bremen, 1961), p. 117.

TABLE 2.3. WEALTH OF EMIGRANTS BY OCCUPATION AND FAMILY STATUS
(Münster and Osnabrück Districts)

	Münster District, 1846–1850			Osnabrück District, 1832–1858		
	Mean	Median	N	Mean	Median	N
Single Women, all	82	50	147	64	50	175
Single Women, occupation not given	97	51	83	71	40	38
Single Women, *Magd* (Maidservant)	58	50	55	62	50	130
Single Men, all	125	80	747	96	59	336
Single Men, occupation not given	170	62	95	105	51	42
Single Men, *Ackerknecht* (farmhand)	107	70	257	84	61	120
Single Men, *Dienstknecht* (chief hand)	—	—	—	104	60	36
Married Men, all	104	67	568	83	50	253
Married *Heuerling* (tenant farmer)	61	63	41	60	50	163
Married *Kötter* (middling peasant)	130	100	62	119	77	20
Married *Kolon*, etc. (full peasant)	377	214	25	255	167	19
Ackersmann (agricultural, status unclear)						
Single	188	101	80	—	—	—
Married	130	70	93	—	—	—
Tagelöhner, Arbeiter (day laborer, worker)						
Single	111	71	26	61	51	44
Married	58	50	79	71	45	4
Artisan						
Single	91	62	254[a]	87	51	57[b]
Married	77	63	188[c]	56	50	29[d]
Professional, Commerce, Government, Service						
Single	259	100	19	148	115	10
Married	191	150	14	236	50	5

SOURCE: Emigrant lists, see Appendix A. [b] Includes 16 journeymen. [c] Includes 3 journeymen and 10 masters. [d] Includes 1 journeyman.
[a] Includes 97 journeymen and 3 masters.

TABLE 2.4. WEALTH OF EMIGRANTS BY FATHER'S OCCUPATION, OSNABRÜCK DISTRICT (1832–1858)

Occupation of Father	Mean Wealth	N
Single Men, no occupation given		
Rural lower class	62.5	4
None given	63.3	29
Propertied peasant	96.0	10
Single Men, farmhands		
Rural lower class	58.6	7
None given	78.9	97
Propertied peasant	109.3	21
Single Women, all		
Rural lower class	49.9	32
None given	62.6	116
Propertied peasant	88.2	25

SOURCE: Emigrant lists; see Appendix A.

in *Kreis* Ahaus and *Kreis* Tecklenburg with the heaviest emigration rates in the District. One would expect wealth figures to fall below average in such areas. This held true in *Kreis* Ahaus, which had little clandestine emigration, but in *Kreis* Tecklenburg, so many poor people emigrated clandestinely that the wealth of those legally registered was about average. Not included in the tables are the few emigrants from the city of Münster, which was in a category by itself in both intensity and wealth of its emigration. Only thirty-eight single men emigrated from Münster during this time period, but they made up in wealth what they lacked in numbers, showing a mean figure of 240 taler, twice that of their rural counterparts. With only three families and one single female, the urban emigration also was distinguished by its predominance of young, single men.

The majority of the emigrating agricultural laborers and servant girls were children of the rural lower classes, but there were some children of landowners, often victims of indivisible inheritance, among this group as well. This was reflected in their financial situation. Children of propertyless parents took along only 60 percent as much money as landowners' children (see Table 2.4). Those who listed no father's occupation fell somewhere in between, but closer to the lower group, suggesting that most of them also stemmed from the lower rungs of society.

In terms of exchange rates, a taler was worth somewhat less than an

CHAPTER II

American dollar at the time. More important, however, are the wage rates prevalent in northwest Germany during the first half of the nineteenth century. Male farmhands earned between 1 and 2 taler per month, or at most 30 taler annually for an experienced *Grossknecht* (chief hand), plus free board and housing, primitive as the latter was. Their female counterparts seldom earned more than 1 taler per month unless they were weavers. Wages for weavers of either sex were quoted at about 2 taler per month plus room and board. Except for a few specialized trades, other artisans hardly earned more. As late as 1861, an official in Tecklenburg estimated that artisans earned only 20 to 30 taler annually above their costs of food and housing. Similarly, the daily wage rate of a *Heuerling* working for a landed peasant came to 2 or 3 taler monthly, meals included. But his work was demanded steadily only for certain seasons, such as harvest, when his own plot also required the most attention. Slack seasons were of course filled in by linen weaving. A sum of 60 taler thus represented several years' savings, though families, even if they were tenants, also converted to cash any livestock they owned and practically all their household goods except what they could carry on their backs. In summary, while it is clear that emigration offered no alternative to those directly threatened with starvation, this is by no means to say that the majority of emigrants were well-to-do. If they had heeded the advice in immigrant guidebooks, discouraging emigration for any family with less than 1,000 taler, 95 percent of the German emigration would have stayed at home.[10]

Related to the issue of wealth is the question of how nearly the occupational structure of the emigrating group mirrored that of the general population. The rural lower classes proved to be most heavily represented, not only in absolute numbers, but also in relation to the total labor force of the region of origin. In *Kreis* Tecklenburg in 1837, for every six *Heuerling* families there were nearly five landed peasants with various sizes of holdings. But the emigration from the years 1832 through 1850 included 175 *Heuerleute*, plus 30 day laborers of the same class, as compared to only 50 full-scale peasant farmers and 30 of middling sort. There were also 30 *Neubauer*, nominally landowners, but of a very marginal type. So the propertyless were overrepresented

[10] Johann Nepomuk von Schwerz, *Beschreibung der Landwirtschaft in Westfalen* (1836; facsimile reprint, Münster, 1979), pp. 112, 339; Wolfgang Mager, "Protoindustrialisierung und agrarisch-heimgewerbliche Verflechtung in Ravensberg wahrend der Frühen Neuzeit," *Geschichte und Gesellschaft* 8 (1982): 462; Gladen, *Kreis Tecklenburg*, pp. 47–49, 53, 130; Adolf Wrasmann, "Das Heuerlingswesen im Fürstentum Osnabrück," *Mitteilungen des Vereins für Geschichte und Landeskunde von Osnabrück* 44 (1921): 113; Ostendorf, "Auswanderung aus Damme," p. 220. Most of the wages are given in *Silbergroschen*, thirty of which equal one taler.

TABLE 2.5. Occupational Structure of Male Emigrants from Lippe-Detmold

	1840–1860	1860–1880	1880–1900
Einlieger (tenant)	31%	37%	23%
Kolon (landowner)	34	29	19
Knecht (farmhand)	0.8	3	11
Ziegler (brick worker)	0.5	4	20
Kaufmann (merchant, etc.)	5	10	9
Handwerker (artisan)	20	17	18
Data missing		— approx. 25% —	

SOURCE: Hitzemann, "Auswanderung aus Lippe," p. 21.

by a factor of nearly two to one. Even among the landowners it appears that those with smaller holdings predominated in the emigration. The tertiary sector was also considerably underrepresented, making up a good 10 percent of all family heads in 1828, but not even 3 percent of the emigration. The emigrants from southern Oldenburg between 1865 and 1880 showed similar patterns. Compared to their share of the labor force, artisans were underrepresented in the emigration by a factor of two, government and professionally employed by a factor of three. The differences with trade and transport workers were negligible. Though agriculture as a whole was only slightly overrepresented, those emigrating were mostly farmhands or tenants, while landowners, particularly those with larger holdings, were rather rare among the emigrants.[11]

The occupational structure of the emigration from Lippe (see Table 2.5) follows the same general outlines as that from other protoindustrial areas, though the categories used here are somewhat different. The number of agricultural laborers seems implausibly low in the early years, but many of the individuals for whom data are missing probably belong in this category. Also, these figures apparently do not include clandestine emigrants, a group consisting largely of draft-age males, the majority of whom were no doubt agricultural laborers.

Perhaps even more surprising at first glance is the number of land-

---

[11] Gladen, *Kreis Tecklenburg*, pp. 203–205; the emigration figures include the towns of Ladbergen and Lienen, those on occupation do not, but since the economic structure of the whole area was so uniform, the differences would be negligible (Ostendorf, "Auswanderung aus Damme," pp. 204, 238–242). According to Kiel ("Grunde und Folgen," p. 7), only about 250 landowners emigrated from the Osnabrück region before 1848; that would come to only about 5 percent of the 4,500 heads of families who emigrated from that area during this period.

CHAPTER II

owners emigrating during the early years. But included in this figure are cottagers and smallholders, many of whose holdings were small indeed, since provisions against division of inheritance were not so strict in Lippe as in Westfalia. In a survey from 1852, nearly three-fourths of the landowners belonged to the categories possessing less than 15 acres of land, often much less, as their designations suggest: *Strassenkötter, Hoppenplöcker* ("road cottager," "hops picker").[12] Thus the great majority of the landowners were just as dependent on linen weaving as were the *Einlieger*, Lippe's equivalent to *Heuerleute*. Though this may be an extreme case, *Amt* Oerlinghausen in 1845 had 1,100 *Einlieger* families and 415 landowners. But even of the latter, only 81 could live on agriculture alone, while 334 were dependent on other income, primarily from weaving and spinning.[13]

Nevertheless, though Lippe was nearly as dependent on the linen industry as Minden-Ravensburg, emigration rates remained relatively low: under five per thousand even during the peak years from 1851 to 1855. The main reason was the development of seasonal migration to work in the brickyards of industrializing cities, a more modern replacement for the old *Hollandgängerei* (migratory laborer in Holland). The rise of migratory labor corresponded very closely with the downfall of the linen industry. From 1838 to 1845, the amount of sales at the main linen market in Lemgo fell by half, while the number of brickworkers doubled; during the next decade, this halving and doubling repeated itself, and from that point on the number of seasonal migrants continued to climb. Thus for many natives of Lippe, migratory labor presented an alternative to emigration, though toward the end of the century brickworkers, too, began to emigrate more heavily.[14]

In discussing causes of emigration, it is important to distinguish between predisposing factors (long-term developments that caused individuals to weigh the alternative of emigration) and precipitating factors (those which led immediately and directly to the decision to emigrate). The decline of protoindustry clearly falls into the former category, so it might not be expected that short-term fluctuations in linen prices would evoke an immediate response in terms of emigration rates.

Still, it is useful to look at the relationship between linen prices and rates of emigration as they developed over time, and also to relate them to grain prices, since many of the areas and individuals under consid-

---

[12] Source of Table 2.5: Herbert Hitzemann, "Die Auswanderung aus dem Fürstentum Lippe" (doctoral diss., University of Münster, 1953), p. 21; Fritz Fleege-Althoff, *Die lippischen Wanderarbeiter* (Detmold, 1828), pp. 32–37.

[13] Peter Steinbach, *Der Eintritt Lippes in das Industriezeitalter* (Lemgo, 1976), p. 66.

[14] Fleege-Althoff, *Wanderarbeiter*, p. 68.

TABLE 2.6. TIME SERIES ANALYSIS
(Correlation between Annual Emigration Rates and Linen Sales and Rye Prices in the Osnabrück District, 1835–1860)

	Emigration Rate, Current Year	Emigration Rate, Following Year	Emigration Rate, Current Year and Next Two Years
Rye Price	.10	−.00	.03
Income from Linen Sales	−.29	−.16	−.26
Income from Lines Sales/Rye Price	−.28	−.11	−.21

SOURCE: See note 15.

eration were not agriculturally self-sufficient. For the region of Osnabrück, there exists a continuous series of statistics on the value of linen sold at the *Legge* (state-regulated grading and marketing establishment), the yearly average rye price, and the annual totals on emigration from the District. Although Hannoverian statistics continue through 1866, the period from 1835 to 1860 was used here to avoid the distorting effects of the American Civl War. The war discouraged immigration to the United States and at the same time boosted linen prices by restricting the supply of cotton; it thus might create a false impression of a direct association between high linen prices and low emigration.

As can be seen in Table 2.6, a certain amount of correlation does exist between economic trends and intensity of emigration, but the weakness of association suggests that there were other important factors involved that are not captured by these economic variables. It is apparent that the rate of emigration was affected more by the market for linen goods than by grain prices. Association with the price of rye was very weak, though the sign is in the expected direction for a population dependent to some extent on food purchases: the higher the grain price, the heavier the emigration. The value of linen sold has a mild negative association with emigration rates, and in contrast to grain prices, its effects continued over several years. Though it would be a mistake to read too much into such small variations in correlation coefficients, it appears that the strongest associations with emigration rates are produced by the linen variable; the terms of trade between rye and linen have less predictive power than linen sales alone. In terms of R^2 values, the latter variable explains about one-tenth of the variation in emigra-

CHAPTER II

tion rates. While protoindustrial decline was clearly more important than bad harvests as a factor behind emigration, there still remains much to be explained.[15]

It is apparent from a graph of the yearly trends of emigration rates (see Figure 2.1) that the relative influence of economic factors varied from time to time.[16] The onset of emigration in the 1830s came at a time when income from linen was still rising, suggesting that other factors, such as propaganda and political convictions, were more important motivations for the initial phase of emigration. The value of linen sales reached its peak in 1838 and then in two years fell precipitously to the level of the early 1830s, and held there for several years. The further downward trend, beginning in 1844, corresponded with the heaviest emigration wave of the period. Similarly, Westfalian linen sales had fallen by 1846 to only one-fourth their 1840 level. The peak of emigration in 1845 occurred when the burden of decreasing income from linen was exacerbated by skyrocketing grain prices, though emigration fell back in 1846 just as grain prices peaked. The end of the decade saw relatively favorable terms of trade and a moderation of emigration rates. Rising grain prices and falling linen sales pushed up the emigration rate again in the early 1850s, though not to the height of the 1840s. But emigration fell sharply from 1854 to 1855, though grain prices reached record heights in the latter years. Apparently, disturbing reports from America had served to dampen the enthusiasm for migration. This is precisely when the nativist movement made its greatest advances, and anti-immigrant riots swept a number of major American cities.[17]

---

[15] Sources of data used in time series analysis: *Zur Statistik des Königreichs Hannover* (Hannover, 1850–1867), vols. 6, 12 for rye prices; vol. 9 for emigration figures; linen sales and production figures from Hermann Wiemann, "Die Osnabrucker Stadtlegge," *Mitteilungen des Vereins fur Geschichte und Landeskunde von Osnabrück* 35 (1910): 59–60. My dissertation also includes a price series for linen, calculated by dividing earnings by production figures. I have since learned from Jurgen Schlumbohm that the units of production were not consistent over time, and thus useless for calculating prices. The figure on emigration in the third column is in effect a three-year moving average, lagged one year. The table in the dissertation and German version includes a column of correlations erroneously titled "Emigration Rate Current Year and Next Two Years"; in fact, it is not a lagged but an *unlagged* three year moving average. See Kamphoefner, "Transplanted Westfalians: Persistence and Transformation of Socioeconomic and Cultural Patterns in the Northwest German Migration to Missouri" (Ph.D. diss. University of Missouri, 1978), p. 85.

[16] For the sources of Figure 2.1, see n. 15 above.

[17] Gladen, *Kreis Tecklenburg*, p. 65; Marcus Lee Hansen, *The Atlantic Migration, 1607–1860* (Cambridge, Mass., 1940), pp. 300–306; Philip Taylor, *The Distant Magnet: European Emigration to the U.S.A.* (New York, 1971), p. 115.

POOR BUT NOT DESTITUTE

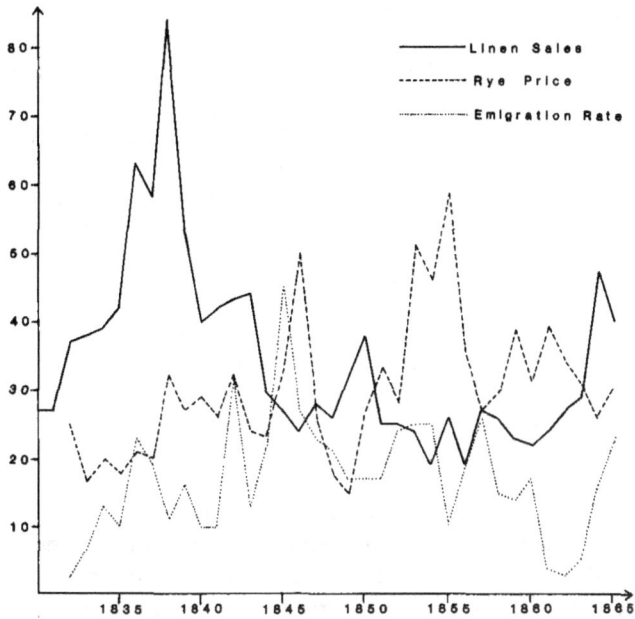

FIGURE 2.1
Time Series Analysis (Yearly Trends of Linen Sales, Rye Prices, and Emigration Rate in the Osnabrück District, 1830-1860)
Source: See note 15.

The American Civil War provides another example of how conditions in the United States could retard or divert emigration. Migration rates were already low in the late 1850s due to an economic slump in America and of a recovery in Germany, but emigration from Osnabrück reached its nadir in 1862 when the fighting was at its fiercest and the Union cause looked darkest. In fact, Peter Marschalck regards much of the heavy emigration in the second half of the 1860s as a delayed response of people held back by the war.[18]

The Civil War also diverted a greater than normal portion of the emigration to destinations other than the United States. This held true for various regions of Germany. During the period from 1856 to 1870, over 60 percent of all emigrants from Württemberg (including those to other German states) had North American destinations, but the proportion fell below 42 percent in 1862 and below 37 percent the next year, not exceeding 50 percent again until 1866. In the Münster Dis-

[18] Marschalck, *Deutsche Überseewanderung*, pp. 40–42.

55

CHAPTER II

TABLE 2.7. DESTINATION OF EMIGRANTS FROM BRUNSWICK
(1846–1875)

	United States	South America	Australia, Africa, Asia	Total Number
1846–1850	98.6%	0.1%	1.3%	1,536
1851–1855	96.7	1.5	1.7	2,581
1856–1860	92.7	1.8	5.5	1,193
1861–1865	88.6	8.5	2.9	446
1866–1870	96.1	3.2	0.7	1,166
1871–1875	91.4	6.5	1.9	415
TOTAL	91.7	2.3	2.1	7,337

SOURCE: Brunswick emigrant lists; see Appendix A.

trict, over two-fifths of those bound for the Western Hemisphere in 1862 and 1863 chose South or Central America, although these destinations attracted less than one-seventh of all emigrants during the decade preceding 1871. In the Duchy of Brunswick (see Table 2.7), the Civil War was the high point of emigration to South America and the low point of emigration to the United States, though generally during periods of low emigration there was a slightly increased preference for other destinations.[19]

Different districts responded with varying intensity to bad news from America; the heavier the emigration, the greater the fluctuations. Figure 2.2 compares yearly emigration totals from three Districts of the Kingdom of Hannover. Since the three are nearly equal in population, the lines are on roughly the same per capita scale. In both the nativist crisis in 1855 and the outbreak of the Civil War in 1861, the drop in emigration was sharpest for Osnabrück and least for Lüneburg, the District of Hannover occupying an intermediate position in both emigration rate and degree of fluctuation.[20]

The greater drop-off in Districts of heavier emigration probably re-

[19] *Württembergisches Jahrbuch* (1870), p. 22; *Preussische Statistik* 26 (1874): 319; source of Table 2.7: emigrant lists, see Appendix A.

[20] Source for Figure 2.2: *Zur Statistik des Königreichs Hannover*, 9: XVI–XVIII. The Districts of Hannover and Lüneburg each had about 360,000 inhabitants, the Osnabrück District only 260,000, so in effect the relative intensity of emigration from the latter is somewhat underestimated in the graph. (Georg Krieg, "Entwicklung und gegenwärtiger Zustand des Auswanderungswesens im Königreich Bayern," in *Auswanderung und Auswanderungspolitik in Deutschland*, ed. Eugen von Philippovich [Leipzig, 1892], pp. 90–93, shows a similar pattern for Bavaria.)

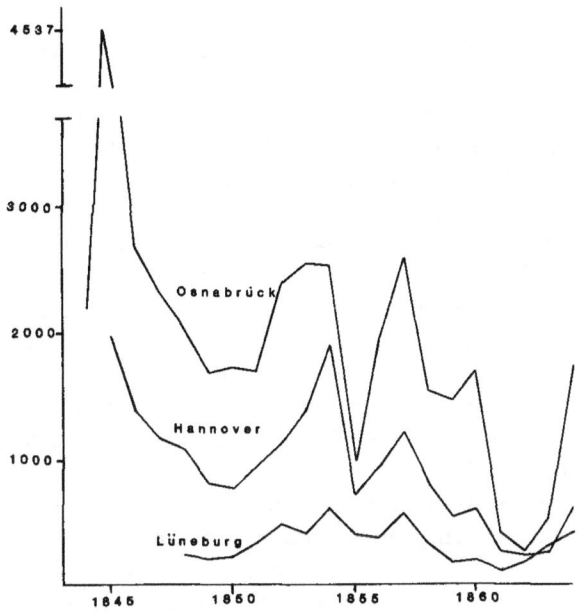

FIGURE 2.2
Yearly Emigration from Three Districts of the Kingdom of Hannover
Source: See note 20.

sulted from chain migration; from such areas there were more potential bearers of bad news in America. The most trusted reports from the New World were those received on a personal basis: letters from relatives and friends. The decline of emigration rates around 1849, however, appears to have been relatively uniform for all three Districts of Hannover, suggesting that conditions within Germany—in this case, lower food prices—were involved.

Another way to look at this is to regard emigration as a combination of two different streams. The first and largest is what Marschalck calls "socioeconomic" emigration, responding mainly to expulsive forces in Europe and fluctuating widely from year to year. The second, smaller stream resembles Marschalck's "business-speculative" category of emigration, a relatively constant background radiation of speculators, adventurers, and persons with idiosyncratic motives. The latter, of course, made up a comparatively greater proportion of the total in regions and in years of low emigration.

It is unlikely that emigration agents and their propaganda had much influence on the volume or direction of migration. The older, nationalistic school of German scholarship put a good deal of emphasis on this factor, often citing statements from local officials, pastors, and the like to support their case. But it was precisely these social groups that perceived emigration as a rejection of their authority and of the existing social order. For them, agents provided a handy scapegoat, a means of asserting that the world was still in order and denying that emigration stemmed from deeply rooted socioeconomic causes. Instead, the network of agents should be viewed primarily as a service organization, which channeled and facilitated the emigration, but did little to convince people who were not already inclined to make the move. During the 1850s, Prussian officials actually kept records on the number of persons booking with agents. These tabulations show that only about one-third of the emigrants from the Münster District availed themselves of such services.

The Germans have a proverb, "Lies have short legs" and this is particularly true in the case of emigration propaganda. Chain migration provided a vigilant control mechanism. If advertisements were not true, they were only effective for one season; thereafter, letters to friends and relatives would set things straight. There is evidence of this just in the bare emigration figures at the *Kreis* or District level. An exotic destination such as Algeria, South Africa, or some South American state is suddenly the rage and attracts a large share of emigrants for one year. But it usually disappears just as quickly from the list once unfavorable reports start trickling back. In 1847, for example, nearly two hundred emigrants from Westfalia and Osnabrück, including thirty-six from the village of Westerkappeln, were recruited to South Africa. However, they met with difficult times and unkept promises upon arrival. As a result, these were apparently the only emigrants from Westerkappeln to South Africa during the whole nineteenth century. Thus, upon closer observation, the influence of emigration agents and recruiters proves to be little more than a myth.[21]

Another of the myths that has been rather effectively laid to rest is that the great surge of German emigration that reached its climax in 1854 was primarily a political reaction to the failed revolution of 1848. As Peter Marschalck points out: "This rise has led many to attribute political motives to the emigration. In this case, the causes of emigration have unquestionably been confused with the events that precipitated it.... The great mass of emigrants at this time left their homes for

[21] Staatsarchiv Münster, Regierung Münster, 131, I–IV; Friedrich E. Hunsche, *Auswanderung aus dem Kreis Steinfurt* (Steinfurt, 1983), pp. 271–286.

other than political reasons." While nearly 240,000 Germans turned their backs on the Fatherland during the peak year of 1854 alone, Marschalck estimates that "the number of politically motivated did not exceed a few thousand."[22]

One must be careful not to take this corrective too far, however. It is apparent that the majority of German emigrants were not politically motivated in the sense that the Forty-eighter intellectuals were. Granting this, however, several important qualifications need to be made. There was a political emigration in response to the unsuccessful revolution of 1830 that had more in common with the Forty-eighters than is generally realized. The bulk of German emigration, however, consisted not of such intellectual and bourgeois types, but of people of peasant stock. Most of the rural emigrants of the 1850s had probably never lifted a hand in anger against the state; few of them had any abstract concept of democracy. But it is important to realize the degree to which the economic problems and the political powerlessness of the rural lower class were interrelated. The revolutionary activity in rural areas and the emigration both before and after 1848 were nourished by many common discontents.

The growing tensions between propertied peasants and the rural lower classes, though of long gestation, first became clearly visible in the revolution of 1830. In the Duchy of Brunswick, the *Häuslinge* (the local equivalent of *Heuerling*) in a half-dozen or more villages publicly protested their difficult economic situation, in several instances threatening local authorities or breaking their windows, though in general they were content merely to "make known rather loudly their dissatisfaction with the hard [*nahrungslosen*] times, the high grain prices, the rents that had jumped sharply, and the taxes with which they were burdened." The class tensions inherent in the situation are illustrated by the decision of the property holders of several villages to form voluntary associations to preserve order.[23]

Whether such sharp confrontations developed in the Münster-Osnabrück region is difficult to say, but similar sociopolitical tensions were centainly present. As early as 1800, a pastor traveling in the Osnabrück region observed, "The *Heuerleute* are often more embittered against their landlords or *Colonus* than the latter may be against their noble estate owners." In another place, he characterizes such peasant proprietors as little tyrants who are often more strict than the big ones,

---

[22] Kollman and Marschalck, "German Emigration," p. 523; Marschalck, *Deutsche Überseewandergung*, pp. 57–58.

[23] Buchholz, *Ländliche Bevölkerung*, pp. 20–21.

CHAPTER II

and refers to the *Heuerleute* as "poor vassals in [the landowner's] miserable shacks." During the first half of the nineteenth century, the situation if anything deteriorated. "There were political disturbances [*Unruhen*] enough in the Osnabrück District," reports a historian of the emigration there, "in 1830 as well as in 1848."[24] The ideology of the 1830 revolution probably reached more of the working class in the villages than is commonly realized. A good illustration of this is an emigrant song of the early 1830s that circulated widely in the region of Osnabrück, southern Oldenburg, and northern Westfalia. It came to the attention of Prussian authorities in Tecklenburg, where, as a concerned administrator noted, it was on everyone's lips and was eagerly grasped by the "rabble." More important than the origins of the song was the receptive chord it struck with the populace. A version of the song turned up in an emigrant letter from Milwaukee to the middle Rhine in 1840, and others made their way into collections of folksongs as far away as Alsace in 1884 and Baden in 1910. Thus the song probably represents the mentality behind much of the emigration of the time.[25]

> Hail Columbus, praise to thee,
> We laud thee high eternally.
> Thou hast shown to us the way
> Out of our hard servitude,
> To save us, if we only dare
> To bid our Fatherland farewell.

So the song begins, and continues through forty-eight stanzas of spiteful and bitter doggerel. It speaks of the chains of slavery, of hunger and cares, of princes "who drive us to despair," their courts "who consume our marrow," their "brood of rats," the ministries, oppressive taxes of all kinds, and a class system of justice.

To this is contrasted the egalitarianism of America, "where the man

---

[24] J. G. Hoche, *Reise durch Osnabruck und Niedermünster in das Saterland, Ostfriesland und Groningen* (Bremen, 1800), pp. 74–83; Kiel, "Gründe und Folgen," p. 119.

[25] There are conflicting accounts of the origins of the Columbus song, but the earliest and most plausible is [H. A.] R[attermann], "Zwei Agitatoren der Auswanderung. II: Franz Joseph Stallo," *Der Deutsche Pionier* 7 (1875): 2–16. A different version, but also attributing authorship to a German immigrant in an American port city, is given by Kiel, "Gründe und Folgen," pp. 127–128. On the song's reception in Germany, see Gladen, *Kreis Tecklenburg*, p. 141; for the complete text, pp. 215–218, the source of all translated citations presented here. Günther Moltmann is conducting a more thorough study of emigrant songs generally and the Columbus song in particular. Preliminary results were presented at the symposium, Amerikaauswanderung im 19. und 20. Jahrhundert: Probleme und Ergebnisse historischer Migrationsforschung, Hamburg, April 1981.

from every station as a true brother is honored high." Class distinctions are unknown: "The wife of the mayor sweeps right along with the wife of the broom maker." If anything, class prejudices are reversed. "Here in the promised land the noble is despised by all / . . . and even the haughty baron counts for no more than the farmer's son." At times an almost millennial vision is evoked of the paradise across the sea.

But American freedom also has its more practical aspects: "Here the man from every station is free to hunt and fish." Guild restrictions (*Gewerbescheine*), too, are unknown, for "Here anyone who wants to can practice a trade if he's able." Taxes, where they exist at all, are moderate, "For we know no excise here / On salt or wine, on schnapps or beer." Military service is purely voluntary, in contrast to Europe, "Where, with his twentieth year, your son / Is drilled by a barbarian." Throughout the whole song, moreover, the perception is very apparent that economic harships are closely entwined with political injustice.

The unsuccessful revolution of 1830 is clearly in the background, as the next-to-last stanza illustrates:

> Brothers, I will not mislead you
> To rebellion, no, for heaven's sake
> If you can just afford the journey
> Come over here, don't miss your chance.
> If you revolt you're bound to lose
> As they've found out in Hesse, too.

If the political and socioeconomic grievances of the rural lower classes to a large extent remained latent in the revolution of 1830, or were given vent harmlessly in songs such as these, this was not the case in 1848. The divisions between haves and have-nots became abundantly clear in confrontations and violence that shattered the accustomed pastoral tranquillity of northwest Germany.

The revolutionary activity in rural areas was apparently strongest in the region around Osnabrück. In March 1848, the people took to the streets in a score or more rural villages, often venting their hostilities by stoning the houses of authority figures: tax collectors, local officials, pastors, and occasionally merchants. Troops were stationed in a number of communities, and where they were not, propertied burghers and landowning peasants often cooperated to establish civil guards. The large Prussian garrison at Minden acted as a damper on revolutionary activity in that region, but even so there were several incidents that required the calling out of troops: one in which 125 persons, and another in which over 60, were arrested. One of the hottest trouble spots was the spinning village of Spenge in the area of Bielefeld, where a crowd as

CHAPTER II

large as 350 men and 400 women and children were involved. As the *Landrat* (a local official) of Minden noted, the uprisings were "primarily in those parts of the *Kreis* where poverty was most prevalent." As late as November 1848, there were still street clashes and "excesses." One demonstration in Lippe involved over a thousand people and resulted in the summoning of troops from Detmold. In Tecklenburg also there was at least one outbreak serious enough to bring out the troops, although here the greatest discontent was found in villages where class tensions were reinforced by confessional differences, the Catholic minority being forced to pay taxes in support of Protestant clergy.[26]

But the rural lower class showed its dissatisfaction not only through street demonstrations against symbolic enemies and toward rather indistinct goals, but also in a number of petitions to authorities that laid out their grievances in specific detail. The *Häuslinge* from 28 villages, nearly one-twelfth of the whole Duchy of Brunswick, combined in a petition to the throne seeking better treatment in renting land.[27] A petition from the village of Engter near Osnabrück, signed by 160 *Heuerleute*, made the following demands:

1. Complete relief from the head tax (*Personensteuer*)
2. Ending of the practice of purchasing substitutes for military service
3. Representation in the state assembly (*Landtag*) and the village council
4. Freedom from the school tax and other ecclesiastical taxes, and improvements in the common schools
5. Ending of all unpaid road work
6. Assignment of sufficient acreage in the divided and undivided common lands for free use
7. Regulation of rental conditions; no more unpaid service: fixed duration and price of rentals
8. Erection of a public institution for the care of old and invalid *Heuerleute*.[28]

[26] Secondary sources on the 1848 revolution in the Westfalia-Osnabrück region include Hans Joachim Behr, "Zur Rolle der Osnabrücker Landbevölkerung in der burgerlichen Revolution von 1848," *Mitteilungen des Vereins fur Geschichte und Landeskunde von Osnabrück* 81 (1974): 128–146; Wilhelm Schulte, *Volk und Staat: Westfalen im Vormärz und in der Revolution 1848/49* (Münster, 1954); Gladen, *Kreis Tecklenburg*, pp. 163–168. Hermann von Laer, "Protoindustrialisierung und Industrialisierung in Ostwestfalen" (undergraduate thesis, University of Munster, 1971), pp. 80–89; Wrasmann, "Das Heuerlingswesen," 44: 102–120. The best primary source is the liberal *Osnabrücker Tageblatt: Von und für Jedermann*, founded in 1848. The Münster *Westfalischer Merkur* also provides some information from a less sympathetic point of view.

[27] Buchholz, *Landliche Bevölkerung*, p. 22.

[28] Behr, "Landbevolkerung in 1848," p. 134, citing from *Osnabrücker Tageblatt*, 16

Most scholars dealing with this subject point out that the demands of the *Heuerling* and *Häusling* involved immediate economic interests rather than any political issues. But the language of the petitions shows how closely the two were intertwined: "We are obliged to pay taxes and render military service, and formerly road work, too, but are not represented in the *Landtag*."[29] Regarding military service: "Those with means can purchase a substitute, but we, the proletariat, must . . . bleed for the so-called Fatherland." The disadvantages of taxation without representation were even more serious on the local level: "We are responsible for school, church, and other taxes, but are neither represented nor consulted in the village council about measures that affect our interests."[30] Foremost among these was the division of common lands, whereby the *Heuerling* lost grazing and pasture land, wood for fuel, and peat for mulching crops—rights previously enjoyed for generations by custom but without legal base.[31]

Theodore Hamerow sees the roots of failure of German liberalism in its timidity, its unwillingness to expropriate the aristocracy and make the peasantry its partner in crime. He quotes a petition similar to those cited above, signed by two thousand persons from Minden-Ravensburg, as a radical demand for government sponsorship to establish peasant proprietors. Hamerow may be right about German liberals, but he fails to see that in northwest Germany, the main class conflict was not peasants against nobility, but the rural lower classes against peasant proprietors, who had less to fear from above than from below. The petition he cites specifically mentions *Heuerleute*, and calls for local governments on the basis of universal suffrage and a progressive income tax, both measures that would redress the political powerlessness of the lower classes and the resulting economic inequities. A closing statement, not cited by Hamerow, stresses the *"principle of popular sovereignty"* (italics in original) as the basis for a new constitution. By 1848, whatever paternalistic *Gemeinschaft* had once existed in rural communities had long since been destroyed, as the tensions between landowners and the propertyless clearly demonstrated. This confrontation was political as well as economic, and was perceived in class terms both by the peasant aristocracy and the rural proletariat. A well-

---

April 1848. For other, similar petitions see Wrasmann, "Das Heuerlingswesen," 44: 102–115.

[29] *Osnabrucker Tageblatt*, 15 April 1848.

[30] Ibid., 16 April 1848.

[31] Christa von Graf, "Johann Carl Bertram Stüve und die Befreiung des hannoverschen Bauerntums," *Mitteilungen des Vereins fur Geschichte und Landeskunde von Osnabrück* 79 (1972): 32–33.

CHAPTER II

known emigrant song begins with the line, "*Hier sind wir nur Bauernsklaven.*" This is usually taken to mean "peasant slaves," but at least in northwest Germany the interpretation "slaves of the peasantry" appears more plausible. As E. W. Buchholz perceptively observes with respect to Brunswick, "We see therefore the real roots of this revolutionary movement not so much in an acute economic crisis but rather in a social crisis, which resulted from the political dominance of the *Reiheeinwohner* [propertied peasants] and their economic monopoly."[32]

Conspicuously rare in all of the petitions of the *Heuerlinge* were references to the depressed price of linen wares, which had persisted since 1840. But there was a similar silence about the price of grain, which had skyrocketed with the bad harvests of 1846 and 1847 before moderating somewhat with the harvest of 1848. Both were regarded, it would appear, in much the same way as wars and natural catastrophies, as the results of impersonal forces that could only be endured with peasant stoicism. One of the few references to the linen industry came in the unsympathetic reply of a local official to one of the petitions from the Osnabrück region, that "the *Heuermann* in his side occupation restricted himself too much to the spinning and weaving of the same articles," instead of diversifying his production.[33] But the *Heuerleute* directed their protests in 1848 against social and political injustices, not against the economic developments that were part cause and part effect of the former.

To the extent that there was revolutionary activity in rural areas of northwest Germany, it was most intense in, and indeed primarily restricted to, regions of heavy protoindustrialization and high emigration. Purely agricultural regions remained largely quiet. In the Osnabrück District a definite hierarchy is apparent. Bentheim, a pastoral region with insignificant rates of emigration, did not produce a single political organization in 1848. In the areas where emigration (and protoindustry) was moderate, in Lingen only the bourgeoisie organized, and in Arenberg-Meppen the only agitation was over such local issues as retaining a *Gymnasium*, rather than for political principles. Only in the protoindustrial *Fürstentum* Osnabrück, source of the heaviest emigration, did the revolution take on a class character. Indeed, emigration and revolution can be regarded as two different responses to the

[32] Theodore S. Hamerow, *Restoration, Revolution, Reaction: Economics and Politics in Germany, 1815–1871* (Princeton, 1958), pp. 160–161; *Neue Rheinische Zeitung*, 16 September 1848; Wrasmann, "Das Heuerlingswesen," 44: 83; Buchholz, *Ländliche Bevölkerung*, p. 25.
[33] *Osnabrücker Tageblatt*, 14 May 1848.

same set of underlying causes.³⁴ But in Westfalia, the revolutionary activity in protoindustrial regions was overshadowed by the violent conflict in some of the cities on the Ruhr, where emigration had been minimal.

The rural revolution takes on added signficance, however, when put into perspective. In the Osnabrück region even the emigration of more than 1 percent of the population yearly and additional losses through internal migration were not adequate safety valves to prevent at least a mild explosion in 1848. By contrast, despite rates of in-migration that had doubled the population of the city of Iserlohn and of Ennepe-Ruhr *Kreis* between 1818 and 1843, a great majority of the newcomers had achieved a relatively successful integration into the economy and the society.³⁵ The social problem in the cities was not primarily home-grown, but rather transplanted from rural areas. Better opportunities for employment and higher wages than they had ever earned before had induced many rural proletarians to join the urban proletariat. But what they lost in the process was a potato patch to fall back on when bread was scarce, friends and relatives who could be counted on for a loan or perhaps a handout, and even an occasional sympathetic landowner who, during slack times, might retain a farmhand he did not really need. Therein lay the revolutionary potential of the industrial cities when boom turned to bust.

Another important difference was that the obstacles to revolution were much greater in the country than in the city. Once again, the remarks of a German historian with regard to Brunswick are very pertinent:

> It is, of course, impossible to make an objective comparison of the extent and significance of revolutionary activities in city and country. But one can draw a certain justification for emphasizing the significance of rural incidents just from the fact that the events in the village took place in full public view.... By comparison, the events in the city of Brunswick take on more the character of an anonymous tumult.³⁶

But to return to the original question, What was the effect of the revolution of 1848 on subsequent emigration, and how important were political motives to the mass of emigrants? The decline of emigration rates in 1848 and 1849 says little about this question. As Mack Walker

---

³⁴ Behr, "Landbevölkerung in 1848," p. 141; Graf, "Stüve und die Befreiung des Bauerntums," p. 34.
³⁵ Schulte, *Volk und Staat*, p. 110.
³⁶ Buchholz, *Ländliche Bevölkerung*, p. 25.

TABLE 2.8. CLANDESTINE EMIGRANTS FROM BAVARIA AND TECKLENBURG
(Number and Percentage)

	Kingdom of Bavaria		Kreis Tecklenburg	
	Number	% of Total	Number	% of Total
1840	1,146	15	79	36
1841	745	17	30	22
1842	885	21	7	7
1843	826	19	15	16
1844	975	17	15	13
1845	3,103	31	33	14
1846	4,605	35	62	16
1847	5,572	36	45	14
1848	3,835	40	172	61
1849	4,258	51	47	32
1850	4,530	54	7	15
1851	5,689	48	—	—
1852	4,821	24	—	—
1853	5,321	26	—	—
1854	5,641	23	—	—

SOURCE: Krieg, "Auswanderungswesen im Bayern," pp. 90–91; Tecklenburg from emigrant lists, see Appendix A.
[a] Fourth quarter of previous year through third quarter of current year.

has pointed out, there were enough reasons for emigration rates to subside without the revolution. After the good harvest of 1848, grain prices had returned to near normal, and in general the economy was picking up. And once the revolution broke out, it temporarily raised the hopes of the have-nots and placed additional obstacles in the way of the haves, adding to the uncertainty of travel and depressing land prices for those who had hoped to finance their journey by disposing of their holdings.[37] One trend that should be noted was the increase in clandestine emigration, observed by Walker in Bavaria and also evident from the Münster data (see Table 2.8). In part this may be attributed to the desire to escape military service, for to the indignity of being harangued by a Prussian drillmaster was now added the immediate prospect of being shot at in Denmark. But for many of the so-called primitive rebels from rural villages who had spontaneously taken to the streets in 1848 without the protection of urban anonymity, emigration was a haven from possible retribution once the old order was back in the driver's

[37] Walker, Germany and Emigration, pp. 153–157.

seat again. As the ranks of emigrants once again swelled in the early 1850s, among their numbers were no doubt a few whose middle-class anxieties had been awakened by the boldness of the lower classes in 1848. But much more numerous must have been those of the rural lower class who were in silent sympathy with the revolution, and who were now voting with their feet against an authoritarian state that demanded much of them and gave them little in return.

A study of the Lüneburg region, where emigration reached significant proportions only after 1848, concludes that the economic preconditions had already been present for some time, but required the catalyst of the revolution before migration would result. In the author's words: "We find the emigration movement ... explained by the *'restless fever of the Zeitgeist.'* Clearly the revolution of 1848 caught the imagination also of the lower classes, waking a sense of dissatisfaction, and if it did not cause the 'restless fever,' then at very least it sharply intensified it."[38]

Another indication that the spirit of 1848 inspired more German-Americans than just the political elite is the reception that the Hungarian revolutionary Louis Kossuth received in the United States, and not only in the large cities. An enterprising salesman in St. Charles, Missouri, tried to capitalize on these sentiments among immigrant farmers in 1852 by prefacing a newspaper blurb for a new shipment of Moline plows with the eye-catching headline "*Kossuth ist gekommen*!"[39]

Immigrant biographies also give occasional glimpses of the motives behind emigration. One St. Charles, Missouri, resident of rather humble artisan origins in Germany explained that he had "come to this country on account of his admiration of the free institutions of America" in 1854, and was not about to let "this free Republic" be broken up in 1861.[40]

Not given to false modesty, a college professor from the same area characterized himself as "a worthy representative of that large and better class of Germans whose fortunes were cast with this country by the events of the Revolution of '48." A merchant's son who had studied medicine in Germany, he went on to become an educator and Methodist minister in the United States. Among the other people he men-

---

[38] Theodor Penners, "Entstehung und Ursachen der überseeischen Auswanderungsbewegung im Lande vor 100 Jahren," *Lüneburger Blätter* 4 (1953): 122.

[39] *St. Charles* (Mo.) *Demokrat*, 3 April 1852. See also issues of 7 February and 13 March 1852 for examples of the attention given Kossuth in this county-seat weekly German newspaper.

[40] *History of St. Charles, Montgomery, and Warren Counties, Missouri* (1885; facsimile reprints, St. Louis, 1969), p. 389.

CHAPTER II

tioned as Forty-eighters were Carl Schurz and Daniel Siegel, and also Arnold Krekel, the last a prominent Missouri politician who had in fact emigrated with his parents in response to the 1830 revolution. But this is illustrative of the affinity that contemporaries perceived between the refugees of the two revolutions.[41]

The sentiments of many of the emigrants after 1830 are captured in one son's description of his father: "He enjoyed in his youth many advantages and was reared in the midst of affluence. But certain restraints were placed as a yoke upon him and weighed too heavily. Thus burdened he determined to turn his face westward to the New World, where liberty is the enchanted word, and where all are born equal."[42]

But such clear-cut expression of political motives were rare, even among the local elite featured in biographical sketches. More unusual yet were immigrants who expressed purely entrepreneurial motives. One such individual had been a banker and broker in Berlin, but suffered reverses and was forced to sell out. He managed to salvage $40,000 and with this fortune emigrated to Missouri. But as his son admitted, such a person "possessed advantages uncommon to the majority of the pioneers." Another entrepreneur on a smaller scale had been "a miller by trade . . . but not being satisfied with the government requirement," he emigrated in 1833. Eventually he became quite prosperous in America, but he began as a wage laborer and did not bring his family over until 1837.[43]

For the majority of immigrants—those of peasant stock—the motives for migrants were perhaps too obvious to require mentioning. Most biographies offered at best only a vague statement about the opportunities of America, often linking them with freedom. Among the typical designations for the United States were "the land of promise and liberty" or "the land of plenty and feedom."[44] Which of the two was more important, or how the two were related, were not questions that occurred to most immigrants. But an immigrant son probably spoke for the great majority in relating the reasons his father, a *Heuerling* and carpenter in Tecklenburg, came to Missouri: "He had left his native land owing to the limited chances there afforded the poor, and the wisdom of his venture was shown very soon after he reached the state, for he at once began to make his way upward."[45]

[41] Ibid., pp. 1100, 107.
[42] *Portrait and Biographical Record of St. Charles, Lincoln, and Warren Counties, Missouri* (Chicago, 1895), p. 407.
[43] Ibid., pp. 343, 395.
[44] Ibid., pp. 320, 554.
[45] Ibid., p. 247.

A German pastor related how he visited the same community in the mid-1830s and was called upon to baptize a child for one of the recently settled immigrants there, almost certainly another Tecklenburger *Heuerling*. After the baptism, the father proudly showed the fields that he had cleared with his own hands, and explained what emigration meant to him:

> You see, *Herr* Pastor, America is indeed a splendid land. Here a person can still acquire something. In Germany, I didn't have as much property as I could hold in my hand, and dared not hope, no matter how hard I worked and saved, ever to acquire any property. What you see here belongs to me. I have had to work terribly hard, that is true, but I have something to show for it, too. Here I have eaten more pork in one year than I have ever seen in Germany my whole life. We have plenty of potatoes, too; what more could we want, if we stay healthy?[46]

When such sentiments found their way back to Europe in immigrant letters, they were a more effective advertisement for emigration than all the books on the subject combined.

[46] J. G. Büttner, *Die Vereinigten Staaten von Nord-Amerika: Mein Aufenthalt und meine Reisen in denselben, vom Jahre 1834 bis 1841*, 2 vols. (Hamburg, 1844), 1: 200.

CHAPTER III

Transplanted Villages: The Effects of Chain Migration on Regional Distribution and Settlement Patterns of German-Americans

The letters that the first German settlers and those immediately following wrote back to their old home towns accomplished more than all the books about America and all the efforts of land agents combined....

When letters made the rounds in the former home towns, telling how the same people whose poverty was known to young and old, had in three or four years become owners of forty or perhaps even eighty acres of land ... it is understandable that these letters made a great sensation, and that everyone who could get away emigrated and sought out his old neighbors.[1]

IT IS CLEAR that immigrants from Germany and other parts of Europe did not scatter randomly across the American continent. Instead they formed very pronounced ethnic concentrations in certain locales. But as yet these patterns have scarcely even been documented in detail for German-Americans, much less adequately explained.[2] Among other ethnic groups, Scandinavians have led the way in migration research, using their excellent source materials to show that affinity between the economic structures of the sending and receiving areas often influenced where a Swedish immigrant settled. A study of Dutch emigration provides further evidence that the occupation of an immigrant affected his locational preferences. A Danish study comes to similar

---

[1] Gert Goebel, *Länger als ein Menschenleben in Missouri* (St. Louis, 1877), p. 49.

[2] A synthesis of theories of location, dealing with differences between groups but not with differences within them, is provided by David Ward, *Cities and Immigrants: A Geography of Change in Nineteenth-Century America* (New York, 1971), pp. 51–83. One indication of the need for work in this area is that most of the literature Ward cites is more than a generation old. Accounts, primarily descriptive in nature, of changing routes and developing technology of immigrant transportation include the following: Marcus Lee Hansen, *The Atlantic Migration, 1607–1860* (Cambridge, Mass., 1940); Mack Walker, *Germany and the Emigration, 1816–1885* (Cambridge, Mass., 1964); Maldwyn Jones, *American Immigration* (Chicago, 1960); Philip Taylor, *The Distant Magnet: European Emigration to the U.S.A.* (New York, 1971); Leo Schelbert, *Einführung in die schweizerische Auswanderungsgeschichte der Neuzeit* (Zurich, 1976).

conclusions, also arguing that the timing of emigration played an important role as a locational factor.³

The contemporary observer quoted above points up one crucial variable in the emigration process that has only very recently begun to gain the scholarly attention it deserves. *Chain migration* is "that movement," according to the definition of one sociologist, "in which prospective migrants learn of opportunities, are provided with transportation, and have initial accommodations and employment arranged *by means of primary social relationship with previous migrants.*"⁴ Since it is difficult for a historian to ascertain the extent of services provided by chain migration in the past, the evidence is of necessity indirect, but the effects of chain migration can be easily recognized from the concentration of an immigrant population of homogeneous origins in a given locality. The first part of this chapter gives an overview of German-American settlement patterns, presenting evidence of extensive chain migration. The second part focuses more closely on one such migration chain, in which several Westfalian villages were practically transplanted to Missouri.

The division of Germany into a number of sovereign states meant that there was no centralized and uniform registration of emigrant destinations either locally or at the ports. But on the American side the fragmentation of Germany has advantages, for it allows a comparison of the distribution of Germans from different regions in individual states and cities of the United States. As will be shown below, it is possible even at this level of aggregation to infer many of the factors influencing the location of German immigrants. One thing is immediately apparent: Impersonal economic forces are inadequate to explain these patterns. This is not to say that economic considerations were irrelevant in migration decisions, but rather that economic information was channeled through the filter of personal ties. Where the first emigrants from a given region happened to settle was of prime importance in determining the path of subsequent migrants. These pioneers and pathfinders have in many cases remained anonymous, so it is difficult to re-

³ Harald Runblom and Hans Norman, eds., *From Sweden to America: A History of the Migration* (Minneapolis, 1976), pp. 250–251; Robert P. Swierenga and Harry S. Stout, "Socio-Economic Patterns of Migration from the Netherlands in the Nineteenth Century," in *Research in Economic History* 1, ed. Paul Uselding (Greenwich, Conn., 1976), pp. 311–312; Kristian Hvidt, *Flight to America: The Social Background of 300,000 Danish Emigrants* (New York, 1975), pp. 173–175.

⁴ John S. MacDonald and Leatrice D. MacDonald, "Chain Migration, Ethnic Neighborhood Formation, and Social Networks," in *An Urban World*, ed. Charles Tilly (Boston, 1974), p. 227. Two exemplary studies of chain migration are the works of Gjerde and Ostergren cited in the Introduction, nn. 14 and 15.

CHAPTER III

construct their motives, but it appears that they often decided on a particular location purely by chance. Sometimes, too, they were swayed by propaganda. The progress of the frontier and the opening up of cheap new agricultural lands also played a role. While Germans were not typically on the cutting edge of the frontier, they were usually not far behind. Thus as a general rule, the later the onset of emigration from a given region of Germany, the farther west its settlers were concentrated. But the important point is that wherever the earliest migrants from a given locality happened to strike roots, a concentration of immigrants from that part of Germany usually persisted for several decades.

Economic ties between certain ports in Europe and America have often been cited as a factor in location. It is clear that Germans from different regions favored different ports. For southwest Germans, the French port of Le Havre was more accessible than the north German coast. The Rhine provided a natural highway to Rotterdam. Post coaches and steamboats on the Weser provided easy access to Bremen for those northwest Germans who could afford to ride. Hamburg was ideally located to serve the needs of East Elbian Prussia. But in the location of immigrants, no clear reflections of the influence of trade patterns can be observed. They were probably most influential during the initial stages of migration, before the emigrant trade became the tail that wagged the dog, the primary cargo instead of the return ballast it had been initially. Technological advances in transportation did play a role, however, in providing easier access to new areas of the American continent.

Even a cursory examination of the composition of the German population in various American states (see Table 3.1), makes it clear that the representation from different regions of Germany is anything but uniform across the United States.[5] With small states such as Brunswick,

[5] The index of representation is a common sociological measurement that permits the easy comparison of groups and units of observation of differing size. The figure can be regarded as the percentage of parity. For example, if 2.8 percent of all Germans in the United States were Mecklenburgers, then a state with 1.4 percent of its Germans being Mecklenburgers would have an index of 50 (half the expected); a state with 5.6 percent would have an index of 200 (twice the expected). For a more detailed explanation, see E. P. Hutchinson, *Immigrants and Their Children, 1850–1950* (New York, 1956), pp. 302–303. The indexes in this and subsequent tables and figures were calculated from the published volumes of the U.S. Census of 1860, 1870, and 1880, excluding "Germans, not specified" from the calculations, and also, in 1860, "Austrian," and in 1870 and in 1880, "Lübeck" and "Weimar." German state of birth was recorded most systematically in 1870, the proportion "not specified" dropping from nearly half in 1860 to only about

Hamburg, Nassau, and Oldenburg, each constituting less than 1 percent of the total, a skewed distribution might be expected. But even such a large group as the Prussians ranges from barely one-half of "parity" to more than double. Furthermore, local and regional patterns of concentration were very stable over time, although the number of Germans in the country grew from 1.25 million to 2 million during the two decades after 1860. Several suspect figures from 1860 receive confirmation from the 1870 census, when information on German state of birth is most complete.

A few of the more striking concentrations bear witness to the role of propaganda. Nassau and Brunswick were among the chief recruiting grounds of the *Adelsverein*, an abortive attempt by a group of noblemen to colonize central Texas in the mid-1840s. The Oldenburgers in Texas were probably recruited by their countryman Friedrich Ernst, who settled east of Austin in 1831 and wrote to publicize the state. The degree of clustering was even greater than it appears from state-level figures. Despite the early and catastrophic demise of the *Adelsverein*, 22 percent of the Germans in west-central Texas hailed from Nassau and another 7 percent from Brunswick in 1860, while in east Texas neither group exceeded 1 percent. Nearly four decades after Ernst's arrival, Oldenburgers still accounted for 6 percent of the Germans in east Texas, but not even 1 percent further west.[6]

Another little-known figure, Franz Stallo, seems to have been the force behind the large concentration of Oldenburgers in Ohio. A small-town radical journalist, harassed by censors, he emigrated in 1831 and founded the village of Stallotown (later Minster) in west-central Ohio. Before he succumbed to cholera in 1833, his letters had attracted a number of settlers from southern Oldenburg and neighboring areas. A few miles down the road from Münster, the village of New Knoxville was settled almost entirely by immigrants from Ladbergen in *Kreis* Tecklenburg, while forty miles to the north, German settlers named Glandorf after their home village a few miles east of Tecklenburg.[7]

---

15 percent the next decade, climbing again to 30 percent in 1880. Despite the Prussian annexation of Hannover and Hesse-Nassau in 1866, these were included as separate categories among the German states in the U.S. Census through 1880.

[6] Terry G. Jordan, *German Seed in Texas Soil: Immigrant Farmers in Nineteenth-Century Texas* (Austin, 1966), pp. 40–48, 65. It should be noted that the *Adelsverein* transported only a small fraction of the emigrants from Nassau and Brunswick to Texas. It was only because the initial settlers continued to draw others that such concentrations developed and persisted.

[7] Johannes Ostendorf, "Zur Geschichte der Auswanderung aus dem alten Amt Damme (Oldenburg)," *Oldenburger Jahrbuch* 46/47 (1942–1943): 167–169; Friderich

TABLE 3.1. RELATIVE CONCENTRATION OF NATIVES OF VARIOUS GERMAN STATES IN THE GERMAN POPULATION OF SELECTED AMERICAN STATES (1860, 1870, 1880)

		Baden	Bavaria	Brunswick	Hamburg	Hannover	Hesse	Mecklenburg	Nassau	Oldenburg	Prussia	Saxony	Wurttemberg
New York	1860	112	130	—	—	—	114	—	76	—	69	—	103
	1870	120	135	37	162	61	125	97	66	24	87	96	102
	1880	130	152	63	179	74	126	97	75	29	79	104	114
Pennsylvania	1860	118	91	—	—	—	129	—	54	—	57	—	187
	1870	137	125	52	52	39	150	16	84	13	61	119	231
	1880	147	139	71	56	39	183	22	73	17	63	131	236
Ohio	1860	127	131	—	—	—	97	—	84	—	56	—	134
	1870	147	143	58	47	136	104	56	132	271	62	68	131
	1880	155	138	80	65	136	147	94	127	241	63	64	136
Illinois	1860	90	89	—	—	—	114	—	167	—	115	—	67
	1870	84	70	122	79	158	100	144	110	106	112	87	56
	1880	77	66	121	75	145	98	128	121	109	114	75	59
Missouri	1860	92	73	—	—	—	88	—	116	—	145	—	49
	1870	99	75	258	84	224	83	21	138	58	106	97	52
	1880	110	74	235	59	203	93	20	126	70	103	88	57
Texas	1860	32	22	—	—	—	72	—	743	—	192	—	34
	1870	29	27	559	117	95	52	75	565	292	149	181	38
	1880	37	33	302	97	86	45	51	386	311	140	161	45
Michigan	1860	70	74	—	—	—	50	—	66	—	132	—	164
	1870	69	73	41	50	29	53	311	61	13	116	97	163
	1880	59	64	44	40	31	51	276	76	11	118	92	144
Wisconsin	1860	37	54	—	—	—	57	—	107	—	202	—	38
	1870	33	51	86	35	41	47	257	94	44	162	126	32
	1880	32	49	66	24	38	49	176	65	37	153	102	29
Base Percentages	1860	16.6	22.1	—	—	—	14.1	—	1.5	—	33.6	—	12.0
	1870	10.7	14.2	0.34	0.54	7.3	9.2	2.8	0.62	0.72	41.5	3.1	8.9
	1880	9.5	12.8	0.34	0.66	7.7	5.4	3.4	0.47	0.74	47.3	3.6	8.1

SOURCE: See note 5.
NOTE: 100 = Same proportion among Germans in the state as among Germans in the U.S.

Hannoverians were overrepresented in Ohio, but they were most heavily concentrated in Missouri, with southern Illinois a close second, thanks probably to the writings of Gottfried Duden. A Prussian magistrate and physician who spent two years in Missouri in the 1820s, Duden wrote back a series of glowing letters that appeared in book form in 1829. The response to his book must have followed immediately, for several accounts in the early 1830s mention flourishing Hannoverian settlements in Duden country.

A more comprehensive view of the patterns of German settlement in the United States is gained in looking at the distribution of immigrants from several different regions of Germany across the whole American continent.[8] Baden-Württemberg, Hannover, and Mecklenburg typify three different regions of Germany, distinctive, too, in dates of the onset of emigration, ports of departure, and principal mode of transportation in America.

Baden and Württemberg are the principal states of southwest Germany. Their emigration patterns were probably shared by the Bavarian Palatinate, Alsace, and Hesse-Darmstadt, and their favored port of departure was Le Havre. Emigration had already begun before 1820, when all major American cities were ocean ports and overland travel was a tedious affair with horse and wagon. As Table 3.2 shows, southwest Germans were principally concentrated in the east, becoming scarce west of Indiana. The opening of the Erie Canal in 1826 improved access to Ohio. It may also account for the concentration of Württembergers in Michigan that dates back to a settlement around 1830. But if trade routes between ports and access to their hinterlands were the only factor in location, one could expect the distribution of Badenese and Württembergers to be very similar. Instead, there are enough differences to suggest that local traditions played an important role. It is also striking that even a half-century after the onset of mass emigration

---

Schnake, "Zwei Agitatoren der Auswanderung: I. Gottfried Duden," *Der Deutsche Pionier* 6 (1874): 390–396; [H. A.] R[attermann], "Zwei Agitatoren der Auswanderung: II, Franz Joseph Stallo," *Der Deutsche Pionier* 7 (1875): 2–16; Wolfgang Fleischhauer, "German Communities in Northwestern Ohio: Canal Fever and Prosperity," *Report* 34 (1970): 23–34.

[8] Relative concentrations in Table 3.2 were calculated as in n. 5, except that, for the states of New York, Pennsylvania, Ohio, Illinois, Missouri, and Wisconsin, indexes represent rural areas only. The South includes the states of Arkansas, Mississippi, Alabama, Georgia, Florida, North and South Carolina, Virginia and West Virginia, Kentucky, Tennessee, and Louisiana minus New Orleans. New England includes Maine, Vermont, New Hampshire, Connecticut, Rhode Island, and Massachusetts minus Boston. Delaware and the District of Columbia were combined with rural Maryland (minus Baltimore). The Far

CHAPTER III

TABLE 3.2. RELATIVE CONCENTRATION OF NATIVES OF VARIOUS GERMAN REGIONS IN THE GERMAN POPULATION OF AMERICAN REGIONS
(1870)

	Baden	Württemberg	Hannover	Mecklenburg
EAST COAST				
Boston	235	91	48	11
Rest of New England	110	137	53	18
New York City	90	74	72	9
Rest of New York	134	116	55	143
New Jersey	152	149	56	31
Philadelphia	148	331	25	5
Rest of Pennsylvania	132	181	47	23
Baltimore	51	64	115	3
Rest of Maryland, Delaware, D.C.	87	122	108	8
LOWER MIDWEST				
Cincinnati	100	73	249	13
Rest of Ohio	166	155	90	74
Indiana	106	109	71	123
Chicago	66	52	75	269
Rest of Illinois	90	57	188	104
St. Louis	98	51	217	12
Rest of Missouri	100	53	234	32
Kansas	79	118	99	62
UPPER MIDWEST				
Michigan	70	163	29	316
Milwaukee	27	35	37	380
Rest of Wisconsin	34	32	42	216
Minnesota	48	54	96	96
Iowa	77	73	139	161
Nebraska	59	41	88	101
SOUTH AND WEST				
New Orleans	168	66	101	3
Rest of South	123	90	146	17
Texas	29	39	95	76
Western Territories	93	117	93	20
San Francisco	57	52	125	12
Rest of California, Oregon, Nevada	94	71	126	14

SOURCE: Calculated from U.S. Census figures; see note 5.

from the southwest, when new areas of the United States had been opened to settlement, the emigrant stream continued to flow largely in the old channels charted before 1830.[9]

The column in Table 3.2 showing the distribution of Hannoverians represents a stream of emigration from northwest Germany, where the first trickles began around 1830. By this time, steamboats on the Ohio and Mississippi rivers had greatly facilitated inland travel. By far the most favored port of embarkation for these emigrants was Bremen. Its heavy tobacco trade with Baltimore may account for the slight overrepresentation from Hannover there, but greater numbers probably traveled by way of New Orleans, which offered the advantage of direct steamboat connections to the heart of the Midwest. That, in combination with the propaganda efforts of Duden and Stallo that appeared just as emigration from the northwest was beginning, accounts for the heavy concentrations in Missouri and Ohio. Away from the great river systems, Hannoverians were underrepresented both in the Northeast and the Upper Midwest.

Mecklenburg, shown at the right of Table 3.2, should be a good surrogate for all of East Elbian Prussia. Here emigration did not begin until about 1850 and did not reach significant proportions until after the Civil War. Hamburg was the favored port, and its connections with New York were apparent, though hardly any Mecklenburgers were stranded on the docks. By this time, the New York–Chicago rail route, supplemented by Great Lakes shipping, provided easy access to the Upper Midwest. Milwaukee could be called the Mecklenburger capital of the United States, but large concentrations were also found in Michigan, Iowa, and northern Illinois. Although greater numbers might have been expected in Minnesota and Nebraska, here they were supplanted by a 50 percent overrepresentation of Prussians, probably from areas east of the Elbe where emigration began slightly later than in Mecklenburg.

Settlement patterns similar to those of immigrants from Hannover were shown by other northwest Germans from Prussian Westfalia, and to some extent from Oldenburg and Brunswick as well. Emigrants from the Münster District in Westfalia during the 1830s and 1840s provide a good example. Missouri was their most popular destination,

---

West includes the states of Oregon, Nevada, and California minus San Francisco. The Territories includes the future states of North and South Dakota, Montana, Idaho, Washington, Wyoming, Utah, Colorado, Arizona, New Mexico, and Oklahoma.

[9] Arnold Scheuerbrandt, "Südwestdeutsche Einwanderung und Siedlungsgründungen

CHAPTER III

with Ohio a close second, each accounting for about 30 percent of the total. Another 30 percent specified merely a seaport, while the remaining 10 percent were bound either for Texas or for widely scattered destinations in the Midwest. Baltimore was the favorite port of Westfalians, followed closely by New Orleans. For every ten who traveled via New York, eighteen went by way of Baltimore and fourteen by way of New Orleans, while Boston and Philadelphia remained insignificant. In all these aspects, the similarity with Hannover is very apparent.[10]

Emigration from Lippe-Detmold, which began later than in Hannover, but earlier than in Mecklenburg, shares some of the distribution characteristics of both. Missouri was first on the list of destinations, followed closely by Wisconsin and northern Illinois. However, Ohio was well down on the list, behind Texas, Iowa, and Indiana. Among the ports, New Orleans led New York by more than two to one, and Baltimore fell behind even Philadelphia.[11]

If trade routes had been the determinant factor in immigrant location, northwest Germans should have been concentrated on the East Coast because of the tobacco trade between Bremen and Baltimore, while southwest Germans, because of the cotton trade of Le Havre, would have been steered via New Orleans to the Midwest. Instead, the two groups show nearly the opposite patterns. The growing importance of the emigrant trade brought about changes in shipping patterns from Bremen. In the early 1830s, when emigration was still negligible, Bremen's trade with Baltimore surpassed even that with New York, and the two stayed about even until the great emigration wave began in 1844. The contrast with New Orleans was even greater. As large-scale emigration began from 1832 to 1834, more than fifty ships and six thousand passengers sailed annually from Bremen to Baltimore,

---

in USA," in *USA und Baden-Württemberg in ihren geschichtlichen Beziehungen* (Stuttgart, 1976), p. 56. Even ignoring the emigrants who traveled via Le Havre, Württemberg still ranked among the top ten German states and Prussian provinces in rates of emigration for the period 1871–1895 (John Knodel, *The Decline of Fertility in Germany, 1871–1939* [Princeton, 1974], p. 195).

[10] Destination was recorded in about 10 percent of the cases in the Munster District emigrant lists described in Appendix A.

[11] Based on tabulations from the geographic index to Fritz Verdenhalven, *Die Auswanderer aus dem Fürstentum Lippe (bis 1877)* (Detmold, 1980). No attempt was made to count the number of persons per emigration case; rather, each entry, whether family or individual, was counted as one, and state and city entries were compared to eliminate duplicates. Section XVII, based on secondary sources rather than emigration permits, was excluded from the tally. Only a small minority of emigrants recorded a destination more specific than North America.

whereas traffic to New Orleans never exceeded nine ships or one thousand passengers per year. In the peak emigration years from 1844 to 1847, shipping to Baltimore remained at about the same level, but it was equaled or surpassed by the Bremen–New Orleans route. By the next emigration wave in the 1850s, New Orleans was clearly leading in passenger numbers from Bremen.[12]

St. Louis was usually the next stop on this immigration route. Of the Germans landing in New Orleans from 1847 to 1860, nearly three times as many continued on to St. Louis as headed up the Ohio River. Similarly, two-thirds of the Germans arriving in the Missouri metropolis from 1848 to 1855 had come by way of New Orleans, the rest via the East Coast. New Orleans' share was usually lowest in the third quarter of the year, when the danger of cholera was greatest. Immigrant biographies from an area of rural Missouri settled mostly by northwest Germans confirm these patterns. Of twenty-two persons who recorded port of embarkation, all had sailed from Bremen except three from Dutch ports and one from Hamburg. Of seventy persons who mentioned port of arrival, forty-five had come by New Orleans, with New York a distant second, Baltimore third, and other ports insignificant.[13]

The Civil War blockade dealt New Orleans a near-fatal blow as an immigrant port. With the expansion and consolidation of the railroad network and the concentration of the Atlantic trade in ever bigger steamships, New York attracted increasingly greater proportions of post-bellum immigration regardless of final destination. Before the Civil War, however, the main long-distance connections from New York were with the Upper Midwest. This is reflected in the destinations recorded by Germans landing in 1855. The state most popular with those traveling beyond New York was Wisconsin, attracting nearly 4,700 immigrants, ten times as many as Missouri. Illinois was in third place, following Pennsylvania. Similarly, New York was the most common stop along the way for Germans in antebellum Milwaukee.[14]

[12] Rolf Engelsing, *Bremen als Auswandererhafen, 1683–1880* (Bremen, 1961), pp. 180–183.

[13] George Helmut Kellner, "The German Element on the Urban Frontier: St. Louis, 1830–1860" (Ph.D. diss., University of Missouri, 1973), pp. 317–320; Frederick M. Spletstoser, "Back Door to the Land of Plenty: New Orleans as an Immigrant Port, 1820–1860" (Ph.D. diss., Louisiana State University, 1978), p. 356; tabulations from *Portrait and Biographical Record of St. Charles, Lincoln, and Warren Counties, Missouri* (Chicago, 1895).

[14] Robert Ernst, *Immigrant Life in New York City, 1825–1863* (Port Washington,

CHAPTER III

It appears at first glance paradoxical that Germans in America were much more urban than either the countrymen they left behind or the inhabitants of the United States in general (see Table 3.3). On the other hand, the proportion of Germans living in America's leading cities was highest in 1850, immediately after the hunger years in Europe, and declined every decade thereafter through 1890. Even when smaller cities are taken into consideration, the urbanization rate of German-Americans decreased during the 1870s, and increased only slightly with the last great German immigration wave of the 1880s. Germans were clearly swimming against the cityward tide of Americans in general.[15]

The urbanization rate of the state of origin was apparently inconsequential for the location of immigrants in America.[16] Even from the maritime city-state of Hamburg, only a bare majority of immigrants were found in cities of over 25,000 in 1870. Among the larger German states, Saxony was in a class by itself in terms of urbanization and industrialization, but Saxons in America were no more urban than Hessians, Württembergers, or natives of Baden. In fact, Bavarians led the list despite low urbanization rates at home. Southwest German origins were apparently a common denominator for urbanization in America, so some cultural factor could be involved. But if it was poverty and

---

N.Y., 1949), p. 190; Kathleen Neils Conzen, *Immigrant Milwaukee, 1836–1860: Accommodation and Community in a Frontier City* (Cambridge, Mass., 1976), pp. 39–40. Judging by the birthplaces of children of German families, as many stopped in New York as in all other states combined en route to Milwaukee.

[15] Knodel, *Decline of Fertility*, p. 143, is correct in his observation that German-Americans were more urban than either Germans or Americans at the turn of the century, but he exaggerates the degree. Only 51 percent of German-Americans, not over 70 percent as he asserts, lived in cities of over 25,000 inhabitants in 1900; the figure Knodel gives is apparently the percentage in cities of over 2,500 inhabitants.

Regarding Table 3.3, the "8 Principal Cities"—New York, Philadelphia, St. Louis, Chicago, Baltimore, Boston, Cincinnati, and New Orleans—were the only ones separately enumerated in 1860 and were among the ten largest cities in the nation through 1880. The "44 Largest Cities" included all those which were among the fifty largest cities in both 1870 and 1880. One problem in making a comparison over time was that, except in 1860, individual German states of birth were recorded more thoroughly in rural than in urban areas. I assumed that the "Germans, not specified" should have had the same rate of urbanization as "all Germans," and that the underenumeration was uniformly distributed over all German states. So I inflated (in 1860, deflated) each column of figures to, in effect, set the urbanization rate for "Germans, not specified" equal to that of "all Germans." The figures on "all Germans" and "Germans, not specified" in the table are unadjusted figures; the rest were adjusted.

[16] Urbanization rates in German states of origin were calculated from figures in *Vierteljahreshefte zur Statistik des Deutschen Reichs* 2 (1873): 152–155.

heavy emigration, it should have affected Mecklenburgers in the same way. Perhaps it was because the southwest was a region of agricultural villages rather than scattered farmsteads, and agriculture was closely entwined with artisanship. However, these urbanization rates reflect specific migration traditions, some going back to the eighteenth century, rather than general urban preferences. Each of the East Coast cities was dominated by a different group: Baltimore by Hessians, Philadelphia by Württembergers, Boston by Badenese, and New York by Bavarians. Only the Saxons, coming from an industrial background, were overrepresented throughout the region. Thus it is more likely that southwest Germans concentrated in cities because they had a tradition of settling in the East than that they located in the East because of urban preferences.[17]

The similarity of the German population of several cities with that of the surrounding states suggests that migration chains often led through a city on the way to the country. The mix of immigrants from various German regions was very similar in Milwaukee and in rural Wisconsin (see Table 3.4). The *Deutschtum* of Philadelphia and of St. Louis also showed a rather close affinity with that of the rural hinterlands.[18] But what of New York, where weak correlation appears, or especially Cincinnati and Chicago, where negative correlation exists between the distribution in the city and in the rest of the state? Neither of the latter two cities was the entrepôt to its respective state. New York City served as the gateway not only to the Empire State but to an entire region. Included in its hinterland was northern Ohio, which was mainly settled by the Erie Canal and Great Lakes route, while Cincinnati served only

[17] In 1870, Württembergers were overrepresented among Philadelphia Germans by a factor of three, and immigrants from Hesse in Baltimore and from Baden in Boston more than doubled their quota. New York City's population was somewhat less skewed, but Bavarians had an index of 126 in 1870, 141 in 1860, and 150 in 1880, leading the larger states in all three decades. Forty percent of all "Bavarian" emigration came from the Palatinate, an exclave of extremely heavy emigration west of the Rhine. According to a tabulation of the financial resources of immigrants arriving at New York during the last five months of 1855, Mecklenburgers fell at the bottom of the list with $23 per capita; Württembergers were also well below average with $43, but Bavarians, with $76, were somewhat above average, and natives of Baden and Hesse both slightly surpassed the Prussian average of $61 per capita. Thus it hardly appears that southwest Germans were stranded in the ports because of poverty. Figures are from a report of the Deutsche Gesellschaft of New York, as cited by Agnes Bretting, *Soziale Probleme deutscher Einwanderer in New York City, 1800–1860* (Wiesbaden, 1981), p. 197.

[18] Index figures in Table 3.4 were calculated as in n. 5; the *r* values in the table are Pearsonian coefficients calculated thus:

TABLE 3.3. PROPORTION OF GERMANS FROM VARIOUS STATES LIVING IN AMERICAN CITIES (1850–1890)

	8 Principal Cities					44 Largest Cities			Urbanization Rate, State of Origin, 1871[a]
	1850	1860	1870	1880	1890	1870	1880	1890	
Index (German-Americans to all Americans)	383	343	304	282	253	268	257	239	
All German-Americans	29.6%	25.8%	24.8%	22.9%	22.4%	38.9%	38.7%	40.4%	32.1%
Baden	—	26.2	24.7	25.5	—	41.4	44.5	—	33.0
Bavaria	—	31.3	27.8	28.5	—	45.5	49.1	—	23.0
Brunswick	—	—	19.5	18.0	—	25.7	25.9	—	35.6
Hamburg	—	—	29.6	37.7	—	51.7	58.4	—	90.1
Hannover	—	—	30.6	26.7	—	39.4	37.0	—	22.3
Hesse	—	29.9	26.2	18.6	—	42.9	43.2	—	29.8
Mecklenburg	—	—	11.4	7.1	—	26.5	25.0	—	36.9
Nassau	—	22.6	16.9	16.7	—	30.5	31.2	—	24.5
Oldenburg	—	—	36.4	24.4	—	41.1	29.6	—	15.9
Prussia	—	21.0	23.2	21.3	—	35.5	34.6	—	32.0
Saxony	—	—	24.1	25.1	—	40.4	43.4	—	49.4
Württemberg	—	24.4	25.5	25.0	—	40.5	42.0	—	27.4
(Not Specified)	—	23.6	39.0	30.1	—	47.8	45.1	—	—

SOURCE: See note 15.
[a] Proportion of population living in communities of 2,000+ inhabitants.

the smaller German contingent in southern Ohio. Illinois presents a similar case. Outside of Chicago, most of the Germans were concentrated in the southern part of the state where St. Louis served as the staging area. Chicago looked much more to the northwest, and the German population of rural Wisconsin resembled that of Chicago ($r = .82$) almost as much as it did Milwaukee ($r = .92$). Meanwhile, the population of St. Louis had almost the same affinity to rural Illinois ($r = .65$) as to outstate Missouri ($r = .69$).

The Mecklenburgers, one of the most recently arrived immigrant groups, provide added evidence of dropping out or stopping along the way. Though most of them escaped the port of New York, they were overrepresented upstate and scattered in large numbers in cities all along the Great Lakes route. Their relative concentration in Buffalo was 168; in Rochester, 186; in Cleveland, 161; in Detroit, 189; in Toledo, a striking 464. But they never strayed far from the route, not reaching 25 percent of parity in Columbus and falling below 5 percent in Syracuse, Pittsburgh, and Dayton. Immigrant biographies in county histories attest to the same phenomenon, often mentioning a stay of anywhere from a few weeks to a decade before proceeding to a farm or rural village. A check of several counties in southern Illinois showed that over 10 percent of the Germans had stopped long enough in Missouri (presumably St. Louis) for one or more children to be born there. Perhaps this explains why Kathleen Conzen found in her study of Milwaukee that between 1850 and 1860 Germans were the least persistent of all ethnic groups. Many of them were on their way to farms in rural Wisconsin.[19]

A comparison of the occupational and demographic structure of Westfalian immigrants with urban and rural destinations provides more suggestive evidence that life-cycle stage was as important as occupation in determining who would settle in cities. The majority of immigrants destined for both rural and urban parts of Missouri and Ohio had previously been engaged in agriculture. Even in East Coast cities, there was a significant minority with an agricultural background, though the proportion coming from the tertiary sector was considerably greater than with immigrants to other areas. But contrasts in de-

---

x_1 = relative concentration of Badenese in Milwaukee
y_1 = relative concentration of Badenese in rural Wisconsin
x_2 = relative concentration of Bavarians in Milwaukee
y_2 = relative concentration of Bavarians in rural Wisconsin, etc.,
giving twelve units of observation upon which each coefficient of correlation is based.

[19] Conzen, *Immigrant Milwaukee*, pp. 42–43, 136.

CHAPTER III

TABLE 3.4. RELATIVE CONCENTRATION OF NATIVES OF VARIOUS GERMAN STATES IN T

	Baden	Bavaria	Brunswick	Hamburg	Hannover	Hesse
Milwaukee	26	58	129	37	37	57
Rural Wisconsin	34	50	79	33	42	46
Chicago	66	57	53	130	74	80
Rural Illinois	90	74	147	59	186	107
St. Louis	98	81	138	102	216	94
Rural Missouri	100	68	382	63	233	71
Cincinnati	100	144	50	74	248	53
Rural Ohio	166	143	62	35	89	125
Philadelphia	149	94	38	89	25	103
Rural Pennsylvania	131	140	59	33	47	173
New York City	90	126	44	161	73	120
Rural New York	135	139	32	116	54	126

SOURCE: See note 18.
[a] Correlation (r value) between index for rural Wisconsin and Chicago.

mographic characteristics were even more striking. Immigrants to New York and Philadelphia were on the average five full years younger than those destined for the Midwest. Age differences between immigrants to the urban and rural Midwest were not striking, but over 70 percent of those destined for rural Ohio and Missouri were married, as compared to less than half of those bound for St. Louis and Cincinnati and not even one-third of the future New Yorkers and Philadelphians. The cities were especially attractive to young, single, and mobile immigrants, with occupation playing only a secondary role. In fact, the demographic profile of Germans in American cities was strikingly similar to that of newcomers to German cities in the late nineteenth century.[20]

The distribution of immigrants from the heavily industrialized Kingdom of Saxony suggests that occupational background may have come to play an increasing role in locational preferences as the nineteenth century progressed. Especially striking is the fivefold overrepresentation of Saxons in the mill towns of New England. But they were also heavily concentrated all the way down the East Coast as far as Baltimore. Moreover, this tendency intensified between 1870 and 1880. Meanwhile, in the rest of the country, almost without exception, the

[20] These figures should be interpreted with caution, since only about 10 percent of all

German Population of Selected Cities and Rural Areas in America (1870)

Mecklenburg	Nassau	Oldenburg	Prussia	Saxony	Wurttemberg	Intercorrelations of Relative Concentrations
375	177	60	145	161	35	.92
213	79	41	163	119	31	.82[a]
264	73	19	132	116	53	−.26
93	123	136	105	74	57	.65[b]
12	139	54	104	103	52	.69
31	137	63	108	94	53	
13	42	708	75	58	73	−.07
75	177	89	57	71	155	
5	34	14	59	136	332	.74
22	108	13	61	110	181	
9	84	19	108	84	74	.38
139	57	26	60	100	116	

[b] Correlation (*r* value) between index for rural Illinois and St. Louis.

proportion of Saxons dropped. Thus it is probable that the last great wave of German immigration in the 1880s included fewer reluctant urbanites and more intentional ones than had previously been the case.

If a high degree of clustering of Germans from a particular region is observed at the state level, it results from even more extreme concentrations at the local level. The fourfold overrepresentation of Brunswickers in rural Missouri, for example, meant 1 percent of the German population in a block of four Missouri River counties and nearly one-fourth of all Germans in a southeast Missouri county. The remainder of this chapter focuses on one such local concentration, using as an example two adjoining Missouri counties: St. Charles and Warren. Located in east-central Missouri, they form part of the "German belt" extending up both sides of the Missouri River from St. Louis. More than one-sixth of the Germans in rural Missouri lived in these two counties in 1860. Both in rank and in absolute numbers, they were among the most German in the state. Together with St. Louis City and County,

---

emigrants specified a destination. On urbanization within Germany, see Walter Kamphoefner, "The Social Consequences of Rural-Urban Migration in Imperial Germany: The 'Floating Proletariat' Thesis Reconsidered," Social Science Working Paper no. 414, California Institute of Technology, January 1982.

CHAPTER III

TABLE 3.5. RELATIVE CONCENTRATION OF NATIVES OF VARIOUS GERMAN STATES IN THE GERMAN POPULATION OF PARTS OF MISSOURI

	1860			1870		
	St. Louis	Rural Missouri	St. Charles and Warren Counties	St. Louis	Rural Missouri	St. Charles and Warren Counties[a]
Baden	84	106	66	98	100	63
Bavaria	84	51	17	81	68	16
Brunswick	—	—	—	138	382	327
Hamburg	—	—	—	102	63	35
Hannover	—	—	—	216	233	461
Hesse	99	68	61	94	71	57
Mecklenburg	—	—	—	12	31	7
Nassau	137	87	9	139	137	14
Oldenburg	—	—	—	54	63	344
Prussia	134	166	221	104	108	110
Saxony	—	—	—	103	94	26
Württemberg	47	53	18	52	53	15

SOURCE: See note 21.
[a] Local figures for 1860 relative to national distribution 1870.

and Franklin, Gasconade, and Osage counties south of the river, they formed a block in which German culture dominated.[21]

While Missouri generally was a haven for northwest Germans, this was especially true of St. Charles and Warren counties (see Table 3.5). New Hannover would have been an appropriate name for this area, for Hannoverians were found in nearly five times the expected numbers. The adjoining German states of Oldenburg and Brunswick provided the next largest concentrations. By contrast, no south German state reached as much as two-thirds of parity. Even Prussia as a whole was hardly overrepresented, though, as will be seen, the Prussian province of Westfalia, bordering on Hannover, turned out in full force.

The most spectacular concentration of northwest Germans, however, came from the tiny Principality of Lippe, nestled between West-

[21] In Table 3.5, indexes for Missouri and St. Louis were calculated as in n. 5. The figures on natives of different German states in St. Charles, Warren, and other Missouri counties in the table and below are based on hand tallies made from the U.S. Federal Manuscript Census of 1860. For exact figures by township, see Kamphoefner, "Transplanted Westfalians: Persistence and Transformation of Socioeconomic and Cultural Patterns in the Northwest German Migration to Missouri" (Ph.D. diss., University of Missouri, 1978), pp. 130–131.

falia and Hannover. Too insignificant for separate enumeration in the U.S. Census, Lippe-Detmold comprised only one-third of 1 percent of the population of Germany. But nearly 20 percent of the Germans in Warren County hailed from Lippe, where they were second in number only to Prussians. In St. Charles County, however, they were represented by five lonely souls just across the border, so localized was the migration chain. Similarly, south of the Missouri, Lippe-Detmolders made up one-eighth of the Germans in Gasconade County but only 2 percent in Franklin County, over half of whom were in one township on the Gasconade border.

Similar patterns occur with other groups. Only four out of nearly one hundred Alsatians were found in Warren County; in fact, they were practically restricted to the township and city of St. Charles. There were 22 Thuringians in the two counties, all of them in one township. Though south Germans were generally few and far between in the area, they dominated the small German settlement in southwestern Warren County to the virtual exclusion of north Germans (see Figure 3.1). They probably looked across the river to the town of Hermann just upstream. In fact, Swiss, south Germans, and Alsatians made up 55 percent of the German stock in the winegrowing areas of Hermann and surrounding Rourk Township, but only 21 percent in the rest of Gasconade County.[22]

Although migration chains often show through in county-level figures, it was really the township level that formed the basis of such homogeneous concentrations. Emigration was so heavy from "Old" Melle to New that 70 percent of the Germans in the town and surrounding Calloway Township were natives of Hannover. Taking Gasconade County again, nearly half of the Lippe-Detmolders lived in Bolware Township, making up over 45 percent of the Germans there. Over two-fifths of that county's immigrants from Hannover settled in Third Creek Township, where they made up a good half of all Germans. One could go on and on with examples. Civil boundaries sometimes obscure the degree of regional clustering. What appears to be a scattering of Brunswickers among several townships on the Warren–St. Charles County border was in fact a rather compact chain migration, also including some families from neighboring parts of Hannover. The selection of marriage partners and godparents in America showed clear influences of common origins.

[22] The town of Hermann had been founded in 1838 by an immigration society in Philadelphia consisting largely of southwest Germans.

CHAPTER III

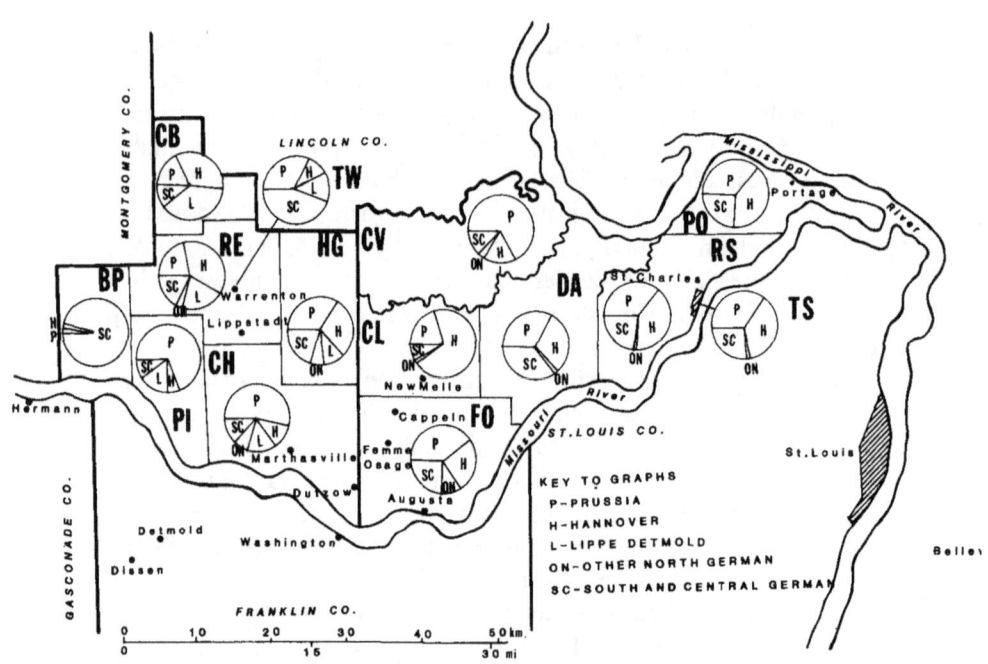

FIGURE 3.1
Regional Origins of Germans by Township (St. Charles and Warren Counties)

Townships of Warren County
BP Bridgeport PI Pinckney
CB Camp Branch RE Rural Elkhorn Twp.
CH Charette TW Town of Warrenton
HG Hickory Grove

Townships of St. Charles County
CL Calloway PO Portage
CV Cuivre RS Rural St. Charles Twp.
DA Dardenne TS Town of St. Charles
FO Femme Osage

The evidence presented so far has been largely circumstantial; but where there is so much smoke, there is usually fire, as the settlers from Oldenburg demonstrate. Of a group of more than one hundred in 1860, all but nine were located in two adjoining townships. But even this figure fails to capture their degree of concentration. They were practically all situated along the Missouri River between Augusta and Dutzow, where they formed the nucleus of a German Catholic parish. All but one of ten successive families in the 1850 census were from Oldenburg, and nearby were two other nodes of two families each. Moreover, all of these families could be traced to a single village in *Amt* Damme, Oldenburg, just across the border from the Osnabrück District.[23]

[23] For details, see Kamphoefner, "Transplanted Westfalians," p. 148, n. 15.

But what of the two states that provided the bulk of the immigration to Duden country: Hannover and Prussia? Large numbers from an expanse of territory that took up over half of Germany are not a sure sign of chain migration. But in rural Missouri, Prussia usually meant the Province of Westfalia, and Hannover usually meant the Osnabrück District. Indeed, at least two-thirds of the Germans in Duden country hailed from an area about sixty miles long and thirty wide, stretching along the Teutoburger Wald from *Kreis* Tecklenburg to Lippe-Detmold, including the *Fürstentum* Osnabrück, *Amt* Damme in Oldenburg, and the intervening part of the Minden District. An even greater proportion—fully four-fifths—was Low German in origin.

Place names were the first clue to this concentration and, supplemented by several parish histories, they were enough to call attention to the Osnabrück region (see Figure 3.2; compare Figure 3.1). Six miles apart in the Femme Osage hills lie the towns of New Melle and Cappeln, with German namesakes Melle and Westerkappeln only twenty miles apart on opposite sides of Osnabrück. Just northeast of that city are two villages, Osterkappeln and Belm, from whence the founders of the Catholic congregation in Washington, Missouri, set out in 1833. A bit further northwest is *Amt* Damme in Oldenburg, source of most of the Augusta Catholic parish. Immediately east of Damme in Hannoverian territory is the village of Menslage, to which the Lutheran congregation in St. Charles traces its roots. The presence of Lippe-Detmolders is betrayed by a Lippstadt in Warren County and a Detmold just south of the river in Franklin. Near the latter is the hamlet of Dissen, which has as its namesake a village just south of Osnabrück.[24]

The success of a given town is not, however, a sure indication of the amount of immigration. New Melle was for a time a thriving market village, while Cappeln never consisted of much more than a store, an Evangelical church, and high hopes; but there were probably more immigrants in the area from Westerkappeln than from Melle. Schluersburg (the name is almost bigger than the town) in St. Charles County does hark back to a place name in the Osnabrück region, but was only the birthplace of the local storekeeper, Wilhelm Horst. Though nearly one-fifth of Warren County's Germans hailed from Lippe, Lippstadt never progressed beyond a since-abandoned churchsite and a few houses. Warren County also has a Holstein that apparently owes its

---

[24] Westerkappeln was also referred to as Kappeln or Cappeln, not receiving its official name until 1884. Emmet H. Rothan, *The German Catholic Immigrant in the United States (1830–1860)* (Washington, 1946), pp. 51–54; Frederic Niedner, "The Long History of a Church," *St. Charles Journal*, 28 September 1967, written for the 100th anniversary of the Immanuel Lutheran Church building, St. Charles, Missouri.

CHAPTER III

FIGURE 3.2
Origins of Emigrants to Missouri (Detail of the
Westfalia-Osnabrück Region)

name to a single Schleswig family, Dr. Charles Ruge and his sons, in an otherwise Westfalian settlement.[25] And Hamburg in St. Charles County must have commemorated someone's port of embarkation, for only one person in all Dardenne Township claimed the Hanseatic city as his birthplace.

The most conclusive evidence of chain migration comes from German emigrant lists and biographical sketches in American county histories. Prussians made up over two-fifths of the Germans in the two-county area. Of these, roughly one-half were from northern Westfalia,

[25] Biographical sketches in *History of St. Charles, Montgomery, and Warren Counties, Missouri* (1885; facsimile reprint, St. Louis, 1969), pp. 1048–1051. Naturalization records of Wilhelm Horst, St. Charles County Court, 25 February 1834, transcript in Work Projects Administration Collection, folder 18094, Western Historical Manuscripts Collection, University of Missouri–Columbia.

primarily *Kreis* Tecklenburg, but with smaller numbers from Halle and Herford as well, according to biographical sketches from county histories. Among 78 first- or second-generation Prussians featured in an 1895 volume, 31 either specified an origin in *Kreis* Tecklenburg or could be identified in emigrant lists. With three others from *Kreis* Halle and a handful of other Westfalian Protestants, they account for a majority of the Prussians. Eight people traced their roots to Rhine Province, and 1 Berliner and 1 West Prussian were the only others who specified a province. So there were probably few East Elbians among the remaining 21 Prussians.[26]

Of 59 local notables with Hannoverian origins mentioned in the 1895 volume, only 26 furnished further detail. Of these, 7 were from around Melle, 6 from Menslage, and 5 more simply listed Osnabrück. Family names and social patterns suggest that most of the unspecified Hannoverians were also from this region. The only other concentration was 5 people from Hildesheim, while three other Districts had 1 representative each. Lippe (6), Oldenburg (5), Schleswig-Holstein (2), and Brunswick (2) bring the proportion of north Germans to over three-fourths of the 191 people who specified town or province of origin. The population of Franklin County, just across the Missouri, must have been very similar. Of 111 immigrants specifying province of birth in 1888 biographies, Hannover (36), Prussia (31), and Westfalia (12) led the list, though the presence of people from Mecklenburg, Saxony, and Silesia suggests a slightly heavier east German representation.[27]

Such county-history data may give a slightly skewed picture of population origins, however, since the elite of a community was probably more heterogeneous than the peasant-stock rank and file. The strongest evidence of chain migration was obtained by linking individual-level data from both sides of the Atlantic. About one-eighth of all Germans in the 1850 census of St. Charles and Warren counties could be linked to the emigrant lists of *Kreis* Tecklenburg, and allowing for imperfections in both sources, probably one-fifth of Duden country Germans were of these origins. There were over two hundred individuals, vir-

[26] Tabulated from *Portrait and Biographical Record*. Additional information on birthplace was gained by matching persons with the Münster emigration lists and with biographical entries in *History of St. Charles, Montgomery, and Warren Counties*.

[27] Tallies from county history biographies made by Charles van Ravenswaay, *The Arts and Architecture of German Settlements in Missouri: A Survey of a Vanishing Culture* (Columbia, Mo., 1977), p. 70. Half of the Hannoverians were Catholic, which would suggest origins in the Osnabrück region. All but two of the Westfalians were Protestant, and since none was from Tecklenburg, they probably originated from the Minden District.

CHAPTER III

tually a transplanted village, from Westerkappeln alone, and over one hundred from the nearby village of Lienen. Their settlements were also tightly clustered, especially in the Femme Osage area, where in one stretch of the 1850 census, all but one of fifteen consecutive families were from Tecklenburg.

The designation "transplanted village" is a slight misnomer, however. The migration chain documented here extended to the whole Protestant half of *Kreis* Tecklenburg with greater or lesser intensity. It involved more than just people who had been in daily contact in the old country, extending also to those who might meet only occasionally at a fair or market. In fact, this was practically the same radius as that from which most peasant marriage partners were drawn. The core of the chain was the village of Westerkappeln. Over one-fourth of its emigration in the two preceding decades was accounted for by people matched to the 1850 census of the two-county area of Missouri. Allowing for poor census coverage and other flaws in the two data sources, at least one-third and perhaps as much as one-half of Westerkappeln's emigration must have settled in Duden country. At the next stage of migration intensity were Lienen, Lengerich, and two smaller villages within a twelve-mile radius of Westerkappeln, each with about 10 percent of its emigration traced to the two counties. A striking illustration of the specificity of migration tradition was the village of Ladbergen, bordering on Lienen and Lengerich, but sending only 3 percent of its emigrants to the Missouri settlement, so strong was the migration chain to its daughter village, New Knoxville, Ohio.[28]

---

[28] For more detail on sources and matching procedures, see Appendix A. Family names in Germany are often very localized. The typical Westfalian name of Schroer was represented by seven families, only three of which could be matched with emigrant lists, though six of seven Bierbaums were linked. Of roughly thirty Tecklenburger immigrants in county history biographies, at least three who were obviously present in the area in 1850 could not be linked to the census. The District-level emigrant lists from Münster were also incomplete; besides the approximately 130 families thus matched, about fifteen more families were matched to local lists from Westerkappeln and Lienen, the two towns responsible for the bulk of the Tecklenburg immigration. Also, several family names appeared in early emigrant lists and were common in the area in the twentieth century, but were not found in the 1850 census. If any member of a nuclear family in the emigration lists was traced to Missouri, it was assumed that all members had located there, although many individuals disappeared through death or, in the case of females, marriage. The *Bauernschaft* of residence was often lacking in the Münster lists, but could usually be ascertained from the local lists or from entries in Wolfgang Leesch, *Schatzungs- und Sonstige Höferegister der Grafschaft Tecklenburg, 1494 bis 1831* (Münster, 1974). Pursuing my own family history, I have found additional evidence of widespread omissions by the census. On this problem, see Richard Jensen, "History from a Deck of IBM Cards," *Reviews in American History* 6 (June 1978): 232–233. A census-recapture study led by Jen-

But if migration chains often spanned village boundaries, in another sense they showed a degree of selectivity going below the village level to the *Bauernschaft*, a neighborhood group of farmsteads that had originally shared the same common fields and pastures. One *Bauernschaft* of the eight in Lienen accounted for over one-third of the tracings to Missouri, and two out of the seven in Westerkappeln accounted for over five-eighths. There were actually three Tecklenburger subsettlements: one in Warren County, a second in western St. Charles County around Femme Osage, and a third in the eastern part of the county near St. Charles. Each had somewhat different origins. The twenty-five families in the latter settlement were all from Westerkappeln save one; in fact, thirteen of them were from a single *Bauernschaft*. By contrast, over four-fifths of the forty-three families traced from Lienen located in Warren County. The Femme Osage settlement, lying midway between the two others, saw more overlap, but here, too, two-thirds of the traced families were from Westerkappeln. What could explain such homogeneity?

The initial impetus for immigration to Missouri clearly came from Gottfried Duden's "Report." A Prussian jurist from Remscheid in northeastern Rhine Province, Duden hoped that emigration might provide a solution to the poverty and crime that he witnessed in his profession. Taking a course in medicine as preparation, he set out in 1824, accompanied by a friend, Louis Eversmann. He arrived in the fall and spent the next two years on a farm that he purchased in what later became Warren County. Possessed of enough means to hire farm labor, Duden could devote his time to observation and writing. In the spring of 1827, he returned to Germany and published his romanticized if not inaccurate observations in a book, the first edition appearing in Elberfeld in 1829.[29]

---

sen using the 1880 Soundex index to trace people throughout the country found that only 20 percent of those people not at their original location five years later could be found anywhere in the United States Census.

[29] One sign of the continuing interest in Duden's book is the recent publication of a complete annotated English translation: James Goodrich et al., eds. and trans., *Report on a Journey to the Western States of North America and a Stay of Several Years along the Missouri (During the Years 1824, '25, '26, and 1827)* (Columbia, Mo., 1980). Selected sections were also translated by William G. Bek, "Gottfried Duden's 'Report,' 1824–1827," *Missouri Historical Review* 12 (1917): 1–21, 81–89, 163–179, 258–270; ibid., 13 (1919): 44–56, 157–181, 251–281. German immigration to this part of Missouri essentially began with Duden. Alfred B. Faust's unsupported statement that in St. Charles County, Germans from Osnabrück and Oldenburg had settled in the beginning of the 1820s is almost certainly erroneous; for details, see Kamphoefner, "Transplanted Westfalians," p. 149, n. 21.

CHAPTER III

The impact of Duden's "Report," reinforced by the political upheavals of 1830, resulted in the formation of several emigration societies composed of intellectuals and people from the higher ranks of society. Because these groups left practically the only written records from this period, they are often accorded an influential role in the settlement of this region. These "Followers of Duden," often referred to as "Latin farmers" because they were more proficient in the classics than in agriculture, were undoubtedly important as a cultural leavening to the peasant community, but as will be seen, they were of limited influence in shaping the patterns of settlement that developed in the area.[30]

At least three groups deserve mention: the Berlin Society, the Solingen group led by the Steines brothers, and the Giessen Society headed by the remarkable Friedrich Muench. Little information has survived about the Berlin Society, but it appears to have been small and loosely organized, with more than its share of eccentric aristocrats. In the pungent words of Gert Goebel, they were "just plain nobility, who seemed to have no other distinction and no other occupation either than just being nobility." Contemporaries always added the qualifier "so-called" when referring to the Berlin Society. According to one such observer, it consisted of only fourteen persons, all relatives and friends, and had already dissolved its communal organization by 1833. It must have been formed very soon after the appearance of Duden's book, for permanent settlers from the Society had began arriving by 1832.[31]

---

[30] Typical in its exaggeration of the importance of emigration societies is the editors' introduction to Goodrich, *Report on a Journey*, p. xviii, which lists among the "colonization societies bound for Missouri" the Mühlhausen Colonization Society organized by E. K. Angelrodt and the Osnabrück Colonization Society of Heinrich von Martels. There is no mention of any society or any larger party of immigrants in Heinrich von Martels, *Briefe über die westlichen Theile der Vereinigten Staaten von Nordamerika* (Osnabruck, 1834). Moreover, as can be seen from ibid., pp. 15–16, 71–72, the Muhlhausen (or Thuringian) Society originally intended to settle in Pennsylvania and was an unmitigated disaster. Only a small remnant, including Angelrodt, went to Missouri.

Much of the primary material on these emigration societies has been collected and translated by William G. Bek, "Followers of Duden," *Missouri Historical Review* 14 (1919) through (1925), passim. Because of my greater knowledge of local detail and occasional disagreements on shades of meaning, I have usually supplied my own translations of primary material below. Other eyewitness accounts from the mid-1830s include J. G. Büttner, *Die Vereinigten Staaten von Nord-Amerika: Mein Aufenthalt und meine Reisen in denselben, vom Jahre 1834 bis 1841*, 2 vols. (Hamburg, 1844), 1: 184–201; Fred Gustorf, ed. and trans., *The Uncorrupted Heart: Journals and Letters of Friedrich Julius Gustorf, 1800–1845* (Columbia, Mo., 1969). A good account of the emigration societies, based largely on Bek, is given by Ravenswaay, *Arts and Architecture*, pp. 32–46.

[31] Quote from Goebel, *Länger als ein Menschenleben*, p. 7. The Berlin Society consisted of Herr von Bock and his two sons-in-law, Radje and Friedrich Morsey, two Blüm-

The Solingen Society was organized around two brothers from Rhenish Prussia, Hermann and Frederick Steines, the latter a liberal-minded schoolteacher who had become fed up with the authoritarian and bureaucratic Prussian government. Following Duden's advice, Hermann was sent ahead in 1833 to prepare the way. The influence of Duden is seen in Hermann's letters, where he often cited chapter and verse with the remark that all is exactly as described in the book. Frederick followed the next year with a party of about 120 persons, most, it seems, of the prosperous middle class. By the time the group reached St. Louis, however, it was beginning to split up. An additional blow was the shocking death of Frederick Steines's wife and children in a cholera epidemic. Of the original party, only Steines remained in Franklin County by 1850, and two other families were located north of the river near Duden's site.[32]

The Giessen Society was organized by two former members of the liberal student movement, Friedrich Muench and Paul Follenius, and also included in its ranks Professor David Goebel, former tutor to the prince of Coburg. After the failure of the 1830 revolution in Germany, the group planned to found a model German republic in the wilds of Arkansas. The one division led by Muench decided while on the voyage to Baltimore to dissolve its organization and divide up the common funds. Nevertheless, they traveled together in a group on the land and river route to St. Louis. By the time they reached Missouri, the other division traveling under Follenius via New Orleans had suffered an outbreak of cholera and given up its original destination, scattering instead to various locations in Missouri and southern Illinois. Muench and Follenius settled on adjoining farms near the spot where Duden had composed his Missouri idyll, Goebel settled south of the Missouri in Franklin County, and the rest of the society scattered about these and other locations.[33]

---

ner brothers, two Huttawa brothers, a Swede named Walke, and Plate from Hamburg, father and son, according to Friedrich Muench, "Die Duden'sche Niederlassung in Missouri," *Der Deutscher Pionier* 2 (1870): 202; counting the wives of the four people presumably married, one would arrive at a figure of fourteen persons, the size of the "society of Rathje and Blumner" given by Martels, *Brief über die Vereinigten Staaten*, p. 175. Letters of the Blümner brothers are included in Wolfgang Helbich, Walter Kamphoefner, and Ulrike Sommer, eds., *Amerika-Auswanderer im 19. Jahrhundert schrieben nach Deutschland* (tentative title, Munich, forthcoming).

[32] One primary source on the Solingen Society is Friedrich Dellmann, ed., *Briefe der nach Amerika ausgewanderten Familie Steines* (Wesel, 1835). Excerpts from this and a sizable collection of other material on the Steines family has been translated by Bek, "Followers of Duden," 14: 29–73, 217–232, 436–458; ibid., 15: 519–544, 660–699.

[33] The main primary source on the Giessen Society is a series of articles by Friedrich

CHAPTER III

Muench was somewhat acquainted with farm life and manual labor from his youth, and adjusted rather successfully, if not easily, to American ways of agriculture. With appropriate but unconscious symbolism, he cut his first corn crop using as a corn knife a sword that his brother had carried against France in 1813, thus combining two very different expressions of that generation's ideals. For the first several years Muench hired the help of a peasant family that had accompanied him, but when his eldest son was but ten years old, he set them up on their own plot of land and dismissed them, thereafter relying solely on his own labor. Still he found time to conduct a school for the neighborhood, and also carried on a lively intellectual life, corresponding with a number of newspapers under the pen name "Far West," and campaigned against slavery in a political career that led him all the way to a seat in the Missouri State Senate. Combining such diverse activities was no easy task, as is shown by the following quote where Muench apologized to his readers for an absence of several months:

> We tillers of the soil are often even envied by others, but they would hardly want to take our places under the blistering June and July sun as we wrestle from the soil bread for us and them. At such times the poetry of rural life is not exactly overwhelming. As for me, I have almost forgotten how to write in the last few months.[34]

Not many of the Latin farmers proved as adaptable as Muench. Follenius died after only ten years in America, a frustrated and disappointed man. For the quixotic adventurers of the Berlin Society, it was even worse. "One after the other went to ruin," observed Muench. "Their wealth had passed into the hands of their day laborers," and the former employers suffered want and misery. Though suicide was in any case not uncommon in immigrant communities, Muench counted no less than twelve in his immediate neighborhood during the first several years.[35]

But if most of these Latin farmers were personal failures, was not their dream of a new Germany in America to some extent realized through the more adaptable peasantry that followed them? A new Ger-

---

Muench in *Der Deutsche Pionier* 1 (1869) through 11 (1880); and Hugo Muench, ed., *Gesammelte Schriften von Friedrich Muench* (St. Louis, 1902), pp. 92–125. Translated excerpts from the above are presented by Bek, "Followers of Duden," 18: 114–129, 338–352, 562–584. Another eyewitness account is Goebel, *Langer als ein Menschenleben*, pp. 9–21. For translated selections, see Bek, "Followers of Duden," 16: 119–145, 289–307, 343–383, 522–550; ibid., 17: 28–56, 331–347.

[34] *St. Charles Demokrat*, 4 August 1855.
[35] Friedrich Muench, "Sonst und Jetzt," *Der Deutsche Pionier* 4 (1872): 231.

TRANSPLANTED VILLAGES

many of sorts was indeed established in Missouri. By 1870, first- and second-generation Germans probably constituted a majority in St. Charles and Warren counties, and in Franklin, Gasconade, and perhaps Osage County as well. In a town such as Washington, Missouri, there were in the 1870s still many Germans "who understood next to nothing of the English language, while there are many Americans, especially children, who can make themselves understood fairly well in German," according to Gert Goebel, the professor's son who had immigrated as a youth with the Giessen Society. But, as Goebel also remarked, the Latin farmers were succeeded by a wave of "peasants, cottagers, and common day laborers who advanced the *material* development of the country much more than the former group."[36] Though this mass immigration began arriving almost simultaneously with the Latin groups, it was apparently separate with respect to both its geographic origins and its leaders and organizations.

The presence of several well-to-do Oldenburgers among the early settlers in Duden country might lead one to believe that they were the influence behind the subsequent peasant settlement from that state, but this does not seem to be the case. Both Count Wilhelm von Bentinck and Hieronymus Ulfers were from Varel near the North Sea coast, and Frederick Rasmus, another local notable mentioned by Muench, was from nearby Brake, whereas the peasants came from the extreme southern tip of Oldenburg, sixty miles away. The pathfinder of the latter migration was probably Johann Heinrich Dickhaus, a shoemaker by trade, who left Germany with his family in 1831. After spending about two years in Kentucky, he arrived in Missouri in 1834. Soon several others from the village began to follow: his in-laws in 1833 or 1834, another Dickhaus (probably a relative) in 1835, a larger party in 1839, and several other groups in the 1840s. By 1860, the settlement numbered over one hundred souls born in Oldenburg, plus a burgeoning second generation. Whether it was Duden's book that led Dickhaus to Missouri is not recorded, though he went on to become a merchant and appears to have had somewhat wider horizons than the average peasant.[37] The important point is that once he made his choice of location, whether by chance or design, the results were decisive for those who emigrated thereafter.

The huge Tecklenburger settlement in Duden country began in much the same way. The first large party left Westerkappeln in 1832 with

[36] Goebel, *Langer als ein Menschenleben*, pp. 137, 47.
[37] *Portrait and Biographical Record*, pp. 247, 286; *History of St. Charles, Montgomery, and Warren Counties*, pp. 1056, 1036–1037; Bek, "Followers of Duden," 18: 578; Ostendorf, "Auswanderung aus Damme," pp. 281–285.

CHAPTER III

Ohio as its stated destination, but at least two of these families, headed by Johann Heinrich Schroer and Steffen Heinrich Freese, went to Missouri instead. They were of undistinguished social origins, both landless artisans, but were probably linked by family ties, since both their wives were Westermeiers. Others from the village began to follow by late March 1833, about the interval required for word to get back from America. The influence of the first migrants doubtlessly precipitated the emigration of a group of fifteen families in late summer of 1833, for among them was a Widow Schroer who stated that her son had already gone to America the previous August. Another Schroer, perhaps a brother, was also in the party. All fifteen families registered for emigration within a ten-day period at the end of July, and most set out together on 7 September. In all, about two dozen of the families traced to Missouri had emigrated before 1834. Another group of families began registering for emigration from Westerkappeln in January 1834, about time that word from the previous party could have gotten back. Family connections are often apparent among these emigrants; another Westermeier emigrated in 1834, and a Freese brother came over in 1835.[38]

Emigration from other Tecklenburg villages began almost as early. Heinrich Forderhase from Wersen arrived in Baltimore in May 1833, proceeding immediately to Missouri, and his brother followed within a few months. Arnold Heinrich Oberhellmann and family from Lengerich also arrived some time in 1833. Two brothers from Lienen, Friedrich and Jacob Ahmann, set out for Missouri in April of that year, reaching Baltimore in June and Missouri by July. Friedrich Wilhelm

---

[38] According to the memoirs of his American-born son recorded a half-century later, Caspar Heinrich Schaaf had emigrated in 1832, which would make him the first of the Tecklenburgers in Missouri, but parish records at Westerkappeln show that his wife bore a child on 16 July 1834, making it unlikely that he had left before September 1833 (*Portrait and Biographical Record*, pp. 395–396).

The main sources on emigration are the District-level lists transcribed by Müller, described in Appendix A. Since this source records the transit of several south German families from 1828 on, if any Tecklenburger emigration had occurred before 1832, one could expect it to have been recorded. Although the Müller transcript shows family no. 29 as emigrating in 1828, a check of the original document shows the correct date to be 1832. For Westerkappeln, there is a supplementary list taken at the village level, and including information on actual date of departure instead of just when the emigration permit was applied for, though it seldom gave destinations more specific than America. Finally, early naturalization declarations on the American side often give birthplace, date and port of arrival, as well as other details of travel. Schroer, emigrant no. 29, was not linked at all to the 1850 census, but was almost certainly the son referred to by no. 78, since the Westerkappeln list shows he emigrated the previous August. Freese, emigrant no. 32, was also missed by the 1850 census, but could be matched to a barn-door inscription recorded by Ravenswaay, *Arts and Architecture*, pp. 272–273.

Oberdalhoff, from the same village, accompanied them the whole way. It is difficult to say how great a role Duden's report played in these migrations. According to family tradition, it led the Ahmann brothers to Missouri. The fact that most of these immigrants followed Duden's tortuous overland route from Baltimore instead of the easier river connections from New Orleans further hints of this influence. But once a migration chain was established, such public sources of information were overshadowed by private ones. Persons applying for emigration permits in Lienen after 1840 were routinely asked whether they had read the Hesse book (a rather pessimistic account by one of the founders of Westphalia, Missouri), and just as routinely replied that they had, but would not change their minds on that account. However, the uniform wording of question and answer for emigrant after emigrant leads one to suspect that this was a mere formality. Officials gave the required warnings, and applicants gave the expected answers. Perhaps most of them did know the Hesse book at least from hearsay, but the reports of relatives and friends were what they relied on in making their decisions.[39]

No individual pathfinder can be singled out in the Hannoverian migration, but it apparently also began in the early 1830s. A group of Catholic peasants from near Osnabrück reached Franklin County in 1833. Associated with the Berlin Society was Count Frederick von Martels from near Osnabrück, who arrived in Missouri in late 1832. But he brought along only three laborers of peasant stock, and soon had a falling out with them, so his influence on later immigration was probably minimal. His son returned to Osnabrück in the spring of 1833, and the next year published his letters in a book similar to Duden's. Included was a detailed map of Duden country showing a settlement of "20 farmers from Osnabrück" between Femme Osage Creek and the Missouri River.[40] The settlement of New Melle began somewhat later, roughly 1838. But within a few years, a thriving community had been established. A Lutheran congregation began keeping baptis-

[39] Bek, "Followers of Duden," 18: 38; *History of St. Charles, Montgomery, and Warren Counties*, pp. 1046–1047. Grover A. Ahmann, *Family Tree of Herman and Sophia Ahmann Covering the Period 1811–1922* (Bakersfield, Calif., 1922). On Hesse, see William Bek, ed. and trans., "Nicholas Hesse, German Visitor to Missouri, 1835–1837," *Missouri Historical Review* 41 (1946–1947): 19–44, 164–183, 285–304, 373–390; ibid., 42 (1947–1948): 34–49, 140–152, 241–248. Emigrants in the Müller lists mentioning the Hesse book include nos. 786, 791–795, 800–803, 887, 1042–1043; for original documents, see Reg. Mü. 130, Bd. 8–10.

[40] Rothan, *German Catholic Immigration*, pp. 51–52; *Portrait and Biographical Record*, pp. 386, 254; Martels, *Briefe über die Vereinigten Staaten*, pp. 40–41 and appended map.

CHAPTER III

mal records in 1840 and was able to support a full-time pastor by 1844. The homogeneity of the community is suggested by the high percentage of the immigrants in the surrounding township who were natives of Hannover.[41]

Thus it is clear that in general emigration societies did little to encourage emigration from northwest Germany. In fact, peasant settlements preceded both the Giessen and Solingen societies. When Hermann Steines traveled toward Bremen in 1833, he noted in his journal, "Especially from Münster on, we found the inhabitants . . . occupied with emigration projects, and so many had already emigrated." One of these groups, the party from Westerkappeln that settled in St. Charles County, landed in Baltimore about the time Steines sailed from Bremerhaven. When brother Frederick arrived in Baltimore in June 1834 with the main Solingen contingent, he was almost a month behind a second party from Westerkappeln.[42] Upon arriving in Missouri in 1834 with the Giessen Society, Friedrich Muench noted that there was already "a considerable number of Westphalian *Heierleute* [sic]" in the neighborhood.[43]

Of the three societies, the Giessen group headed by Muench probably attracted the largest peasant following. It is no coincidence that most of the immigrants from Hesse-Darmstadt were clustered in Femme Osage and Charette townships near where Muench lived. Approximately ten families who had made the ocean crossing with him could be located in the census of the two counties in 1850, along with a half-dozen families from the other division of the Giessen Society under Follenius. There was at least one instance of chain migration. Three grown children of a village shoemaker in the town where Muench's brother had been pastor emigrated with Follenius; their widowed mother and younger siblings followed several years later. There were probably other examples. In recounting the prominent families of the Latin settlement, Muench mentioned several individuals from the region of Upper Hesse near his home town, and county-history biogra-

---

[41] *St. Charles Demokrat*, 24 September 1857; historical sketch of St. Paul's Lutheran Church, New Melle, Mo., in possession of the author.

[42] Dellmann, *Briefe der Familie Steines*, p. 8; Bek, "Followers of Duden," 14: 36, 40–49; ibid., 18: 37–38; ibid., 15: 523; Naturalization Records, Warren County Court, 30 June 1836, transcript in Work Projects Administration Collection, folder 21438, Western Historical Manuscripts Collection, University of Missouri–Columbia, declarations of intention to become citizens, F. Henry Bierbaum and Frederich Bierbaum (emigrants nos. 108 and 109 in the Münster lists). The Bierbaum party landed in Baltimore on 14 May 1834; the Steines party on 6 June.

[43] F. Muench, "Die Duden'sche Niederlassung," p. 199; Bek, "Followers of Duden," 18: 575.

phies included several people from this region who emigrated as late as the 1850s. By contrast, not a single person gave the Solingen region as his place of birth in these biographies. In fact, besides Frederick Steines, the only persons who could be linked to the passenger lists of the Solingen Society were two families in St. Charles County.[44] The Berlin Society, the most aristocratic of the three, was probably the least influential in attracting subsequent immigration.

In conclusion, then, it was peasant families acting on their own initiative who constituted the bulk of the immigration to Duden country. Here they settled in very homogeneous groups, apparent already at the township level, but even more so in the church congregations that developed. For instance, of the twenty founders of the Lutheran parish in St. Charles, all eighteen who could be located in the census or county histories were from Hannover, and several who were more specific all named Menslage as their birthplace. Of the eleven founders of the Evangelical church at Lippstadt, one may have been from Hannover, but the other ten all showed up in the census with Lippe as their birthplace. Moreover, they were tightly clustered, three families following successively in the census, and four others grouped within another cluster of eight families.[45] As a result, many of the first and second generation in America married descendants of the same village in Germany.

A striking example of local cohesiveness is presented by immigrants from Brunswick and the adjacent Hildesheim region of Hannover, who were somewhat outsiders in the area of study. Natives of Brunswick numbered only thirty-five souls scattered across three adjoining townships in a settlement composed largely of Westfalians and Osnabrückers, or less than 1 percent of the Germans in the two-county area. Jacob Diederich, hailing from Duderstadt in extreme southeastern Hannover,

[44] The Steines party arrived in Baltimore on the ship *Jefferson*, 6 June 1834; the Muench party on the *Medora*, 24 July 1834. Follenius arrived in New Orleans on the *Oelbers*, 2 June 1834 (National Archives, Baltimore passenger lists, microcopy 255, roll 2; New Orleans Quarterly Abstracts, microcopy 272, roll 1). Not all passengers on the *Oelbers* were with the Giessen Society; apparently only the first 259 on the list. Many of the others also settled in St. Charles County, but at the opposite end, northeast of St. Charles. A number of south Germans, about the last 40 on the passenger list of the *Jefferson*, were not members of the Solingen Society. Shoemaker's son Conrad Weinrich, his mother, and siblings could all be identified in the parish records of the Evangelical Church of Alten Buseck near Giessen. Weinrich's biography is found in *Portrait and Biographical Record*, p. 371. Two other Hessians emigrated in 1857: Henry Schweissguth, who had attended school in Alfeld, and a native of Nidda, Theodore Borberg, with the same family name as Muench's wife (*History of St. Charles, Montgomery, and Warren Counties*, pp. 240, 1054).

[45] *History of St. Charles, Montgomery, and Warren Counties*, pp. 350, 1012; *Portrait and Biographical Record*, pp. 210, 561.

CHAPTER III

would appear to have been even more of a loner. However, his journeyman years as a shoemaker probably brought him to the Hildesheim area before emigration, for he married Dina Staake, from a village just east of that city, shortly after arriving in St. Louis in 1855. By the time their first child was baptized in March 1857 they were living near the Tecklenburger settlement around Femme Osage. Christened on the same day in this congregation was a child of Christoph Wildschuetze and Friederike, nee Ohlendorf, both natives of rural Brunswick who had married in Missouri. Conrad Langemann, serving as godparent for both couples, was of the same origins, as was Dorothea Paul, the other godparent for the Diederichs. Except for Mr. Diederich, all these people stemmed from an area just ten miles in diameter on the Brunswick-Hannover border. The Diederichs and a Staake brother-in-law each had a child baptized on 12 June 1870, with Christoph Wildschuetze serving as godfather for both. The Diederichs and Wildschuetzes had settled near one another (and the Ohlendorfs) in Warren County, but later moved to adjacent farms near Langemanns a few miles away in St. Charles County. In the next generation, a Diederich son married a Wildschuetze daughter, and it was not until the following (third) generation that the German-American melting pot finally combined the Brunswicker-Hildesheimers with the Tecklenburger-Osnabrückers, although both groups were Low Germans and originated little more than one hundred miles apart in Germany. One might argue that it was proximity rather than regional affinity that led to this intermarriage in the second generation, but it was affinity that led to the proximity in the first place.[46]

But how typical was Duden country of German-American settlements generally? If anything, the nationwide publicity provided by the Duden book should have attracted a population more heterogeneous than usual. Detailed investigations on this subject are rare, but the existing information suggests that homogeneity on the local level was the rule rather than the exception in rural areas.

In both Clinton County, Michigan, and Osage County, Missouri, a town named Westphalia appears to have been taken over by later arrivals from the Rhineland, but in each a very homogeneous settlement developed. In the Michigan example, 97 of 133 German heads of fam-

[46] St. Louis Marriage Records, book 7, p. 425; parish records of the German Evangelical Church at Femme Osage; 1860 and 1870 U.S. Federal Manuscript Census of St. Charles and Warren counties; Brunswick emigrant lists published by Gruhne (see Appendix A). Wildschuetze and Paul were from Bleckenstedt, Ohlendorfs from Berel, Langemann from Vallstedt in Brunswick. Several of these matches to emigrant lists were confirmed in German parish registers.

ily specified Prussia as their birthplace in 1860. But 47 heads of families, nearly one-half of all Prussians, could be traced to *Kreis* Adenau west of Koblenz in Rhine Province. In the town of Westphalia, Missouri, not a single family was headed by a native-born American in 1860. Moreover, seven-eighths of the town's Germans were from Prussia. In two adjoining townships, Prussians accounted for nearly three-fourths of the Germans, and most of the rest were Bavarians concentrated in a rival parish at Rich Fountain. But except for the original party of about ten families, none could be traced to the emigrant lists of the Münster District, so if most Prussians were Westfalian at all, they must have come from the other two Districts of the province. In 1837, a dispute "between the hard-headed Westphalians and the light-hearted Rhinelanders" over the ordination of a priest was won by the former, but most likely the newly arrived Rhinelanders soon came to dominate the community.[47]

The early settlements were not the only ones to develop such a strong regional coloring. Similar homogeneity at the local level was characteristic of other German centers that developed later. "No, I'm at home here," wrote Jürnjacob Swehn, who had emigrated from Mecklenburg in 1868 and settled in Iowa. "Here most everybody is Low German and from Mecklenburg." His letters to his old schoolmaster were full of references to friends and acquaintances who had emigrated from the old home town and the surrounding villages and were living in the neighborhood.[48]

The colonies of Oldenburgers, Westfalians, and Hannoverians in west-central Ohio, all inspired by the writings of Franz Stallo, have already been cited. After Missouri, the leading destination for Lippe-Detmolders was Sheboygan County, Wisconsin. Although Lippe is barely thirty miles across at its widest point, the sources of migration to the two states were geographically distinct. The Sheboygan settlement began as a religiously influenced group migration, but it was hardly atyp-

[47] Joseph Scheben, *Untersuchung zur Methode und Technik der deutschamerikanischen Wanderungsforschung* (Bonn, 1939), pp. 39, 91. Hand tallies from manuscript census of 1860 of Germans in the town of Westphalia, and Washington and Jackson townships, Osage County. Entries in emigrant lists published by Müller (see Appendix A) were checked against the 1850 census of Osage County. Quotation from John Rothensteiner, *History of the Archdiocese of St. Louis*, 2 vols. (St. Louis, 1928), 1: 689–690. Rothensteiner (2: 363) adds parenthetically that the inhabitants of Westphalia, Missouri, "were not Westphalians."

[48] Johannes Gilhoff, *Jürnjacob Swehn der Amerikafahrer* (Berlin, 1919), p. 50. For other examples of homogeneous rural settlements, see Hildegard Binder Johnson, "The Location of German Immigrants in the Middle West," *Annals of the Association of American Geographers* 41 (1951): 1–41.

CHAPTER III

ical in its homogeneity, as the names of neighboring townships suggest: Rhein, Mosel, Holland, Schleswig, and New Holstein, the last boasting a village of Kiel named after the provincial capital of Schleswig-Holstein.[49] Likewise, in southern Illinois there were a number of homogeneous settlements from northwest Germany. The Osnabrückers who founded Washington, Missouri, in 1833 were the remnant of a larger party of Catholics and Protestants who had sailed from Bremen bound for Illinois. Several place names in southern Illinois bear witness to northwest German origins, among them New Minden in Washington County, Paderborn in St. Clair County, the town and township of Bremen in Randolph County, the hamlet of Oldenburg since engulfed by Wood River, and perhaps most appropriately, the town and township of New Hannover in Monroe County just southeast of St. Louis.[50]

The naming of Germantown, Illinois, is cited by Oscar Handlin as an example of how emigration broke down regional barriers and forged a national consciousness that had not existed in Europe.[51] Instead, it is a perfect example of how local and regional groupings persisted in America. The settlement had its beginnings in 1834, when two Germans from Osnabrück bought land on Shoal Creek and sought friends and relatives in St. Louis and in Germany to help found a German Catholic colony. They attracted a number of immigrants, "mostly Catholics of Low German stock," as an ecclesiastical history relates. When the time came in 1837 to name the place, the Hannoverians and Westfalians each favored the name of their native province, though some were willing to hyphenate the two. However, all agreed on Germantown.[52] But this is almost as if natives of Alabama and Mississippi had moved west and named their new settlement Dixie. The people of Germantown were practically all Catholic, they spoke the same Low German dialect, they came from areas with similar patterns of agriculture and inheritance. It is doubtful that they had lived more than fifty miles apart in Germany; in fact, some of them must have been acquainted in the old

[49] Immigrants from Lippe were traced back from the 1860 Federal Manuscript Census in Missouri to the emigrant lists published by Verdenhalven, *Die Auswanderer aus Lippe*. On Sheboygan County, Wisconsin, see Jerome C. Arpke, *Das Lippe-Detmolder Settlement in Wisconsin* (Milwaukee, 1895); Richard M. Bernard, *The Melting Pot and the Altar: Marital Assimilation in Early Twentieth-Century Wisconsin* (Minneapolis, 1980), pp. 13–15, 42–43; *Portrait and Biographical Record of Sheboygan County, Wisconsin* (Chicago, 1894).

[50] Rothan, *German Catholic Immigrant*, p. 51; August R. Suelflow, *The Heart of Missouri* (St. Louis, 1954), p. 32.

[51] Oscar Handlin, *The Uprooted*, 2d ed., rev. (Boston, 1973), pp. 166–167.

[52] Rothan, *German Catholic Immigrant*, p. 42; Rothensteiner, *Archdiocese of St. Louis*, 1: 772.

country. Natives of the two provinces regularly intermarried along the borders. In American cities, the situation may have been different, though, as has been seen, the *Deutschtum* of a particular city usually had a distinct regional coloring. But particularly for settlers in rural areas, emigration was less an uprooting than a transplanting.

CHAPTER IV

Native and Adoptive Americans: The Extent of Acculturation in Social Patterns and Agricultural Practices

Recognizing that which is good and better here, which is not hard to find, we Americans of German extraction should make it our own, without thereby thoughtlessly and childishly throwing overboard the genuine good of the old homeland. If we instead . . . make the effort to hold up before the eyes of our fellow citizens of English extraction that which was really better in Germany, our skill, our diligence, our festivities, our schools, then these will certainly also find recognition.[1]

AT FIRST GLANCE, the self-designation "Americans of German extraction" above might suggest an attempt to play down ethnicity, adopt an attitude of Anglo-conformity, and assimilate as quickly as possible. A closer look, however, reveals instead an espousal of cultural pluralism, the idea that German immigrants could contribute more to America by retaining and cultivating institutions and customs of their cultural heritage that were lacking in the New World than by denying their heritage and attempting to submerge themselves in the Anglo-American mainstream. The first part of this chapter examines in greater detail the self-image of Missouri Germans and their attitudes toward other ethnic groups. The second part then investigates the degree to which these attitudes were translated into behavior, using indicators such as intermarriage patterns, religious affiliation, neighborhood segregation, occupational structure, and agricultural specialization.

The statements left behind by Missouri Germans show how much they considered themselves to be a people apart, different and in many respects superior to other groups. This is particularly apparent in their image of the Old French, a group that kept mostly to itself and remained culturally distinct despite the fact that many of these families had been in Missouri since the eighteenth century. The *St. Charles Demokrat*, in an 1857 series on different settlements in the county, observed that the residents of the French village of Portage "supported themselves less from agriculture and artisanship than from hunting, fishing, and boating on the . . . rivers." "A log cabin with a few acres of

[1] *St. Charles Demokrat*, 21 August 1852.

cleared land to plant vegetables and some corn was the most property the easily satisfied Frenchman accumulated," the account continued. "It is unbelievable how little influence the change of the last fifty years has had on them."[2] Gustave Koerner made a tour of Missouri in 1833 and also commented on the French he encountered: "Indifferent farmers they were, fond of hunting and particularly fishing ... [living] in villages, where they could have music and dancing and could play at cards. They were a gay and harmless people, and indolent, though their young men would frequently hire themselves out to the fur companies for a year or two as hunters or trappers."[3] Both Koerner and Heinrich von Martels, a Hannoverian officer who visited them about the same time, commented favorably upon French hospitality, but the latter also noted "their whitewashed cabins, their well-kept gardens, their poorly fenced, poorly tilled, mediocre corn fields" and flatly stated that "their young men ... hate all work, and spend the greater part of their lives in the woods or on the rivers as hunters, trappers, and fur traders."[4] Obviously, none of these observers had ever helped drag a keelboat two thousand miles up the Missouri River, but these antimodern attitudes they described were very real even if they did not stem from laziness.

Toward the Irish the Germans displayed a different kind of ambivalence. Both the Enlightenment ideology of German liberalism and the common threat that nativism posed for all immigrants made it necessary to defend the Irish. For example, the *Demokrat* reported as "disgraceful" an incident in which four Irishmen were badly mistreated by a steamboat crew without any provocation. But mixed with this support in principle was an image of the Irishman as a drinking, brawling rowdy. One typical ethnic joke in the newspaper involved an Irishman who, asked in court for a certificate of his marriage, showed the judge a wound in his scalp inflicted by a fire shovel. Fights among Irishmen were often related with a mixture of superiority and tolerant bemusement characteristic of earlier reports of petty crimes by blacks. One example is sufficient to illustrate: "Fight: Two Irishmen, who despite the cold weather were still too hot blooded, found it advisable for their health to open a few veins for one another."[5]

[2] Ibid., 17 September 1857.
[3] Thomas J. McCormack, ed., *Memoirs of Gustave Koerner, 1809–1896*, 2 vols. (Cedar Rapids, Iowa, 1909), 1: 321–322.
[4] Heinrich von Martels, *Briefe uber die westlichen Theile der Vereinigten Staaten von Nordamerika* (Osnabrück, 1834), pp. 72–73.
[5] *St. Charles Demokrat*, 6 October 1855; 31 January 1852; 10 February 1855. For similar examples of German ambivalence toward the Irish, see Walter D. Kamphoefner,

CHAPTER IV

The image of native-born Americans was still more complicated, for it involved at least three competing stereotypes, each with different negative aspects: the sharp-trading Yankee, the aristocratic planter, and the shiftless frontiersman. One article in the *Demokrat* spoke of the dark side that "grows out of the pursuit of the dollar among the Yankees, such as the deceit and corruption in the present legislature and in trade, the destruction of human life on exploding steamboats for the sake of money, the systematic swindling of immigrants." Nativism could be found among Southern-stock "border ruffians" as well, but there were other aspects that made the New England Yankee character especially suspect: "his religious hypocrisy, his temperance movement, his spirit-rapping and the like."[6] Americans of Southern origin were represented by two contrasting stereotypes. One was the "aristocracy" that was especially concentrated in one of the settlements featured in a newspaper series describing the county. "The farms are more like plantations, and all are inhabited and worked by Virginians, who almost all own Negroes. They ... seem to resist stubbornly the 'invasion of foreign elements.' The families constitute a kind of closed society among themselves, and from here the fate of St. Charles County is determined, or at least so they believe." If this group and the Germans had little to do with one another by mutual choice, there was another type of Southern-stock American with whom Missouri Germans competed more directly. The frontiersman was seen as a product of the American environment that often brought out the worst in people, even in those who stemmed from an earlier generation of German immigrants. The *Demokrat* observed that family names, however corrupted, bore witness to the German origins of a significant number of early settlers. "Their descendants who were still here in 1832 and were bought out by the more recent German settlers were mostly Americans in the worst sense of the word: rough, brutal, ignorant, and ashamed of their ancestry if they were still aware of it."[7]

These German images of the American character seem to have established themselves very early in the period of settlement. A diary entry by a Femme Osage pastor's wife, Adelheid Garlichs, from June 1836, only five months after her arrival, includes all the stereotypes, though they must have been based as much on hearsay as on personal observation. First of all, the Americans were sharp traders: "such free spenders, not at all frugal, and still so interested in dealing and so egoistic that

---

"St. Louis Germans and the Republican Party, 1848–1860," *Mid-America* 57 (1975): 85–86.

[6] *St. Charles Demokrat*, 2 September 1854; 13 September 1856.

[7] *St. Charles Demokrat*, 10 January 1857; 13 December 1857.

they hardly consider it a sin to cheat in business or to swear a false oath." Second, they were rootless: "Today with great effort they establish themselves on a farm; tomorrow they may sell it for a petty profit." The image of the lazy backwoodsman was rounded out by this version of the Arkansas Traveler tale: "For they can often live for years in a house where it rains in very badly without ever thinking of making some minor repairs and doing away with this nuisance."[8]

German Americans often expressed more admiration for "the true American spirit, the spirit of its free institutions" than for the American people. In fact, Germans sometimes intimated that they understood the ideals of this country better than those who were citizens by accident of birth rather than choice:

> Whoever conducts himself in his opinions and actions according to the republican Constitution of our new fatherland, which by no means excludes reforms, is an American in the sense in which it is honorable to be called an American, and not all native born are necessarily through chance of birth Americans in this sense.[9]

A resolution from the height of the nativist crisis lectured on Americanism in similar terms: "Resolved, that those who make use of the catch phrase 'America must be ruled by Americans' either are ignorant of the history of their own country or conceal behind this catch phrase goals they do not dare to acknowledge openly."[10]

These same elements of superiority with touches of condescension are apparent in German self-characterizations. The features of the German self-image that stand out most prominently are their hard-working perseverance and their craftsmanship, but above all their determination to strike roots in the country. Descriptions of three different German settlements in St. Charles County follow almost identical stereotyped phrasing as this description of New Melle: "The land in the vicinity is second class . . . the diligence and frugality of the inhabitants has made this into a flourishing settlement despite the stepmother-like treatment of nature."[11]

Along with this diligence went the determination to stay in one place and make the best of the situation. Seven years after the founding of Hermann, Missouri, on a site more picturesque than productive, the

---

[8] Diary of Adelheid Garlichs, nee von Borries, 1835–1840 (typescript transcript by W. D. Kamphoefner). My thanks to the Reyner von Borries family, who generously loaned me the original.

[9] *St. Charles Demokrat*, 21 August 1852.

[10] *St. Charles Demokrat*, 29 March 1856.

[11] *St. Charles Demokrat*, 21 August 1852; 24 September 1852.

CHAPTER IV

editor of the local *Wochenblatt* surmised that "if our settlement were inhabited by Americans instead of Germans, Hermann would now ... have been reduced to just a few stores doing business with the farm population, while most of the other inhabitants would have long since sought their fortunes somewhere else." A German politician expressed a similar view of his people's virtues: Germans "do not always push on like the Yankees from the cleared farm to the unbroken virgin forest, but once they have won an inheritance they remain there, and develop the feeling of hearth and homestead, and this gives their children the opportunity to uplift themselves to a higher civilization."[12]

While it is easy to ascertain the attitudes of German Americans, or at least of their articulate elite, records of everyday behavior, particularly of the peasant stock, are more elusive. There are only a few scattered references from contemporaries that give some clues to the extent of contacts between immigrants and natives. Gert Goebel, from just south of the Missouri in Franklin County, gives an amusing account of a German greenhorn's initiation into the secrets of rail-splitting by his backwoods neighbors. He also tells of participating in hunting parties and dances with Anglo-Americans. But he may have been an exception, since his was the only German family in a six-mile radius, and his sister represented a one-in-one-hundred case of a German woman married to an American. Heinrich Meinershagen, a prospering storekeeper from Tecklenburg, actually employed at least one American. The circumstances under which this was recorded, however, lead one to question how widespread or cordial such relationships were: The employee, Thomas McGough, shot Meinershagen dead after being knocked to the floor in a fight that grew out of a financial dispute. Similarly, Adelheid Garlichs mentioned in her diary a dance attended by both Germans and Americans, but it ended up in a brawl (*Schlägerei*) between them. When Pastor Garlichs first brought his young bride to America in 1836, she recorded that they visited all their neighbors, German and American. Over the next five years, however, only four American names appear among roughly four hundred persons listed as guests or hosts in her diary, which often reads more like a social calendar. If contacts were this rare at the upper levels of immigrant society, they were probably even less common among the peasant stock.[13]

More enlightening than such fragments of literary evidence, however, are empirical measures of German assimilation. Intermarriage is

[12] *Hermanner Wochenblatt*, 19 December 1845; *St. Charles Demokrat*, 13 March 1852.

[13] Gert Goebel, *Länger als ein Menschenleben in Missouri* (St. Louis, 1877); *St. Charles Demokrat*, 26 November 1853; Adelheid Garlichs diary, p. 30 and passim.

perhaps the most demanding test of acceptance, but there are others. Institutional affiliations, especially to religious denominations, both facilitate integration into a host society and serve as badges of this integration, while transplanted denominations often serve as a focus for ethnicity and an agent of language preservation. Residential segregation is just as important in rural as in urban areas. Patterns of immigrant occupation different from those of the host society may result from the negative factor of prejudice, but may just as often reflect a positive factor—special skills brought along from Europe. Agricultural specialization may likewise reflect the influence of cultural baggage. All these aspects will be considered with respect to the Germans of St. Charles and Warren counties and their neighbors.

Two of the most famous residents of this area were Daniel Boone and Gottfried Duden. Boone left Kentucky and settled on Femme Osage Creek in St. Charles County before 1800 when the territory was still under Spanish rule. Thousands of other settlers followed in the old pioneer's footsteps, especially after the Louisiana Territory came under American rule in 1803, so that the population of the area was principally of Southern stock, mostly from Virginia and Kentucky. Gottfried Duden lived for several years on a farm in what was to become Warren County. His "Report" provided the impetus for the large German migration to Missouri beginning in 1830. By 1850, the followers of Duden had not yet taken over from the followers of Boone, but they constituted a strong minority. Germans made up 44 percent of the heads of families in the two counties, as compared to 49 percent who were native-born. In fact, if one excludes those born in Northern states, the groups are almost evenly matched. The category "German" as it is used in this chapter includes Swiss and Alsatians, both German-speaking groups that were well integrated into the German community. About 5 percent of the free population was Old French, a group that remained culturally distinctive despite a long tenure in the New World. Many of these families had been in Missouri since the eighteenth century, but they had been augmented by some migration, principally from Canada. The scattering of immigrants of British stock includes a few born in Canada. If there were any Ulster natives, they are subsumed under "Irish" since the census does not specify religion. These are the ethnic groups that constituted as much as 1 percent of the free population, and together they accounted for more than 99 percent. The rest were either free blacks or a few people from other states of Continental Europe whose main contacts were with Germans.[14]

[14] In the two counties in 1850 there were more men aged eighteen and older born in

CHAPTER IV

TABLE 4.1. PROPENSITY TO MARRY WITHIN ETHNIC GROUP
(Couples Not Married Abroad; St. Charles and Warren Counties, 1850)

Men by Ethnic Origin	Women by Ethnic Origin						
	American	German	Old French	Irish	British	Other Foreign	Total
American	1,034	12	—	2	5	—	1,053
German	41	569	—	—	2	—	612
Old French	—	2	91	1	—	1	95
Irish	6	—	—	5	1	—	12
British	10	—	—	—	8	—	18
Other Foreign	1	2	2	—	—	1	6
TOTAL	1,092	585	93	8	16	2	1,796

SOURCE: See Appendix B.

By 1850, some of the Germans had been living in Missouri for nearly twenty years, but the amount of intermarriage that took place between Germans and natives was still negligible. In fact, it may even have decreased over the years as more prospective German spouses became available. Only one German woman in one hundred had an American husband, and despite the unbalanced sex ratio, only 4 percent of the German men married outside their ethnic group. Americans were nearly as endogamous as the Germans, with only 5 percent of the women and 2 percent of the men taking spouses from outside their group. Calculating intermarriage rates on the basis of the whole immigrant group is somewhat inappropriate, however, since some people were already married when they came to this country and thus were not at risk, so to speak, for intermarriage. Likewise, potential foreign partners for Anglo-Americans were limited before mass immigration began around 1830. Thus, Table 4.1 is restricted to couples who had no children born abroad, a rough approximation of those who had married in the United States. There was no easy procedure for eliminating natives who were married before 1830, however, so the table includes all American spouses and gives a somewhat exaggerated picture of their endogamy. A similar problem arises with the Old French, who were identified primarily on the basis of family name. Some Frenchwomen

---

Virginia than in Missouri. Of the men in the "German" category, 2.1 percent were Alsatian and 1.3 percent were Swiss. Among the Old French, about one-fourth of the men aged eighteen and older were born in Canada, but two-thirds were native to Missouri. Only one in twelve in the British category was Canadian-born.

TABLE 4.2. SEX RATIO AND PROPORTION MARRIED BY ETHNIC GROUP
(Persons 18 and Older, St. Charles and Warren Counties, 1850)

	Women 18 and Older		Men per 100 Women	Men 18 and Older	
	Married or Widowed	Number		Married or Widowed	Number
American	76%	1,679	112	65%	1,873
German	87	1,262	132	70	1,660
Old French	76	169	116	65	196
Irish	43	28	243	33	68
British	72	32	144	57	46
All	80	3,177	121	67	3,859

SOURCE: See Appendix B.

who married Anglo-Americans doubtless went undetected, and at least two men in this category were listed as non-Catholics, a good clue that they were not French. Nevertheless, the cohesiveness of this group appears impressively high in view of its small size. The melting pot likewise held little attraction for Germans who had married in Missouri. Only 7 percent of German men and less than 3 percent of German women looked outside their own group for partners. The handful of people from the rest of Continental Europe also avoided partners of English stock. Only the tiny group of English-speaking immigrants—the Irish and particularly the British—appear to have been well accepted by Americans, and one suspects that the exogamous Irish were mostly Protestant.

Table 4.2, showing sex ratios and proportions married among various ethnic groups, points up some of the dynamics of the intermarriage patterns. The German fondness for home and hearth, observed by other researchers also, comes through clearly from the table. Despite a sex ratio more unfavorable than that facing Americans or Frenchmen, German men married in greater proportions than the men of any other group. Yet, only 4 percent of them turned to Americans for wives. The extraordinarily high proportion of German women who married made this unnecessary. Of all those eighteen and older, fully 87 percent were either married or widowed. This is similar to the patterns of Swedish immigrants in rural America, where the same proportion of Swedish men were able to marry as in the old country despite an unfavorable sex ratio because a considerably greater than normal proportion of Swedish women married. Another interesting feature regarding the Germans

CHAPTER IV

TABLE 4.3. RELIGIOUS AFFILIATION OF FIRST- AND SECOND-GENERATION GERMANS
(St. Charles and Warren Counties, 1895)

	Catholic	Lutheran	Evangelical	Methodist	Other	None or None Given
Germany unspecified	12	12	20	6	2	7
Prussia unspecified	11	6	3	3	2	—
Rhineland	3	—	—	—	1	3
Westfalia unspecified	4	1	4	—	—	1
Tecklenburg	—	1	18	2	2	4
Hannover unspecified	10	21	3	—	3	—
Osnabrück District	4	10	3	—	—	—
Lippe-Detmold	—	—	1	7	—	1
Oldenburg	4	—	—	—	—	—

SOURCE: See note 16.

is that while men made up nearly 62 percent of the migration to America from 1846 to 1850, nearly 60 percent from 1841 to 1845, and even greater proportions before that, in these two rural counties only 57 percent of the Germans eighteen or older were men. Evidently a larger proportion of unattached men would be found in cities. The Irish appear to have been new arrivals and very transient, for only 43 percent of their women were married despite a huge imbalance in sex ratio.[15]

In religion as in marriage, Germans preferred to stay among their own kind. Table 4.3 reflects the situation in 1895, after the forces of assimilation had been at work for fifty years, among a group of people featured in county-history biographies, a local elite that may have been more acculturated than the general population. Ecclesiastical histories often emphasize the hostility toward religion in the early settlements, but the most striking feature in the table is the degree of religious continuity from Germany to America. Like the Saxons who founded Missouri Synod Lutheranism, some East Elbian Prussians emigrated in protest of government attempts to unify the Lutheran and Reformed

[15] Harald Runblom and Hans Norman, eds., *From Sweden to America: A History of the Migration* (Minneapolis, 1976), pp. 287–290; Peter Marschalck, *Deutsche Uberseewanderung im 19. Jahrhundert* (Stuttgart, 1973), p. 72. Tables 4.1 and 4.2 are both based on the 1850 census data set explained in Appendix B. A comparison with data from the Osnabrück region where many of the immigrants originated (*Zur Statistik des Königreichs Hannover* [Hannover, 1850–1867], vol. 11), shows that in 1858 only 77 percent of all women over age twenty had ever been married, although the rate for such men, 80 percent, was somewhat higher than in America.

churches, but Westfalian Prussians established virtually an American counterpart of the Prussian Union Church.[16] The great bulk of Protestant Westfalians, including most Tecklenburgers, were solidly Evangelical in their affiliation, with only a slight spillover to the more ritualistic Lutherans and the more pietistic Methodists. In neighboring Osnabrück, the Protestants had been overwhelmingly Lutheran, though there was a strong minority of Catholics. These loyalties are very much in evidence among immigrants from this region, many of whom simply gave Hannover as their state of origin. The Catholic antecedents of immigrants from Oldenburg are also very apparent. The only Anglo-American denomination with much appeal to the Germans was the Methodist, but even here a carry-over of German pietism played an important role. Natives of Lippe-Detmold were heavily concentrated in the Methodist church, and it is significant that in their homeland a strong grass-roots pietist movement had developed within an unsympathetic conservative Lutheran state church and may have helped motivate emigration. The Methodist church early developed a German-language branch that helped to attract many German pietists in America.[17] The few persons attracted to other denominations, mostly Presbyterians, represent practically the only case of adoption of American ways. Even those individuals with no religious affiliation usually reflect the anticlerical, freethinking ideology of many German intellectuals rather than the godlessness of the American frontier.

Ownership of slaves, a practice unknown in Germany, is another indication of adoption of American ways. The number and the identity

[16] For example, Carl E. Schneider, *The German Church on the American Frontier* (St. Louis, 1938), pp. 32–41; Walter O. Forster, *Zion on the Mississippi* (St. Louis, 1953), pp. 238–264; Wilhelm Iwan, *Die Altlutherische Auswanderung um die Mitte des 19. Jahrhunderts*, 2 vols. (Ludwigsburg, 1943). On the other hand, a pastor who visited the area in 1835 reported, "Muench had also preached once, but since he did not mention the name of Jesus or pray the Lord's Prayer, his sermons were not attended any more by the Osnabrückers." The people referred to were, in fact, probably Tecklenburgers. (J. G. Büttner, *Die Vereinigten Staaten von Nord-Amerika: Mein Aufenthalt und meine Reisen in denselben vom Jahre 1834 bis 1841*, 2 vols. [Hamburg, 1844], 1: 185). Table 4.3 is based on a hand tally from *Portrait and Biographical Record of St. Charles, Lincoln, and Warren Counties, Missouri* (Chicago, 1895).

[17] W. Lohmeyer, *Die Erweckungsbewegung in Lippe im 19. Jahrhundert*, 2d ed. (Detmold, 1932); Kate E. Levi, "Geographical Origins of German Immigration to Wisconsin," *Collections of the State Historical Society of Wisconsin* 14 (1898): 365–367. According to Levi, immigrants from Lippe often joined Methodist, Baptist, and Presbyterian churches, although some remained Evangelical-Reformed. On German-American Methodism, see Paul F. Douglas, *The Story of German Methodism: Biography of an Immigrant Soul* (Cincinnati, 1939); Carl Wittke, *William Nast: Patriarch of German Methodism* (Detroit, 1959).

CHAPTER IV

of Germans who owned slaves shows that the degree of assimilation was often a function of social class origins. German slaveholders were few, however, for out of more than one thousand German heads of family, only seventeen in St. Charles and eleven in Warren County owned slaves in 1850. Nor were their slaveholdings large, in half the cases involving only one slave. The largest German slaveholders were three with seven slaves each. Of approximately three thousand slaves in the two counties, only about seventy-five were in the hands of Germans.[18]

Many of the German slaveholders were of the type who would state for their biographies in county histories that they were of the "better class of Germans" in the county. Of the eleven slaveholders in Warren County in 1850, one was Duden's traveling companion, Louis Eversmann, and seven others were Latin farmers of either the Berlin or the Giessen Society. Many of the German slaveholders in St. Charles County were also of upper-middle-class origins, though few if any could be traced to emigration societies. However, poverty alone does not account for the low level of German slaveholding. A breakdown by wealth categories shows that over one-fifth of all American farmers without real estate owned slaves, but not a single German in this category. Likewise, among persons with less than $1,000 worth of real estate, 28 percent of all native farmers owned slaves, but only three such Germans or less than 1 percent. At every category of wealth from bottom to top the proportion of slaveholders was lower among Germans than among natives.

There was a considerable overlapping between Germans who owned slaves and those marrying Americans. Seven people in St. Charles County fall into this category, and one in Warren. Moreover, there were several slaveholders among the Germans who belonged to American churches. Although three of the slaveholders in 1850 and two others in 1860 were among the immigrants from Tecklenburg, none of them had been of the propertyless classes in Germany.

An ironic note is that the slaveholders of St. Charles and Warren counties included several people who became prominent and even radical Republicans. In 1850, the brothers Georg and Friedrich Muench were listed with one female slave each in the manuscript census. In 1860, the Muench brothers had apparently given up slaveholding, and Friedrich had taken up the antislavery crusade. Among the slaveholders

[18] Slaveholdings were enumerated on a separate schedule of the census, but names of slaveholders could be matched with those in the population schedule of the 1850 and 1860 census to determine nationality.

in 1860 in St. Charles County were Gustave Bruere and Arnold Krekel, both lawyers, editors, and politicians closely associated with the soon-to-become Republican *St. Charles Demokrat*. But both slaveholding and participation in public life were functions of social class with these people, for all were of upper-middle-class origins in Germany and had enjoyed the benefits of higher education.

One of the factors affecting assimilation was the presence or absence of an immigrant group of sufficient size, a "critical mass" that could sustain community life. People who had emigrated before 1830 and had spent some time in the East, or who had arrived with the first German settlers in Missouri, were much more likely to take American wives, own slaves, or join American religious denominations. A good example is Louis Eversmann, Duden's traveling companion, who remained in Missouri and had, as Gert Goebel observed, "Americanized himself very quickly; he married an American woman . . . and soon became the first *German* slaveholder."[19] Perhaps this early immigration was also of a different type than the later mass migration, motivated more by the business opportunities of America and more inclined to become part of its society than the rural lower classes set in motion by expulsive forces in Europe. Social class played an important role in assimilation. Among the Germans in Table 4.1 for example, those who married Americans showed average real estate holdings about 70 percent higher than those who remained within their own group.

Second-generation sons of Latin farmers were often fully integrated into the host society. Thomas Morsey, whose father immigrated with the Berlin Society, married an American woman and was either unchurched or attended Presbyterian services with his wife. He was working as the editor of an English-language newspaper in the Warren County seat and never even mentioned his German antecedents in a biographical sketch in 1895. By contrast, John Dickherber, one of the few third-generation Germans featured in the same 1895 volume of biographical sketches, but of peasant stock, hardly stood out from the majority of immigrants and their children. He grew up in a German-Catholic parish, was reared to farm life, married a woman with the Teutonic name of Schulz, and had recently left farming to take over a village store with a brother-in-law named Meyer.[20]

Reflecting the patterns of ethnic cohesion and also serving to perpetuate them were the tendencies toward geographic segregation. Though it is not apparent at the township level, Germans and Americans lived

[19] Goebel, *Länger als ein Menschenleben*, p. 6.
[20] *Portrait and Biographical Record*, pp. 325, 555.

CHAPTER IV

TABLE 4.4. DEGREE OF RESIDENTIAL CLUSTERING BY ETHNIC GROUP IN THE 1850 U.S. CENSUS OF ST. CHARLES AND WARREN COUNTIES

	Number of families	Two preceding and two subsequent families all of same ethnicity	Both preceding and subsequent family of same ethnicity	At least one of two adjacent families of same ethnicity
American	1,242	44.7%	61.6%	90.4%
German	1,104	42.1	59.2	88.7
Old French	127	30.7	51.2	90.0
Irish	20	0.0	5.0	45.0
British	23	0.0	0.0	8.7

SOURCE: See Appendix B.

relatively isolated from one another (see Table 4.4). Nine families in ten of each group could count at least one compatriot among the two nearest neighbors in the order the 1850 census taker went down the road, and six in ten had someone of the same ethnicity on either side. In fact, over 40 percent of both Germans and Americans lived in ethnic enclaves of at least five families. North of St. Charles, there was one string of over one hundred native families in the 1850 census without so much as a German hired hand, and there were other areas, especially around New Melle and Femme Osage, that were almost as solidly German. Despite the small numbers of Old French, they were almost as highly segregated as natives or Germans, being mainly restricted to St. Charles and Portage des Sioux townships. The scattering of immigrants of British stock, including a few born in Canada, was well integrated into the native society. Irish family heads were no more numerous but stuck together more, probably in response to the prejudice they encountered.

Occupational distribution is perhaps the least demanding criterion by which to measure acculturation. Particularly where a large ethnic group is involved, the occupational structure of the host society may be duplicated by the immigrant group without much social contact taking place. And in a community not very far beyond the frontier stage, the economy may not have reached a level of development that allowed much occupational specialization. Nevertheless, even though two-thirds of the adult males in St. Charles and Warren counties were engaged in farming, a good deal of specialization is evident in the German occupational structure.

TABLE 4.5. RELATIVE CONCENTRATION OF VARIOUS ETHNIC GROUPS IN NONAGRICULTURAL OCCUPATIONS
(St. Charles and Warren Counties, 1850)

Occupational Strata	American	German	Old French	Irish	British	N of Cases
1 Professional, High White-Collar	121	81	24	67	234	164
2 Proprietary, Low White-Collar	117	80	87			90
3 Skilled Artisan	68	139	87	75	130	450
4 Unskilled Laborer	81	81	357	195	329	204
No Occupation Given, Owning Real Estate	80	97	273	166	0	36
No Occupation Given, without Real Estate	94	86	243	208	0	219
All Occupations outside Agriculture	87	105	161	122	159	1,163
% of Total Labor Force	48.5%	43.0%	5.1%	1.8%	1.2%	

SOURCE: See Appendix B.

The reputation of Germans as skilled artisans is born out in Table 4.5, where occupations are grouped by broad categories.[21] Although nearly half the nonagricultural jobs were in crafts, the Germans were the only group, except for the handful of British, who were overrepresented there. The contrast is especially sharp compared to Anglo-Americans, who reached only two-thirds of their quota in skilled labor whereas Germans accounted for one-third more than a uniform distribution would lead one to expect. In the upper levels of society, Ger-

[21] Source of Tables 4.5 through 4.10 explained in Appendix B. The figures in Tables 4.5 and 4.10 are indexes of representation, showing the degree of deviation from a uniform distribution of all ethnic groups over all occupations. For more detail, see Chap. 3, n. 5 above. In Table 4.5, the unskilled-labor category includes 13 French hunters; but even without these, the French would have shown an index of nearly 250 in this category. Besides persons designated in the census as farmers and laborers, the agricultural groups in Table 4.10 include 22 tobacconists, 2 drovers, 2 dairymen, and one overseer. They were allocated to the three categories of owner, renter, and laborer by the same criteria as persons designated as farmers.

CHAPTER IV

TABLE 4.6. OCCUPATIONS IN WHICH OLD FRENCH PREDOMINATED
(St. Charles and Warren Counties, 1850)

Strata[a] and Occupation	Number of Persons	% Old French
3 (River) Pilot	5	80
4 (Buffalo) Hunter	13	100
ALL OCCUPATIONS		5

SOURCE: See Appendix B. [a] See Table 4.5.

mans were somewhat underrepresented, Americans overrepresented, but the differences were not extreme. At the bottom end of the scale, the Germans were no more likely to be unskilled laborers than the Americans. The Old French are the only other group large enough to warrant much attention. Their concentration at the bottom end of the scale is apparent, though they nearly held their own in low-white-collar and artisan categories. As might be expected in view of the pattern elsewhere, there was a double portion of Irish among the unskilled laborers, but as a group they were perhaps somewhat better off in Missouri than in most parts of the country. The British were overrepresented in all nonagricultural pursuits, at both the bottom and the top of the social ladder. The effects of missing data—highest for French and Irish—apparently caused little bias in either a positive or a negative direction.

The patterns of specialization become even more apparent when one isolates the individual occupations in which a particular ethnic group predominated. The Old French, accounting for only 5 percent of the labor force, were too small a group to dominate many occupations. Yet their fondness for the woods and rivers is evident (Table 4.6). The Germans' perceptions were not totally inaccurate, though the motives they attributed to the French may have been.

Occupations dominated by the Germans were restricted entirely to the artisan sector. Some of the less common trades, among them weaving, cigar making, tin smithing, and as might be expected, watchmaking, brewing, and distilling, were monopolized by the Germans (see Table 4.7). They also accounted for nearly twice their share of bakers and cabinetmakers. Three of four persons employed in such common trades as shoemaking and tailoring were German. In fact, carpentry and coopering were about the only major crafts where the native population was holding its own, and 60 percent of all the people employed in skilled labor were German (see Table 4.8).

TABLE 4.7. OCCUPATIONS IN WHICH GERMANS PREDOMINATED
(St. Charles and Warren Counties, 1850)

Strata[a] and Occupation	Number of Persons	% German	Strata[a] and Occupation	Number of Persons	% German
Distiller	4	100	3 Gunsmith	8	75
Blacksmith	61	64	3 Baker	7	86
Shoemaker	46	74	3 Cigar Maker	7	100
(Stone) Mason	26	81	3 Tinner	4	100
Tailor	24	75	3 Weaver	3	100
Wagonmaker	22	68	3 Brewer	3	100
Miller	19	63	3 Watchmaker	3	100
Cabinetmaker, Joiner	12	83	3 Surveyor	3	100
			ALL OCCUPATIONS		43

SOURCE: See Appendix B.   [a] See Table 4.5.

Thus it was in the solid middle class that Germans were most concentrated. The handicaps of a foreign language, and perhaps also the lack of higher aspirations than a secure and independent life, are reflected by a number of occupations that were primarily left to the native-born (see Table 4.9). Of course, where people were free to choose their own pastors, they usually favored someone of their own group. But the rest of the professions were dominated by natives, medicine the least so but it was perhaps the least respectable in this generation. Few Germans had a command of the language required for the English

TABLE 4.8. OCCUPATIONS WITH APPROXIMATELY EQUAL PROPORTIONS OF GERMANS AND AMERICANS
(St. Charles and Warren Counties, 1850)

Strata[a] and Occupation	Number of Persons	% American	% German
1 Pastor, Clergyman	18	44	50
1 Merchant / 2 Grocer	67	43	49
3 Carpenter	86	44	45
3 Cooper	30	53	43
3 Saddler	11	45	55
ALL OCCUPATIONS		49	43

SOURCE: See Appendix B.   [a] See Table 4.5.

CHAPTER IV

TABLE 4.9. OCCUPATIONS IN WHICH AMERICANS PREDOMINATED
(*St. Charles and Warren Counties, 1850*)

Strata[a] and Occupation	Number of Persons	% American	Strata[a] and Occupation	Number of Persons	% American
1 Physician	47	64	2 County Official	3	100
1 Professional and Secondary Students	22	82	3 Tobacconist	22	86
			3 Printer	7	86
			3 Engineer	4	75
1 Lawyer	12	83	4 Woodchopper	63	71
2 (School) Teacher	22	68	4 Boatman, Ferryman	10	80
2 Clerk	22	64			
2 Justice of Peace	9	67	ALL OCCUPATIONS		49

SOURCE: See Appendix B. [a] See Table 4.6.

press, and a German newspaper was not established until 1852. The concentration of natives in clerking and professional studies suggests that Germans would not quickly make up their deficit in the upper classes. Merchandising was one prestigious occupation where Germans did rather well, even outnumbering natives slightly. Natives were heavily represented at the low end of the scale as well. The designation "boatman" is somewhat ambiguous but probably involved manual labor, and woodchoppers were mostly employed in the woodyards that kept steamboats supplied with fuel.

Despite the contrasts that different ethnic groups showed in the secondary and tertiary sectors of employment, the great majority of persons in every group made their living from agriculture. But in this sector also there were some subtle differences to be observed between Germans and their neighbors. One of these was the way different groups were distributed among the various categories of farmers and agricultural laborers. The designations used in the 1850 census were not very specific, so some assumptions had to be made about what constituted a farm owner or a farm laborer. Fully two-thirds of all men aged eighteen and above were simply designated as farmers (see Table 4.10). One-half of these, or one-third of the male labor force, both owned real estate and were enumerated in the agricultural schedule of the census. These are classified as landowning farmers. Men in the agricultural schedule but lacking real estate were classified as renters, although there may have been other forms of tenure involved, such as an heir waiting to inherit. Those not in the agricultural schedule, many of them dependent sons, are considered to have been farm laborers. Men des-

TABLE 4.10. RELATIVE CONCENTRATION OF VARIOUS ETHNIC GROUPS IN AGRICULTURAL OCCUPATIONS
(St. Charles and Warren Counties, 1850)

	American	German	Old French	Irish	British	N of Cases
Laborer (Farm Laborer)	70	77	101	1,211	309	136
Farmer (Farm Laborer)	112	88	115	35	69	979
Farmer (Renter)	122	86	26	74	102	308
Farmer (Owner)	101	111	51	18	46	1,273
Other Occupation, (in Agricultural Census)	94	116	56	0	144	160
% of Total Labor Force	48.5%	43.0%	5.1%	1.8%	1.2%	

SOURCE: See Appendix B.

ignated as laborers present a similar ambiguity. Whenever they resided in the household of a farmer or renter, they are considered as farm laborers; otherwise these men are classified as general laborers.

The German's desire for an independent farmstead is clearly reflected in the table. Despite the recent arrival of many, Germans constituted the highest proportion of farm owners of any group, but were underrepresented to a greater or lesser degree in all other agricultural categories except part-time farming combined with another occupation. The Old French were the most heavily represented group in the farm labor category. Natives were most prevalent among renters and "farmers" who were actually farmhands. One wonders whether the large number of Irish designated as laborers rather than as farmers reflects anything more than the fact that they were usually boarding hired hands rather than sons or other dependent family members. Half of all Irishmen aged twenty-one and over fell into the boarder category, compared to only one German in seven and one American in nine. Some of the apparent differences between Germans on the one hand and Americans or Frenchmen on the other may be a result of family structure. German households tended to be smaller and less commonly headed by females than was the case with the other two groups. Northwest Ger-

TABLE 4.11. REAL ESTATE HOLDINGS OF MALES 18 AND OLDER BY ETHNIC GROUP
(St. Charles and Warren Counties, 1850)

	Mean $ Value of Real Estate	Number of Individuals	% Owning Real Estate
American	$870	1,873	41%
German	371	1,660	50
Old French	337	196	31
Irish	93	68	12
British	2,046	46	26

SOURCE: See Appendix B.

man inheritance customs dictated that when a father turned his estate over to a son, the former would move out of the main house to a specially erected cottage across the farmyard. This custom seems to have persisted to the extent that older Germans turned farms over to sons while still living. Only about half of all German men over age sixty were still heads of families, compared to three-fourths of such Americans.

The high proportion of Germans who owned real estate, notwithstanding other contributing elements, suggests that the principle factor involved was the land hunger of the rural lower classes, who finally had a chance to be satisfied (see Table 4.11). Landownership had a different meaning for those who had known population pressure and land scarcity than for people who viewed it as an unlimited commodity.[22] The mean real estate value of Germans was not even half that of the native-born and barely exceeded that of the antimodern French. But more than half of all German men owned at least a small plot of land or a house, giving them a broader distribution of property than any other ethnic group. In every occupational group, the Germans were the ethnic group with the highest proportion of property holders. As will be seen in the next chapter, for all the success German artisans enjoyed, a substantial number who had been artisans in the old country eventually turned to agriculture in America.

With the predominance of Germans in artisan trades one might expect them to have left indelible traces on the cultural landscape. But many aspects of German material culture seem to have succumbed

[22] Terry G. Jordan, *German Seed in Texas Soil: Immigrant Farmers in Nineteenth-Century Texas* (Austin, 1966), pp. 115–117, also reported higher rates of landownership among Germans than among other groups.

rather quickly to the geographic realities of Missouri. Examples of anything resembling a north German house-barn, or indeed any housing of people and cattle under the same roof, were extremely rare—only one or two examples are known anywhere in the state. The reasons are not difficult to imagine. In the early years, settlers were happy enough to have a roof over their own heads, usually just a log cabin, and found that their cattle got along well enough American style, with only the forest for shelter. The original cabin was often demoted to a barn when Germans were well enough situated to build a more substantial residence. In house architecture, there were scattered examples of half-timbered construction, but in a region where there was literally wood to burn, it is understandable that these were not common. Wooden shingles seem to have been preferred to thatched or tile roofs from the very beginning—not surprising, considering the force of Midwestern thunderstorms and the abundance of wood. It is only in the stone barns and churches and to some extent in brick structures that the hand of German craftsmen can be clearly discerned, but such materials were not nearly so common as wood.

With furniture and smaller household articles, German styles and patterns were better able to assert themselves. In Warren County there was even a former Negro slave who produced chairs in the German style taught him by his former master, Jonathan Kuntze. But even with such products it seems that local craftsmen succumbed to cheaper urban, factory competition more quickly than their counterparts in the old homeland. However, it is reported that locally made wooden shoes were still in use in Westphalia, Missouri, on the eve of World War I.[23]

German immigrant farmers have enjoyed a reputation for practicing a type of agriculture distinctive from and in many respects superior to that of their Anglo-American counterparts. Because of the greater population density in Europe, agriculture was more labor-intensive than in America. Since most fields had been in cultivation for generations and new land was seldom available and usually of marginal quality, Germans put great emphasis on maintaining soil fertility. By the era of emigration, peasants in Tecklenburg were already familiar with such progressive techniques as planting clover for nitrogen and applying lime to

[23] Charles van Ravenswaay, *The Arts and Architecture of German Settlements in Missouri: A Survey of a Vanishing Culture* (Columbia, Mo., 1977), pp. 111–294 on building methods, 301–484 on artisanship, 379 on Jonathan Kuntze. Russel L. Gerlach, *Immigrants in the Ozarks: A Study in Ethnic Geography* (Columbia, Mo., 1976), pp. 74–96. In west Texas, where wood was more scarce, *Fachwerk* and stone construction were apparently more widespread among Germans (see Jordan, *German Seed in Texas Soil*, pp. 166–167).

CHAPTER IV

reduce soil acidity. They already practiced a complicated system of crop rotation. They were more aware than their American counterparts of the value of animal manure. "Prayer and manure will not be in vain"—such was the pragmatic piety summed up in a Tecklenburg proverb; the punch line, whether explicit or implied, was that "manure will help for sure." Later on, the Germans would also take the lead in agricultural chemistry and artificial fertilizers, but by the mid-nineteenth century this was still in its infancy.[24]

Also, northwest Germans concentrated on different crops, for corn (maize) was practically unknown, rye rather than wheat was the principal small grain, and barley was more common there than in America. The potato, originally introduced from the American continent, had become an important staple in the European peasant diet. Many of the immigrants from the rural lower classes had also grown flax and hemp and worked at spinning and weaving their fibers. Specialized, intensive forms of agriculture, such as viniculture and fruit orchards, had developed in some parts of Germany, but winemaking was just as foreign to northwest Germans as to their English-speaking neighbors in Missouri. In most respects, however, the cultural baggage of immigrant farmers contrasted rather sharply with the system of agriculture they found in the New World.

In the 1850 census, American officials for the first time took a detailed inventory of crops and livestock on the individual level. Combined with personal information from the population census, this makes it possible to test how distinctive the agricultural practices and productivity of Missouri Germans were in comparison to Anglo-American farmers. The German group includes a handful of slaveholders, but since they are so few in number and usually owned only one or two slaves, they hardly influence the averages. With the Americans, however, there is a noticeable difference in the scale of operations between those with and those without slaves, so that the latter group is probably more appropriate for comparison with the Germans.

As can be seen from Table 4.12, the Germans were at somewhat of a disadvantage in terms of farm size. This is not a sure sign of more intensive cultivation, however, since German households also tended to be smaller. The median German holding, twenty-five improved acres, could not yet compare with the proud farmsteads of the peasant aristocracy, but it was a far cry from the acre or two of rented land from which a *Heuerling* had to eke out an existence. In addition to the im-

[24] Jordan, *German Seed in Texas Soil*, pp. 33–38. For a detailed contemporary report, see Johann Nepomuk von Schwerz, *Beschreibung der Landwirtschaft in Westfalen* (1836; facsimile reprint, Münster, 1979), pp. 46–134; for proverb, see p. 133.

TABLE 4.12. AGRICULTURAL PRODUCTION OF GERMANS AND AMERICANS
(St. Charles and Warren Counties, 1850)

	All Germans		Nonslaveholding Americans		All Americans	
	Median Amount[a]	% with Any[b]	Median Amount[a]	% with Any[b]	Median Amount[a]	% with Any[b]
Number of Improved Acres	25	99.5%	30	96.6%	40	97.6%
% of Total Acreage Improved	33.1	99.5	35.3	96.6	33.4	97.6
Value of Land per Acre (Total) ($)	5.49	99.6	5.56	97.0	6.46	97.9
Horses	2.6	96.8	2.5	97.0	3.5	98.3
Mules	1.9	1.8	1.5	4.7	1.8	10.4
Oxen	2.1	28.3	2.2	28.0	2.4	39.6
Improved Acres per Draft Animal	10.0	97.8	10.0	99.4	10.0	96.4
Milk Cows	2.2	97.5	2.9	96.6	3.8	97.7
Other Cattle	2.9	83.3	4.7	81.5	6.6	86.3
Sheep	6	53.4	12	57.6	16	61.2
Swine	15	93.5	20	92.3	25	94.7
Value of Livestock per Acre (Total) ($)	1.80	99.2	2.16	96.8	2.02	97.8
Wheat (bu.)	50	76.1	50	53.8	80	63.2
Rye (bu.)	10	3.0	18	0.6	21	1.7
Oats (bu.)	40	71.4	100	57.2	100	67.7
Corn (bu.)	201	91.6	398	90.5	501	92.9
Tobacco (lb.)	960	2.5	1,800	15.1	2,030	18.0
Value of Implements per Improved Acre ($)	2.27	96.4	1.70	92.0	1.72	94.8
Value of Principle Crops per Improved Acre ($)	4.69	94.5	5.69	90.3	5.62	92.7
N of Cases	833		535		972	

SOURCE: See Appendix B.
[a] Median amount among those farmers reporting a given article.
[b] Percentage of the group reporting any amount of a given article.

CHAPTER IV

proved acreage, farmers of all groups had on the average twice as much unimproved land, mostly forest that would be gradually cleared for cropland and pasture. Judging by the price per acre, German landholdings were of somewhat lower quality than those of Americans, especially slaveholders.[25]

Draft animals were almost a must on a nineteenth-century farm, so that practically every farmer had at least one horse, or usually a team of them. Mules were hardly known in Germany, and just beginning to gain popularity in America. Germans were much more wary of this innovation, but even among Americans only one farmer in ten owned any mules. Though many Germans had previous experience with draft cattle—even if it only involved hooking the family milk cow to the plow—Germans were no more likely to use oxen than their American neighbors, especially if the latter were slaveholders. But the general similarity is reflected in the ratio of total draft animals to improved acreage, which was practically identical for all three groups: one animal for every ten acres.

There was also little difference between natives and ethnics in the proportion who kept other forms of livestock. Nearly every family had a milk cow or two, and four-fifths or more raised some additional cattle. Over 90 percent of the farmers raised swine, and a good half of them also kept some sheep. The differences between natives and Germans were merely in the number of animals kept—not surprising considering the larger size of American farms. However, even when the value of livestock is measured per acre, natives, especially nonslaveholders, maintained a moderate lead. But if the differences between Germans and their American neighbors were slight, the contrast with the former situation in Germany was all the more striking. Of the *Heuerleute* of the Osnabrück region, only 3 percent of the families owned a horse, and a few were even impoverished to the point of substituting a goat for a milk cow. A single butcher hog usually had to last all year. Thus even a quick glance at these agricultural figures gives some idea of the motives for emigration.[26]

The former German peasant was apparently happy to trade his black bread for white. Only 3 percent of the Germans in the two counties

[25] This is also confirmed by least-squares estimating, regressing land price per acre on percentage of acreage improved. For all farms larger than five acres in Warren County in 1850, this procedure yielded an estimated value of $2.70 per acre unimproved land held by Germans, and a value of $3.40 for all unimproved land in the county, where $r = .38$ and .33 respectively.

[26] On the former living conditions of emigrants, see Goebel, *Länger als ein Menschenleben*, p. 49; *Zur Statistik des Königreichs Hannover*, 2: 66.

grew any rye, but over three-fourths of them reported wheat in the census, even though it was not a very good crop for new ground. Oats were also rather common, but were probably used mostly as livestock feed. Germans reported all these small grains somewhat more often than natives, but production figures were usually higher for the latter. The leading agricultural crop, however, was corn (maize). Twice as much corn was grown as all other grains combined, and only 8 percent of the farmers were without it. Despite their inexperience, Germans were just as likely to grow corn as their American neighbors. The advantages of the crop were numerous. It could be planted between the stumps on newly cleared land; it could be used as food for man or beast; it could be harvested at a leisurely pace without much danger of weather damage; and it was easy to grow. Even such an amateur as Friedrich Muench claimed never to have suffered a crop failure, not even in the first year.[27] With a specialized cash crop such as tobacco, however, immigrant farmers were very cautious. Only one German in forty grew the aromatic weed, as compared with nearly one-fifth of the Anglo-Americans. However, this was the only major crop where the differences between native and immigrant practices outweighed the similarities.

Because of untrustworthy data in Warren County, information on minor commodities from the second page of the census form was analyzed only for St. Charles County (see Table 4.13).[28] Except for the higher proportion of Americans who were slaveholders, the differences between the two counties were not very great.

The practices of Germans were most distinctive in matters involving their own stomach. Only 5 percent could get along without potatoes, in contrast to 15 percent of their American neighbors, and the smaller German farms produced just as many bushels. But only one German in fifty was willing to try sweet potatoes, though they were grown by one American in four. Barley and buckwheat were both familiar to Germans from the homeland, and the few persons who grew them were mostly German, but they were negligible commodities in Missouri. A German specialization in the dairy industry was not in evidence at this time and place. Hardly anyone produced cheese, and five-sixths of all farmers reported butter, but this was true for natives as well as immigrants, and production figures were higher for the former. Hay produc-

[27] Friedrich Muench, "Sonst und Jetzt," *Der Deutsche Pionier* 4 (1871): 229.
[28] The schedule of the agricultural census consisted of two pages, with the name of the individual recorded only on the first page. Figures from the second page in Warren County contained serious errors, if indeed they were not simply invented by the census taker.

CHAPTER IV

TABLE 4.13. AGRICULTURAL PRODUCTION OF GERMANS AND AMERICANS
(St. Charles County, 1850)

	All Germans		Nonslaveholding Americans		All Americans	
	Median Amount[a]	% with Any[b]	Median Amount[a]	% with Any[b]	Median Amount[a]	% with Any[b]
Potatoes (bu.)	20	94.6%	15	77.7%	20	84.2%
Sweet Potatoes (bu.)	10	1.8	10	25.0	10	30.3
Barley (bu.)	20	4.4	12	1.8	15	1.0
Buckwheat (bu.)	5	5.6	1	0.5	17	1.6
Butter (lb.)	51	86.4	101	85.5	150	89.2
Cheese (lb.)	200	3.6	640	4.6	203	3.8
Hay (t.)	1.5	43.0	3.4	28.2	4.3	46.5
Value of Orchard Products ($)	10	21.5	25	27.7	30	39.9
Value of Market Gardening ($)	18	0.8	—	0.0	58	1.2
Wine (gal.)	11	1.4	12	0.9	10	1.0
Hops (lb.)	—	0.0	—	0.0	9	1.2
Hemp (t.)	—	0.0	—	0.0	2	1.8
Flax (lb.)	30	4.6	29	3.2	49	5.4
Wool (lb.)	12	39.8	30	37.3	40	48.3
Value of Home Manufactures ($)	10	6.8	20	32.7	25	43.5
Value of Total Production per Total Acerage ($)	2.77	99.0	3.42	99.1	3.01	99.4
N of Cases	498		220		499	

SOURCE: See Appendix B.
[a] Median amount among those farmers reporting a given article.
[b] Percentage of the group reporting any amount of a given article.

tion might indicate better care of livestock through the winter, though the main feed was doubtlessly corn fodder. Here the Germans came off better than Southern yeomen, but not as well as slaveholders.

It was the Americans rather than the Germans who appear to have dominated the production of most specialty crops. Perhaps because of the recent arrival of many Germans, not even one-fourth of them reported sales of orchard products. With natives, the proportion was nearly two-fifths, and the average value of sales was also considerably higher. Market gardening was hardly worth mentioning in 1850, but here, too, Anglo-Americans made up the majority of growers. Moreover, even the dozen winegrowers were almost evenly split between natives and Germans. Perhaps most surprising, German brewers apparently had to depend on six American growers for their supply of hops. Emigrating German artisans appear to have been happy to leave weaving behind. The nine hemp growers in St. Charles County were all native slaveholders. Flax culture was not much more significant, though here Germans held their own. Wool production was fairly common, but the degree of participation hardly differed between the two groups, and native production figures were somewhat higher. And despite their traditions of artisan sidelines, Germans reported significantly lower figures for home manufacturing—whatever that may have encompassed—than did their neighbors.

About the only evidence at all for a more intense agriculture among Germans was that the value of implements per unit of improved land was higher than with natives, but even this may have been primarily a reflection of smaller farm size. Nearly all other indicators go in the other direction. Since the acreage devoted to individual crops was not indicated in the census, it was impossible to compare the per-acre yields of various crops achieved by natives and immigrants. A rough estimate of productivity can, however, be obtained by using commodity prices for each crop to calculate the total value of output.[29] This was possible only for St. Charles County, but a similar figure was calculated for both counties, restricted to the major crops of corn, wheat, oats, rye, and tobacco in relationship to improved acreage. By both measures, Germans appear to have been considerably less productive than their American neighbors. This was probably to some extent due to differences in land quality. In their determination to have a piece of land they could call their own, Germans were not particularly choosy, and much of the best land had already been taken. "These guys will clear any land where the rocks aren't lying three feet deep," remarked Gert Goebel's father-in-

[29] Prices were the same as those used in the county-aggregate data set assembled by Thomas B. Alexander at the University of Missouri–Columbia. A comparison with market reports from 1852 in the *St. Charles Demokrat* confirmed the general accuracy of these figures. Prices applied to various commodities are as follows: corn, $.30/bu.; wheat, $.65/bu.; rye, $.40/bu.; oats, $.25/bu.; tobacco, $.06/lb.; wool, $.25/lb.; Irish potatoes, $.40/lb.; sweet potatoes, $.60/lb.; barley, $.40/bu.; buckwheat, $.40/bu.; butter, $.10/lb.; cheese, $.09/lb.; hay, $5.00/t. Only the first five commodities from the first page of the schedule were used in computing the output per improved acre in Table 4.12. All the commodities plus the values of orchard products, market gardening, home manufactures, and animals slaughtered were used to compute the output per total acreage in Table 4.13.

CHAPTER IV

law with bemusement. He may have exaggerated, but land values per acre do show an apparent contrast, especially with American slaveholders.[30]

In summary, the similarities of immigrant and native agricultural patterns clearly outweigh the differences. There is little evidence to suggest that Germans at that time practiced a more intensive style of agriculture, nor was there much evidence of concentration on specialty crops. The differences were mainly in the numbers of livestock and amounts of various crops produced per farm, but these in turn were closely related to the size of the farm, and probably to household size as well. Whether this would continue to hold true in the following decades is an open question.

Investigations of other areas have disclosed a number of instances of "cultural rebound": the reappearance of ethnic traits not found at the time of first settlement. The early years of clearing land and getting a foothold were not the time for experiments. Later on, however, more risks could be taken and more diversity achieved. Thus, a study of Anglo-American and German patterns of agriculture over several decades might reveal diverging rather than converging trends. Pertinent to this point, a recent study of Missouri Germans has identified some distinctiveness in their agricultural patterns persisting into the 1970s.[31]

One distinctive agricultural specialty that was developed later by Missouri Germans was winegrowing, most spectacularly around Hermann, but also on a substantial scale in the Augusta and St. Charles areas. Before Prohibition, Missouri ranked among the top four wine-producing states in the United States, accounting for one-twelfth of the national output in 1904 according to one report. All but 3 percent of the 3 million gallons came from Gasconade County—the town of Hermann and its surroundings. But much of the rest came from in and around the town of Augusta, which at one time claimed eleven wine cellars in a town of 250 inhabitants.

In 1850, only a dozen individuals in St. Charles and Warren counties reported wine production, in quantities suggesting mostly home consumption. By 1860, the number of producers had doubled, and the average production was reaching commercial proportions, over 100 gallons per cellar. In the following decade a real boom set in, with production by 1870 six times that of a decade earlier. In all, over 18,000 gallons was produced in the two counties, two-thirds of it in

[30] Quote from Goebel, *Länger als ein Menschenleben*, p. 49.
[31] On the concept of cultural rebound, see Jordan, *German Seed in Texas Soil*, p. 199. On Missouri Germans, see Gerlach, *Immigrants in the Ozarks*, pp. 97–109.

August and surrounding Femme Osage Township on the fertile southern exposures of the Missouri River bluffs. Appropriate enough, this region is often called the Missouri Rhineland.[32]

A closer look at winegrowing in Duden country reveals the importance of cultural factors in its development. The town of Hermann, which had been settled mostly by southwest Germans and Swiss, took the lead in viniculture, celebrating its first winefest as early as 1848. Most of the innovators in the Augusta area also had some acquaintance with winegrowing from their homeland. In 1860, only two Americans were still producing wine, and that in insignificant quantities. Despite their predominance in the population, natives of Prussia and Hannover accounted for only one-fourth of the wine producers and even less of the production. There was apparently not a single person from Tecklenburg or Melle among them. Three winegrowers were from the southwest or Switzerland. But half of the twenty-two Germans involved were from Hesse, and together they accounted for over four-fifths of the roughly 2,500 gallons produced. Most of these, including such prominent people as the Muench brothers, had been members of the Giessen Emigration Society. But since Giessen lies just at the edge of the German wine regions, one suspects that education, access to information, and adequate initial capital were more important than previous experience with winegrowing. Two of the leading vintners, Wilhelm Follenius, son of one of the Giessen Society leaders, and Johann Schmidt, would have been under six years of age when they emigrated. Among the other winegrowers was Julius Mallinckrodt from Dortmund, and someone from Saxe-Meinigen who had probably belonged to an emigration society. Both were members of the educated middle class and neither came from the winegrowing regions of Germany. In view of this, it appears that the concept of cultural rebound needs to be rethought and further specified in terms of the mechanisms through which it came about.

The image of German assimilation that emerges from this chapter is somewhat contradictory. On the one hand, Germans adjusted rather quickly to the geographic conditions of their new home. Their adoption of many American crops and farming techniques suggests that at least some Germans had enough personal contacts with Americans to

---

[32] Alfred Bernhardt Faust, *The German Element in the United States: With Special Reference to Its Political, Moral, Social, and Educational Influence*, 2 vols. (1909; reprint, New York, 1969), 1: 41–47; Goebel, *Länger als ein Menschenleben*, pp. 141–146. A comparison with figures from the United States Census of Agriculture suggests that some of the claims as to the national ranking of the Missouri wine industry may be exaggerated.

CHAPTER IV

have learned from them. On the other hand, the intensity of contact seems to have been limited. Even in agriculture most Germans drew the line when it came to adopting slavery and tobacco culture. In other sectors of the economy, the Germans used artisan skills from the homeland to fill specialized niches, serving Americans as well as their own countrymen. But where it came to more intensive personal contacts, most Germans preferred to keep to themselves—in their own families and their own church parishes. As soon as resources permitted, German congregations of all denominations also erected parochial schools, which helped to preserve the language and foster group consciousness. Assimilation was to some extent a function of social class, with immigrants of peasant origins more resistant to change than the educated bourgeoisie.

The rural German community in Missouri was in many respects similar to its urban counterpart in Milwaukee. In both cases the institutional completeness of ethnic representation at all levels of the social scale meant that Germans seldom had to go outside their community to fulfill their economic and cultural needs. They led an existence parallel to and often not very different from that of Anglo-Americans, but with few intensive points of contact. This was, if anything, strengthened after 1860 by the Civil War, when the Germans in Missouri almost unanimously supported the Union, whereas many natives were in active or silent sympathy with the South. Thus individuals who fully assimilated into the native society were few. Instead it was the ethnic community itself that gradually, almost imperceptibly, became Americanized, and that only in the course of two or three generations.[33]

[33] Kathleen Neils Conzen, *Immigrant Milwaukee, 1836–1860: Accommodation and Community in a Frontier City* (Cambridge, Mass., 1976), esp. pp. 225–228.

CHAPTER V

Detours and Shortcuts on the Way to a Farm: Occupational and Geographic Mobility from Westfalia to Missouri

Most of the Germans who came to America with money lost it by injudicious speculation in land, but those who came poor generally prospered on their small beginnings, and soon became money-loaners and landowners.[1]

THIS statement from an 1885 St. Charles County history is typical of much of the booster literature of that period, but it is too strongly imbued with the egalitarian myth to enjoy complete credibility. While it is true that many of the Latin farmers were unsuited to agricultural pursuits and went to ruin, it would be surprising if immigrants of peasant stock who emigrated with some means typically failed to prosper.

This chapter will test the egalitarian rhetoric of American society against its economic and social reality. Central to the investigation is the question whether a secure existence as an independent farmer was open also to emigrants from the rural lower classes in Germany, or whether it could normally be attained only by trading a small, expensive plot of land in the Old World for a large, cheap tract in the New. By linking individual-level data in German emigrant lists with that in American censuses, one can shed light on this and a number of other important questions relating to social mobility.

The limitations inherent in studying overseas migration from only one side of the Atlantic are readily apparent. Mobility studies that begin on the American side are forced to make assumptions about the European background on the basis of an aggregate profile that may or may not hold true for a given individual. Moreover, such studies often suffer from a veiled American ethnocentrism, assuming the same value system and aspirations on the part of immigrants as in the host society. Mere vertical mobility is a narrow and artificial criterion with which to measure the success of immigrant adjustment; more revealing are the horizontal job sectors chosen. The occupational route followed is as important as the final destination. By identifying migrants at their place of origin, one gains clues as to what the newcomers' goals actually were

---

[1] *History of St. Charles, Montgomery, and Warren Counties, Missouri* (1885; facsimile reprint, St. Louis, 1969), p. 106.

CHAPTER V

and to what extent they were achieved. For example, scholars in Germany still place great emphasis on the "frontier thesis" and the availability of free land as a motive for emigration. But paradoxically, although nineteenth-century German emigrants were predominantly rural in origin, German-Americans were more urbanized than either their compatriots back home or the American population as a whole. Was this urbanization primarily the result of positive factors, such as the demand for artisan skills, or does it reflect a negative factor, the lack of sufficient funds to travel further or acquire land? It has been argued that many artisans emigrated to preserve traditional skills that were being undermined by industrialization in Europe. But the heavy clustering of immigrants of the same local and regional origins suggests that cultural ties and chain migration were more important than impersonal economic forces as locational factors. Not that labor-market considerations were inconsequential in migration decisions, but employment information was often obtained through private rather than public sources. These are some of the main issues that will be explored below.[2]

Social mobility from Westfalia to Missouri was examined on the basis of two very similar groups. The first was a group of about 150 adult males who were traced from Tecklenburg to St. Charles and Warren counties by 1850. The second involved a somewhat larger group originating sixty miles further east from Lippe-Detmold, who intermingled with the Tecklenburgers in Warren County and also extended their settlement to the south side of the Missouri River in Gasconade and Franklin counties. While the Tecklenburgers were buried in the census among the many thousand Prussians, Lippe-Detmolders were separately identified in the 1860 census. This "tracer element" made it possible to deal with all the immigrants originating from Lippe, the unmatched as well as the matched. It also facilitated the identification of

---

[2] The volume of mobility studies has become too large to cite individually, but two of the most sophisticated works of this genre also provide guides to the literature: Stephan Thernstrom, *The Other Bostonians: Poverty and Progress in the American Metropolis, 1880–1970* (Cambridge, Mass., 1973), chap. 9; and Gordon W. Kirk, Jr., *The Promise of American Life: Social Mobility in a Nineteenth-Century Immigrant Community— Holland, Michigan, 1847–1894* (Philadelphia, 1978), chap. 7. Two other mobility studies that deal extensively with Germans are Clyde Griffen and Sally Griffen, *Natives and Newcomers: The Ordering of Opportunity in Mid-Nineteenth-Century Poughkeepsie* (Cambridge, Mass., 1978); and Dean R. Esslinger, *Immigrants and the City: Ethnicity and Mobility in a Nineteenth-Century Midwestern Community* (Port Washington, N.Y., 1975). Although both focus on small cities, the social mobility of rural Germans still remains practically unexamined, and studies of transatlantic social mobility of any group are rare.

a comparison group that settled in St. Louis rather than in these rural clusters. The 1860 census has the added advantage of recording personal property rather than just real estate, thus providing a more appropriate basis for comparing rural wealth with urban, or farmers with artisans.

Many of the emigrants in these traced groups were indeed victims of industrialization, linen weavers crowded out by machine production. But in most respects, such rural industry does not fit the image commonly associated with European crafts. Linen weaving was not a highly skilled craft, and usually fell outside guild regulation. Most linen weavers worked their trade only part time, and still had at least one foot firmly planted in agriculture, a fact of importance for their future in America. Indeed, most are designated in the emigrant lists as *Heuerleute* or *Einlieger* (tenant farmers), not as weavers. Similarly, emigrating artisans from other traditional village trades were not so highly skilled or so clearly delineated from the agricultural population as one might imagine. Although the rural lower classes predominated in the migration, peasant proprietors were not totally immune to "America fever," especially during the early years of settlement. Such was the background of the majority of Germans coming into Missouri before the Civil War.[3]

Table 5.1 examines how the European social background affected the real estate and wealth holdings reported by traced immigrants in the 1850 and 1860 censuses. It is restricted to those who came over alone or as heads of families, excluding dependent children who subsequently started out on their own. Obviously, one of the main factors influencing wealth is the recentness of arrival of a person in the country. Therefore, for each occupational category in each traced group, the

[3] Emigrant list sources, tracing procedures, and details of the occupational classification are detailed in Appendixes A and B. I have attempted to construct similar occupational categories for Tecklenburg and Lippe-Detmold, aided by the fact that the rural social structure, and the form of the emigrant lists, are very similar for both areas. Matches were rated as either sure, probable, or doubtful, and all important computer runs were repeated with the exclusion of doubtful matches. Nowhere, except for one minor instance noted below, did this seriously alter the conclusions. With Lippe-Detmolders in particular, it was lack of information on family members, ages, and sometimes even names, that usually caused doubt, not discrepancies between the sources. Since family information was often incomplete in the lists, and since people often married just before or just after emigration, the distinction between married and single was made on the basis of whether someone had any children born in Germany, which often had to be determined from the census rather than from emigrant lists. The birth of the first child had a much more important impact than mere marriage as a factor affecting income or location.

TABLE 5.1. MEAN VALUE OF REAL ESTATE AND OTHER WEALTH OF ADULT MALE EMIGRANTS
(Traced from Tecklenburg and Lippe-Detmold to Rural Missouri, by Former Occupational Group)

Occupational Category	Tecklenburgers, Real Estate, 1850				Lippe-Detmolders, Real Estate, 1850			
	Actual Deviation	Group Mean	Adjusted Deviation	N of Cases	Actual Deviation	Group Mean	Adjusted Deviation	N of Cases
All		$503		123		$154		82
Ag. Labor or Unspec., Single, Poor Family	−193		−155	32	−79		−80	8
Ag. Labor or Unspec., Married, Poor Family	−124		−135	14	+15		+16	5
Tenant Farmer (*Heuerling, Einlieger*)	−150		−107	22	−32		−32	19
Artisan	+31		−5	23	−108		−105	12
Smallholder	—		—	—	+33		+32	17
Ag. Labor or Unspec., Single, *Kolon* Family	+177		+156	21	−10		−12	8
Peasant Proprietor (*Kolon*)	+616		+550	11	+153		+154	13

Occupational Category	Lippe-Detmolders, Total Wealth, 1860				Lippe-Detmolders, Real Estate, 1860			
	Actual Deviation	Group Mean	Adjusted Deviation	N of Cases	Actual Deviation	Group Mean	Adjusted Deviation	N of Cases
All		$1,414		140		$900		140
Ag. Labor or Unspec., Single, Poor Family	−262		−300	15	−58		−97	15
Ag. Labor or Unspec., Married, Poor Family	+40		−4	7	+70		+24	7
Tenant Farmer (*Einlieger*)	−323		−315	30	−191		−183	30
Artisan	−673		−621	24	−392		−338	24
Smallholder	−28		−28	32	+72		+72	32
Ag. Labor or Unspec., Single, *Kolon* Family	+1,073		+1,071	8	+636		+634	8
Peasant Proprietor (*Kolon*)	+910		+885	24	+339		+314	24

SOURCE: See Appendix B.

table presents two wealth figures: first, the mean wealth as recorded by the census, and second, an "adjusted" figure expressing what the wealth would be if all groups had the same duration of residence in the country. Furthermore, the figure for each occupational subgroup expresses not the absolute wealth, but rather the amount by which this subgroup falls above or below the mean for the total group. Thus in terms of the upper left quadrant of Table 5.1, Tecklenburg immigrants in 1850 owned an average of just over $500 in real estate. Among those who had been tenant farmers, the figure was $150 below average, or about $350; for peasant proprietors, it was $616 above average, or over $1,100. If one takes into account the length of residence, the disadvantage of tenant farmers falls to $107, while the advantage of peasant proprietors shrinks to $550.[4]

Differences between Tecklenburgers and Lippe-Detmolders, or between census years, are uncontrolled for length of residence, however. Thus the threefold wealth advantage of Tecklenburgers in 1850 came largely because they had an average tenure of eleven years, while the average Lippe-Detmolder had been around only two and one-half years. Also, the latter resided in somewhat poorer and less settled areas. Nevertheless, 1850 real estate figures for Tecklenburgers were surpassed by the 1860 values for Lippe-Detmolders even though the latter still had an average tenure of only nine years.

It is perhaps useful at this point to consider what such a property holding represented in material terms. A large proportion of all real estate consisted simply of farmland. The cheapest prices were for "government land," which could be purchased for a minimum of $1.25 per acre in plots of forty acres and up. Thus a settler with only $50 in his pocket could become a landowner. Land in private hands, especially if it was already cleared, was considerably more expensive. By 1850, un-

[4] See Frank Andrews et al., *Multiple Classification Analysis* (Ann Arbor, 1973), for an introduction to the technique used here. Theoretically, it would have been possible to use multiple classification analysis to investigate simultaneously the relative effects of occupation, age, and family status at emigration on social mobility in America. As it turns out, however, German occupational designations are closely tied to age and life-cycle stage, so that the results would have been distorted by multicolinearity. Most occupational titles were at the same time designations of marital status. The only exception was in the artisan group, where the lists seldom distinguished between journeymen and masters. But an *Einlieger*—or his Tecklenburger counterpart, a *Heuerling*—was almost always a married tenant farmer. There was also a small category of the rural poor who were married but not specifically designated as tenants. A person designated as a *Kolon* was almost invariably a married peasant proprietor. This leaves unmarried farmhands, who in Lippe usually listed no occupation at all, and in Tecklenburg were usually designated *Knecht*, implying a boarding farmhand.

CHAPTER V

improved land owned by Warren County Germans was worth about $2.70 per acre, while improved land was going for nearly $7.00. Overall in Warren and St. Charles counties, land owned by German farmers was valued at $5.50 per acre, although only one-third of it was improved. So one can assume that the $500 holding of the average Tecklenburger meant about eighty acres, with perhaps twenty-five in cultivation, and some type of dwelling, if only a log cabin. The $150 holding of a Lippe-Detmolder in 1850 was probably not much smaller, but simply farther from civilization and markets, and still largely forest. The increases by 1860 reflected not only improvements, but inflation in land values as well.[5]

The variations in wealth across occupational groups are generally in the direction one would expect on the basis of their financial resources when leaving Germany (cf. Tables 2.3 and 2.4). Peasant proprietors and their sons were better off than the rural lower classes. These differences also remained rather consistent across time and were similar regardless of place of origin. There were a couple of exceptions. Artisans from Tecklenburg fell right at the mean, while those from Lippe consistently brought up the rear. As will be seen below, the former may have had more opportunites for employment around the town of St. Charles, while the latter were in less developed areas where their skills were not so much in demand. In 1860, the sons of propertied peasants from Lippe led all occupational groups in wealth, but two wealthy individuals inflated the average for this small group, while two others were actually propertyless. The relaxation of impartible inheritance laws in Lippe had produced a class of smallholders not present in Tecklenburg. Despite having been landowners, this group was barely above average in its attainments in America. While it might appear that family emigration was more prevalent from Lippe-Detmold, the difference may be simply that Prussian officials in Tecklenburg were more thorough in recording clandestine emigration (mostly of young, single men).

Contrary to the opinion cited at the beginning of this chapter, money brought along from Europe did no harm. Peasant proprietors from both Tecklenburg and Lippe consistently showed real estate holdings well above that of the average immigrant. But it does appear that their

[5] Land prices in Warren County for all German farmers owning at least five acres of land were estimated from individual level agricultural census data by regressing value per acre with percentage of acreage improved, thus obtaining least-squares estimates of land prices where all or none of the acreage was improved. The overall median value of German-owned farmland and percentage of acreage improved in St. Charles and Warren counties was calculated from the agricultural census data presented in Table 4.12.

advantage over the tenant-farmer class steadily narrowed over time. At the time of emigration, the average wealth of a *Heuerling* from Westfalia was only one-third or one-fourth that of a *Kolon*. In 1850, tenant farmers from both Tecklenburg and Lippe were worth about two-fifths as much as their compatriots from the propertied peasant class. With Lippe-Detmolders in 1860, the ratio had narrowed to nearly 1:2 in total wealth and 3:5 when real estate alone is considered. These cold statistics are substantiated by more subjective indicators. Whereas marriage between children of a *Kolon* and a *Heuerling* was almost unthinkable in the old country, this barrier appears to have fallen almost immediately in the New World.[6]

While both optimists and pessimists in the debate over social mobility might feel themselves vindicated by the above evidence, the optimists' case is strengthened when one examines what proportion of each occupational group had attained landowning status (see Table 5.2). Most of the difference between groups was merely in the size of landholdings, and not, as in Germany, whether one possessed land at all. Only with the newly arrived Lippe-Detmolders in 1850 were the rural lower classes at a considerable disadvantage. Over three-quarters of both peasant proprietors and smallholders had obtained land, but not quite half of all tenant farmers. Landowning rates exceeded 80 percent for Tecklenburgers in 1850 and for Lippe-Detmolders ten years later. *Heuerlinge* fell exactly at the mean of the Tecklenburg group, while their counterparts, *Einlieger* from Lippe, had a 70 percent ownership rate, the worst showing by any group except the new arrivals in 1850, but still a considerable improvement from the old country. Although in 1850 few artisans from Lippe owned land, in 1860 their low average wealth obscures widespread, though doubtless modest, landholdings. While propertied peasants failed to improve their standing between 1850 and 1860, this was probably because some of them had reached retirement age in the interim.

Related to the issues of retirement and inheritance is the degree to which socioeconomic status is passed down from one generation to the next. In fact, intergenerational mobility is perhaps the most important

[6] Dieter Sauermann, *Knechte und Magde in Westfalen um 1900* (Münster, 1972); idem, "Das Verhältnis von Bauernfamilie und Gesinde in Westfalen," *Niedersächsisches Jahrbuch* 50 (1978): 27–44. See also the investigation of a village in eastern Westfalia by Josef Mooser in Jürgen Kocka et al., *Familie und soziale Plazierung: Studien zum Verhaltnis von Familie, sozialer Mobilität und Heiratsverhalten an westfälischen Beispielen im späten 18. und 19. Jahrhundert* (Opladen, 1980). One Tecklenburg peasant son had to emigrate in order to be able to marry a *Heuerling*'s daughter (Grover A. Ahmann, *Family Tree of Hermann and Sophia Ahmann Covering the Period 1811–1922* [Bakersfield, Calif., 1922]).

CHAPTER V

TABLE 5.2. PERCENTAGE OF ADULT MALE EMIGRANTS OWNING REAL ESTATE *(Traced from Tecklenburg and Lippe-Detmold to Rural Missouri, By Former Occupational Group)*[a]

	Tecklenburgers	Lippe-Detmolders	
	1850	1850	1860
All Occupational Categories	82%	56%	81%
Ag. Labor or Unspec., Single, Poor Family	75	38	87
Ag. Labor or Unspec., Married, Poor Family	86	60	100
Tenant Farmer (*Heuerling, Einlieger*)	82	47	70
Artisan	78	25	83
Smallholder	—	76	91
Ag. Labor or Unspec., Single, *Kolon* Family	85	63	75
Peasant Proprietor (*Kolon*)	100	77	75

SOURCE: See Appendix B.
[a] Number of cases as in Table 5.1.

test by which the openness of a society can be judged. Table 5.3 examines this issue by focusing on immigrants who had come over as dependent children and had reached age twenty-one by the census year. Some were still under the parental roof, some were boarding farmhands working for others, and some had started out on their own. The gap that was observed among the older generation appears to have narrowed greatly with their children. Among Lippe-Detmolders, sons of propertied peasants had an advantage of about $210 in real estate value and $280 in total wealth when length of residence is taken into account, although this comes out to about the same 3:5 ratio observed with the parents above. But with the Tecklenburg group in 1850, children of Germany's tenant class were actually about $150 better off than scions of the peasant aristocracy. Nor can this be explained by age or length of residence, since the groups are rather evenly matched in these respects. Instead, it appears that the sons of lower-class origins made a virtue of necessity and struck out on their own at a younger age. In part, this is a reflection of cultural baggage. In both the Old World and the New, sons of peasant proprietors enjoyed the luxury of remaining longer in the households of their fathers, who owned enough land to profitably employ them. One such immigrant in this group, Henry Groenemann, claimed in a biographical sketch that he "did not earn a dollar that he could call his own until he was twenty-eight years old," when he married and started farming on his own. When the father died five years later, he inherited an eighty-acre farm. Thus the wealth ad-

TABLE 5.3. MEAN VALUE OF REAL ESTATE AND OTHER WEALTH OF DEPENDENT MALE EMIGRANTS
(Traced from Tecklenburg and Lippe-Detmold to Rural Missouri, by Occupational Group of Family)

	Actual Deviation	Group Mean	Adjusted Deviation	N
TECKLENBURGERS, REAL ESTATE, 1850				
All Dependent Emigrants		$246		33
From Poor Family	+49		+52	22
From *Kolon* Family	−99		−104	11
LIPPE-DETMOLDERS, REAL ESTATE, 1860				
All Dependent Emigrants		$394		37
From Poor Family	−152		−106	19
From *Kolon* Family	+160		+107	18
LIPPE-DETMOLDERS, TOTAL WEALTH, 1860				
All Dependent Emigrants		$551		37
From Poor Family	−203		−136	19
From *Kolon* Family	+215		+144	18

SOURCE: See Appendix B.

vantages shown by Tecklenburg peasants in Table 5.1 must be relativized somewhat, since they had more adult sons contributing to the family economy.[7]

An analysis of extremes—that is, persons in the highest categories of wealth or those with none whatsoever—shows that valuable holdings were less the result of capitalistic enterprise than of happening upon a location where land values climbed rapidly, while at the other end of the scale, lack of real estate was by no means synonymous with destitution.

Of the fourteen Tecklenburgers reporting more than $1,000 in real estate, only two were from Warren County, and ten were farmers in the same neighborhood near the city of St. Charles.[8] Early arrival had allowed many of them to buy when land was cheap. While two of the group had emigrated in 1842 and one in 1837, eleven of the fourteen were in the country by 1835. Friedrich Schafer, with $5,000 the richest man in the group, shows three mutually reinforcing characteristics that

[7] *Portrait and Biographical Record of St. Charles, Lincoln, and Warren Counties, Missouri* (Chicago, 1895), p. 385.

[8] Most of the information in the section below was obtained from emigrant lists, the U.S. Federal Manuscript Census, and sketches in *History of St. Charles, Montgomery, and Warren Counties*, pp. 246, 250; *Portrait and Biographical Record*, pp. 195, 198, 375, 385, 395, 485.

CHAPTER V

contributed to his prosperity: He was a peasant proprietor in Germany; he emigrated early, in 1835; and he located near St. Charles. But wealth in Germany was not a necessary precondition for getting ahead in America. Of the fourteen, one appeared in the emigrant lists as a laborer, and at least five had been tenant farmers in Germany, though three of them had artisan sidelines of wagonmaking or stonemasonry that may have induced them to locate near town. The only ones among the successful who could be described as entrepreneurs were three of the four who lived outside the vicinity of St. Charles. Two were storekeepers and one was a miller, but all farmed enough to be listed in the agricultural census.

Henry W. Gerdemann emigrated in 1833 after the death of his father, a prosperous peasant, but it is doubtful that Henry took a large inheritance with him, for he left a mother and five siblings behind, while one brother accompanied him. He spent seven years in St. Louis, probably clerking, saving money, and learning the mercantile business. In 1841, he moved to rural St. Charles County and established a store, the nucleus of a struggling village he named Cappeln in honor of his home town. Henry Knippenberg came from more modest circumstances in Germany. He and his father were employed as miners, and he no doubt helped till the family's tiny plot of land. He arrived in St. Charles County in 1836 after having worked for three years in St. Louis, and as he prospered as a blacksmith, he invested his earnings in land. Henry Schaaf was among the first emigrants from *Kreis* Tecklenburg to Missouri, coming over in 1833. He was the only one of the three whose German occupation had a direct association with his career in America, having been a miller in both his old and new homes. He was also the only one in the traced group whose enterprise was large enough to be listed in the 1850 manufacturing census. But his path upward was anything but direct. "Few immigrants have had a harder beginning in this country," commented Friedrich Muench, "and few have known how to work themselves up with equal energy." Initially working at a mill in St. Charles for a year, he was forced to seek employment at a tannery in Warren County when the mill closed for lack of grain. It was 1837 before he felt secure enough to bring over his wife and children, though he was ultimately able to set himself up in milling. But even his European experience may have been of limited usefulness in America, for it led him down the blind alley of experimentation with windmills, which he abandoned for ox power and eventually steam.[9]

The thirty-six adult males without real estate were a much more het-

[9] *Portrait and Biographical Record*, p. 395; Friedrich Muench, "Die Duden'sche Niederlassung im Missouri," *Der Deutsche Pionier* 2 (1870): 231.

erogeneous group. Several were from families prominent enough toward the end of the century to rate a biography in a county history, among them brothers of the Gerdemann and Knippenberg mentioned above, and Schaaf's son-in-law, Hermann Bierbaum. In fact, Bierbaum and Hermann Knippenberg were themselves featured in biographies, as were sons of two other Tecklenburgers who were without real estate in 1850. The most spectacular story was that of John Borgmann. Apparently an orphan, he had emigrated in 1836 at the age of twelve with an older sister, and learned brickmaking in St. Louis. In 1850, he was living with his young wife, their infant son, the wife's parents, and several boarders in a rented house in St. Charles, and there was nothing to suggest that he would go on to become a prominent brick manufacturer and a member of the St. Charles city council.[10] But Borgmann's case is clearly exceptional, with respect to both the low level at which he began and the heights to which he rose.

More commonly, people showed no real estate in 1850 because they were part of family enterprises. Eleven of the thirty-six were single men over age twenty-one still living in the households of their parents, who were in every case property holders. Similarly, three single men were living with propertied brothers, and two older men resided with married children who were likewise landowners. There were also five widows among those traced from Tecklenburg, but two of them held substantial real estate, while the other three were comfortably situated with daughters and sons-in-law. Only six of the propertyless men boarded with unrelated families. Three of them had arrived within the past two years, while another had come over as a dependent child in 1837. However, the other two had been around for ten years, if indeed they were correctly matched. Only one-third of the landless group—twelve individuals—were heads of households. Four of these were relatively recent arrivals, having emigrated in 1845 or later. But four others had left Germany by 1835. One of them, Hermann Knippenberg, was a prospering merchant who simply had invested in other goods instead of land. Johann Heinrich Bierbaum, at sixty-nine ripe for retirement, may have followed Westfalian custom and turned his farm over to his son, living next-door on a farm worth $700. But the other two people appear to pose clear-cut cases of extended hard times. Both had toiled for over fifteen years in the New World with little to show for it besides a houseful of children.[11]

[10] *History of St. Charles, Montgomery, and Warren Counties*, pp. 246, 364, 391, 407, 1033; *Portrait and Biographical Record*, pp. 198, 247, 337, 385, 408.

[11] In addition, Fredrick Schowengerdt, who emigrated in 1835, is shown without real estate in the 1850 census of Warren County, family no. 863. However, this is clearly an

CHAPTER V

Biographical information for Lippe-Detmolders is less plentiful, but the richest and poorest among them exhibit many of the same characteristics as the Tecklenburgers. The nineteen persons claiming more than $2,500 in wealth in 1860 represented about the top decile of the group traced from Lippe. Only four of them left biographies in county histories, none particularly revealing. Timing and location often proved to be the key to fortune. Although there had been only a trickle of immigration from Lippe before 1847, the average year of arrival of their elite was 1850. While three-fifths of those traced from Lippe lived south of the Missouri in the rugged Ozark borderlands of Gasconade and Franklin counties, over three-fifths of this elite subset farmed the more productive soils of Warren County. Even more so than with the Tecklenburgers, agriculture was the chief basis of wealth—except for one merchant also listed in the agricultural census, the group consisted entirely of farmers. The presence of one person worth $4,100 who had just arrived in 1860 shows that some fortunes were imported rather than accumulated in America. But this was not the only way. Among these nineteen wealthiest were three from the tenant-farmer class in Lippe and five others who were smallholders of a very marginal nature. Two of them had recorded no real estate a decade earlier. As late as 1860, then, opportunities in agriculture remained relatively open in this area.

Propertyless Lippe-Detmolders in 1860 show much the same pattern as Tecklenburgers a decade earlier, with life-cycle stage playing a crucial role. The forty-four adult males in the traced group who reported no wealth in 1860 consisted largely of people who had emigrated as dependent children and were still living in their parents' household. Over half the group, twenty-four men in all, fell into that category. All but three of them were single. Most of these young men were part of thriving family enterprises, for there were only three instances where the father was worth less than $500. Only one of these families, which had emigrated in 1856, was entirely without real estate, reporting just $200 in personal property. There were two adult males living in the households of married, landowning brothers, and seven older men who were probably retirees. Ranging in age from fifty-seven upward, all except one were living with sons or sons-in-law worth upwards of $1,000. Again, this seems to reflect the northwest German custom of retiring and settling the inheritance while one is still alive. There were six others among the propertyless men who were relatively recent arrivals, having

---

error because he was worth $5,000 in 1860, and a family history states that he purchased land soon after arrival. Thus he was excluded from the data set.

come over within the last five years. This leaves only five other cases of long-term poverty. Three involved persons of tenant-farmer origins, all of whom had emigrated in 1855. But there was at least one landholder's son among the propertyless, an 1848 immigrant, and perhaps another who had come over in 1851. In most cases, however, such poverty was probably temporary. Four young men who had emigrated with their parents and were among the have-nots in 1860 subsequently prospered enough to be featured in county-history biographies, and two of these had been of tenant-farmer origins in Lippe. Thus even if cheap land was becoming scarce in St. Charles County by 1860, opportunity still beckoned a short distance upriver.[12]

These favorable rates of social mobility and property accumulation achieved by rural Germans would appear in an entirely different light, however, if impoverished immigrants were disproportionately clustered in American cities. An investigation of the distribution of wealth in nineteenth-century America showed that in rural areas, immigrants enjoyed practically the same level of prosperity as the native-born. In the cities, however, there was a glaring inequality favoring natives over immigrants, and affecting Germans as much as Irish. One factor that that study could not take into account, however, was length of residence in America. Individual-level tracing can shed additional light on this matter, and also test the influence of background factors, such as previous occupation and life-cycle stage, on immigrant urbanization.[13]

Attempts to pursue this issue on the basis of the Tecklenburger group proved disappointing. Only thirteen families could be located in St. Louis in 1850. Judging by their real estate holdings, immigrants to the city were at a clear disadvantage, for eleven of the thirteen reported none in the census. The most prosperous was the son of a *Heuerling* now in the grocery business with his brother and showing real estate worth $4,000. The other property holder was a former blacksmith who just four years after immigration owned a bar and boardinghouse valued at $2,000. One of his tenants, a former peasant proprietor calling himself a "Gentleman," can probably be counted among the prosperous.

The other ten immigrants were evenly divided between artisans and unskilled laborers. German occupational background played only a minor role. Two tailors did persist in their trade, and a gunsmith failed

[12] *History of Franklin, Jefferson, Washington, Crawford and Gasconade Counties, Missouri* (1888; facsimile reprint, Cape Girardeau, Mo., 1970), pp. 510, 1100, 1127; *Portrait and Biographical Record*, pp. 254, 287.

[13] Lee Soltow, *Men and Wealth in the United States, 1850–1870* (New Haven, 1975), pp. 39–44.

CHAPTER V

to list an occupation upon emigrating. But a carpenter and a wagonmaker had been recruited from the ranks of farmhands and laborers, as had four of the five unskilled laborers traced to St. Louis. The latter were joined by a former landowning peasant working as a drayman despite having emigrated with 700 taler in 1846. A more striking contrast with immigrants to rural areas than occupational background was the recent arrival of those in the city. Only two of the thirteen Tecklenburg families in St. Louis had emigrated before 1840, and eight had arrived since 1845.

These tentative conclusions were greatly strengthened by a comparison of immigrants from Lippe-Detmold in St. Louis and rural Missouri in 1860. There were only eighty-one Lippe-Detmolders in St. Louis in 1860, only one-tenth as many as in the three rural counties, and about the same ratio as obtained for the Tecklenburgers in 1850. While rural immigrants showed more modest levels but a broader distribution of wealth, urbanites showed more extremes of both wealth and poverty. Despite the small size of the urban contingent, two of the three Lippe-Detmolders worth over $10,000 lived in St. Louis. The mean value of real estate and total wealth was higher in the city than in the country, but so was the proportion that reported no holdings. Since only fifteen urbanites could be linked to emigrant lists, comparisons made on this basis are rather shaky. Compared to the traced group as a whole, these St. Louisans showed a disadvantage of $69 in real estate and $116 in total wealth, but when one controls for length of residence, the gap narrows to just $34 for total wealth, while in terms of real estate, St. Louisans traced from Lippe were actually $16 better off than their rural counterparts. Thus it does not appear that focusing on rural areas gives an unrealistically optimistic picture of immigrant prosperity or transatlantic social mobility in general.[14]

More than wealth or occupation, demographic characteristics and life-cycle stage explain the difference between immigrants locating in urban and rural regions (see Figure 5.1). Immigrants in the city were primarily young adults, especially males, while those in the country showed a broader age and sex distribution. Barely one-third of rural immigrants, but nearly one-half of the urbanites, were in their late teens

[14] The rural average is lowered somewhat by a larger share of young men who emigrated as dependents and subsequently attained majority, but even if the comparison is restricted to those who emigrated as adults, St. Louisans only fall 4 percent below the mean of $889 in real estate and 8 percent below the $1,394 mean total wealth, controlling for length of residence. Persons who emigrated as parents consistently show the highest wealth figure, those who emigrated as children the lowest, while singles and newlyweds fall somewhere between.

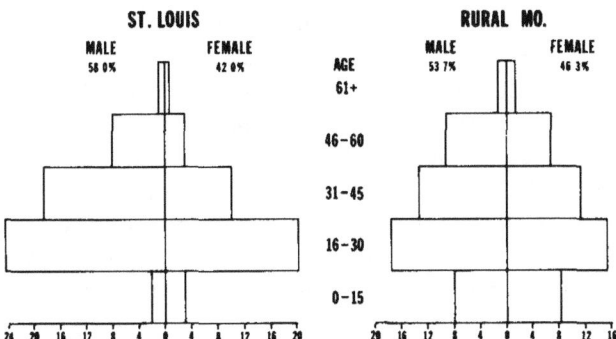

FIGURE 5.1
Age and Sex Profile (Natives of Lippe-Detmold in St. Louis and Rural Missouri, 1860)

and twenties. St. Louisans were also overrepresented, though to a lesser extent, in the group aged thirty to forty-five, while in the oldest age categories, rural immigrants had the upper hand. The greatest contrast, however, was among children under fifteen, who were almost three times as prevalent in the rural group as in the city. What this suggests is that family migration was concentrated in the country, while single migrants were more likely to stop in St. Louis. Among adult males from Lippe in the 1860 census, nearly three-quarters of those in the city had come over as single migrants or newlyweds, while the figure was twenty points lower in the country. Family migration also made for a more even sex ratio, with the surplus of males a good 4 percent higher in the city than in the country. Although there was some evidence of chain migration also in the city—40 percent of all Lippe-Detmolders resided in the Eighth Ward, nearly three times the expected proportion—they never dominated a neighborhood as they did in the country, and the immigrant community seems to have been less closely knit. Not only were more rural immigrants married when they arrived; those who married in America were also more likely to stay within the chain migration group. Considering only Lippe-Detmolders with no children born abroad, in rural areas, over two-thirds of the men chose partners of the same origin, but in St. Louis the figure was below one-third.[15]

[15] German population by ward was obtained from the city census of 1858, as published in the *St. Louis Anzeiger des Westens* (weekly ed.), 24 October 1858. Strikingly similar contrasts in intermarriage patterns could be found between immigrants from Brunswick in St. Louis and their compatriots in a homogeneous settlement in rural Missouri (see Kamphoefner, "Chain Migration and Local Homogeneity of Immigration:

149

CHAPTER V

As with the Tecklenburgers, Lippe-Detmolders in St. Louis tended to be relatively recent arrivals. The mean and median year of arrival was 1852, whereas over half of those traced to rural areas had arrived before 1850. The biggest surge of rural settlers had come in 1847 and 1848, with thirty-three and forty-five male adults traced from those years, while 1854, the peak of antebellum immigration in general, brought only nineteen. While this might suggest a shift from rural to urban destinations, aggregate-level data shows that the proportion of Missouri Germans residing in St. Louis hardly changed in the two decades after 1850.[16]

The recentness of arrival of most Germans in the city suggests that urban residence was often a transitional stage, especially for immigrants lacking money to buy land, on their way to the farm. In America as in Germany, the life-cycle stage also came into play, with city life holding most attraction for young, single adults and for newlyweds. None of the Lippe-Detmolders in the city had more than two children born abroad, but over 40 percent of rural immigrants who came with children had three or more. Those who had older children tended to go directly to rural areas, even if they had to be satisfied for the first few years with renting a plot and letting the children hire out to neighbors. This made good sense considering the trade-off between higher wage levels in the city and the higher cost of living there. Nicholas Hesse had advised in the late 1830s: "The unmarried joiner finds a better income in the larger cities. The father of a family, however, in the smaller towns and in the country, especially if he has grown sons and likes farming, which he can pursue as a side line and can thus procure lodging and maintenance in an easier way than in the expensive large cities." He offered similar advice for carpenters, smiths, cartwrights, tailors, and shoemakers; in fact, for nearly every trade he discussed. Immigrants from Brunswick provide a striking example of the life-cycle effect in their choice between destinations in St. Louis and rural Missouri. Over two-thirds of the predominantly single journeymen preferred the city, whereas two-thirds of all master artisans, for the most part family heads, opted for the country.[17]

Cape Girardeau County Germans in Comparative Perspective," in *French and German Folk Landscape in the Mississippi Valley*, ed. Michael Roark [Cape Girardeau, Mo., 1986]).

[16] The proportion of Missouri Germans living in St. Louis was 51.2 percent in 1850, and 52.0 percent in 1870; the published U.S. Census figures for 1860 combine the city and county of St. Louis, making it impossible to obtain a comparable figure for that year.

[17] William Bek, ed. and trans., "Nicholas Hesse, German Visitor to Missouri, 1835–

Immigrant biographies from the area of study often mentioned an urban sojourn of anywhere from a few weeks to a decade, usually in St. Louis, but occasionally in other cities along immigration routes. If Tecklenburgers stopped at all along the way, it was almost always in St. Louis. Only one Tecklenburg family had a child born anywhere in the United States outside Missouri, and a biography characterized their stay in Cincinnati as a "short sojourn," followed by three years in St. Louis. In the census, children born in St. Louis are indistinguishable from those born elsewhere in the state. In southern Illinois, however, one can assume that Missouri as the birthplace of a child usually meant St. Louis. A check of the Belleville, Illinois, area from the 1860 census revealed that over 10 percent of all German families there had stopped in St. Louis long enough to show one or more Missouri-born children. The tendency was somewhat more pronounced among families begun in the United States than among those that already had children born in Germany, again reflecting the life-cycle effect.[18]

Probably more people remained permanently in the cities than had intended to when they emigrated, restrained either by poverty or by prosperity. The two brothers in the grocery business, sons of a tenant farmer, are probably cases of the latter. A contrasting example would be John Henry Gerlemann, a propertyless laborer in St. Louis in 1850, no more than he had been when he emigrated in 1833 with a large group bound for rural Missouri. From the baptismal records of his children, it appears that he returned to the city after at least five years in the country. More commonly, however, the paths of immigrants led in the opposite direction. Another Tecklenburger, who was working as a laborer in St. Louis in 1850, not only made the transition, but was successful enough at farming to afford a biography in the St. Charles County history. None of the Lippe-Detmolders in St. Louis in 1860 could be traced back to the rural settlement a decade earlier.[19]

For many German immigrants, then, the paths of migration led from

---

1837," *Missouri Historical Review* 42 (1947–1948): 141–143; Kamphoefner, "Chain Migration and Local Homogeneity."

[18] *Portrait and Biographical Record*, p. 518; see Kamphoefner, "Transplanted Westfalians: Persistence and Transformation of Socioeconomic and Cultural Patterns in the Northwest German Migration to Missouri" (Ph.D. diss., University of Missouri, 1978), pp. 190–191, for more detail on Illinois Germans.

[19] A chance discovery revealed that one of Gerlemann's children was baptized in 1841 and another in 1846 at Femme Osage in rural St. Charles County. It is possible that the family lived in St. Louis the whole time, and only took the children to be christened among the rural relatives and friends, since one child was six months old and the other eleven weeks old when it was baptized. Sketch of John Henry Stiegemeier in *Portrait and Biographical Record*, p. 511.

CHAPTER V

American cities to the countryside, and in career patterns, an artisan trade often gave way gradually to agriculture. As Charles van Ravenswaay has documented in such sympathetic detail, German craftsmen continued to produce many articles in the traditional patterns they had known from the homeland. But few showed any exclusive loyalty to a trade, and given the opportunity, most also established themselves in agriculture. Perhaps, too, the community was not yet developed enough to support many full-time artisans.[20]

Both groups of traced immigrants bear out this discontinuity. Including those traced to St. Louis, there were only seven Tecklenburg artisans—three tailors, two smiths, a wagonmaker, and a miller—who remained with their trades, while an equal number of craftsmen had been recruited from agricultural labor. For every artisan who persisted in his trade, there were at least two who had turned to farming. Although mass immigration from Lippe to rural Missouri had only begun in 1847, the shift from artisanship to agriculture was already evident in the 1850 census. None of the eight Lippe-Detmolders who were artisans in 1850 could be linked to the emigrant lists, and of the twelve former artisans who were traced, not a single one stuck with his trade. Four of them owned farms, while five rented, and the other three had to settle for agricultural labor.

The sixty-nine adult men from Lippe persisting in the rural area from 1850 to 1860 showed an even greater affinity for farming. The proportion of landowning farmers increased from 55 to 90 percent in the course of a decade, twenty-six new recruits being offset by only two dropouts or retirees, while thirty-six people remained farm owners in both censuses. Only one of the five artisans present in 1850 stuck with his trade in 1860, the other four becoming farm owners. They were offset by three artisan recruits, one each from the ranks of renters, farmhands, and laborers. Farming was apparently the highest aspiration for most of these immigrants; only one person who had been a renter in

---

[20] Charles van Ravenswaay, *The Arts and Architecture of German Settlements in Missouri: A Survey of a Vanishing Culture* (Columbia, Mo., 1977). Similar instances of artisans turning to agriculture were found among a group of Germans traced to Michigan by Joseph Scheben, *Untersuchung zur Methode und Technik der deutschamerikanischen Wanderungsforschung* (Bonn, 1939), pp. 100–101. Likewise, about one-third of the "urban blue-collar" workers among a group of Dutch immigrants traced to America achieved farm ownership—this American occupational designation apparently includes village artisans and manual laborers who were not specified as agricultural (Kirk, *Promise of American Life*, pp. 88–91). Similar results were reported in the much larger, as yet unpublished, tracing study by Robert P. Swierenga, "Dutch International Migration and Occupational Change: A Structural Analysis of Multinational Linked Files," paper presented at the Social Science History Conference, Bloomington, Ind., November 1982.

TABLE 5.4. OCCUPATIONAL MOBILITY OF ADULT MALE EMIGRANTS
(Traced from Lippe-Detmold to St. Louis and Rural Missouri through 1860)

American Occupation	St. Louis or Rural	German Occupation			
		Ag. Labor or Unspec., Poor Family,		Tenant Farmer (Einlieger)	Artisan
		Single	Married		
Nonmanual	R	—	—	1	—
	S	1	1	—	1
Farmer, Owner	R	10	7	19	12
Farmer, Renter	R	—	—	4	1
Artisan	R	2	—	2	10
	S	—	—	1	3
Laborer	R	—	—	1	—
	S	—	1	1	2
Total	R	12	7	27	23
	S	1	2	2	6
Rural + St. Louis Total		13	9	29	29

American Occupation	St. Louis or Rural	German Occupation			
		Smallholder	Ag. Labor, Kolon Fam., Single	Peasant Proprietor (Kolon)	Total
Nonmanual	R	—	2	—	3
	S	—	—	—	3
Farmer, Owner	R	28	5	18	99
Farmer, Renter	R	—	—	1	6
Artisan	R	1	—	1	16
	S	—	—	1	5
Laborer	R	2	1	3	7
	S	1	—	1	6
Total	R	31	8	23	131
	S	1	—	2	14
Rural + St. Louis Total		32	8	25	145

SOURCE: See Appendix B.

1850 achieved white-collar status in 1860. The Tecklenburger community was very similar in its occupational makeup, although it did include a few more rural merchants.

Table 5.4 examines the occupational continuity of adult men who were traced from Lippe to the 1860 census, in this case also including

CHAPTER V

St. Louis. The most striking feature of these mobility patterns is again the strong concentration of people, regardless of background, in the category of landowning farmers. Over two-thirds of all traced adults, and three-fourths of those in the country, fall into this group. Except for those of artisan backgrounds, at least five-eighths of every occupational group turned to farming in America. Even with artisans, the rate of continuity is rather low. Fewer than half persisted in their trades, while an equal number turned to farming. "Backward looking" continuity was greater than "forward looking" for artisans; over two-thirds of those practicing a trade in America had also done so back in Lippe. The nonmanual ranks of the immigrant community were rather thin, and were recruited from a wide variety of backgrounds. The renting of farms was often a transitional stage for those with origins in the rural lower class. Few adults over twenty-one were confined to agricultural labor; in fact, most of those in the table who seem to be were probably retired, since they had been landowners in Lippe. Most of the urban laborers, on the other hand, seem to have suffered genuine downward mobility through emigration. But for the most part the picture appears positive—just how positive depends on how favorably one regards farming.

Like the choice between urban and rural location, the choice between retaining an artisan occupation or abandoning it for farming was related to life-cycle stage. The thirteen rural dwellers who had abandoned artisanship for agriculture had been fully five years older on average when they left Lippe than the ten who still persisted in their trades in 1860. Family status also played a role: only half of the persisters arrived as parents, compared to eleven of the thirteen who turned to agriculture. There were also thirty-two artisans in the group, about equally divided between country and city, whose occupation in Lippe was unknown. Except in three cases, they could not be linked to the emigrant lists, though no doubt some practiced their trades before emigrating. But clandestine emigrants such as these were also predominantly young and single. Regardless of whether such people were trained as craftsmen in Germany, life-cycle stage as much as previous experience influenced their career choices in America. Their age at emigration is of course unknown, but in 1860 they averaged nearly twelve years younger than artisan dropouts and four years younger than persisters. Furthermore, in all three categories, those in the city were from two to five years younger than those in the country. Thus urban residence and artisan occupations were interrelated and played similar roles in the immigrant life cycle. There were only six Lippe-Detmolders who traded agriculture for artisanship in the process of emigration.

Even this may be an exaggeration, for in four of the cases the links with the emigrant list were doubtful, and the one sure link had just arrived in 1860.[21]

Although life-cycle stage was the prime factor in determining whether immigrants stuck to their old trades, the demand for various artisan skills in America also came into play. Table 5.5 examines the individual trades practiced by Lippe-Detmolders either in Germany, in America, or both. Although background information is missing for nearly half the people in the table, it is clear that patterns of continuity varied considerably from trade to trade.

One exception to the general tendency of artisanship giving way to farming was the tailoring trade. German tailors appear to have found a strong demand for their skills in America. Angela Heck, a young tailor's wife, wrote home from New York in 1854 enthusiastically relating how her husband was hired right off the boat, and advised two friends, still toiling as unmarried servant girls in the steep vineyards along the Moselle, "Burn up your grape baskets and get yourself a tailor, even if he's just a windbag!" Her advice had some validity for the Midwest as well. Tailoring was the most common trade among Lippe-Detmolders in Missouri, and was well represented in both city and country. The low tracing ratio obscures the degree of continuity, but it was probably high. The three apparent recruits from the *Einlieger*, or tenant class, simply may have failed to record their trades in the emigrant lists although they practiced them on the side. Of six tailors in the Tecklenburger group, two remained in St. Louis and one in St. Charles working their trades, while three became landowning farmers.[22]

The shoemaking trade was also well represented among immigrants from Lippe, and showed equal if not greater continuity than tailoring. While mass production was making rapid strides in the shoemaking industry, particularly in New England, it had not yet reached the point of driving out the hand trade. Also, the traced group may well include

---

[21] Questionable matches with emigrant lists cannot account for the large number of artisans turning to agriculture; of thirteen emigrants in this category, only three were doubtful matches; there were more doubtful matches (five of thirteen) among those persisting at their trades—occupation not having been used as a criterion in matching. Among roughly fifteen county-history biographies linked to the emigrant lists from Lippe, there were six cases where artisan occupations were indicated in the biographies but not in the emigrant lists. Three were listed as tenant farmers, the others as proprietors; carpenters predominated, but there was also one tailor.

[22] Letter of Angela Heck, nee Spoo, New York, 1 July 1854 (transcript in the Joseph Scheben Collection, Library of the Verein für geschichtliche Landeskunde der Rheinlande, Bonn, and in the Immigrant Letter Collection, Wisconsin Historical Society, Madison).

CHAPTER V

TABLE 5.5. OCCUPATIONAL CONTINUITY OF MALE ARTISANS
(From Lippe-Detmold to St. Louis and Rural Missouri, 1860)

		\multicolumn{4}{c}{Employed as Artisan in}		
	Rural or St. Louis	Germany, not U.S.[a]	Germany and U.S.	U.S., Ger. unknown	U.S., not Germany
Tailor	R	3	2	4	2[f]
	S	—	—	5	1[f]
Shoemaker	R	1	3	3[e]	—
	S	—	2	1	1[g]
Locksmith, Nail maker, Blacksmith	R	1	2	—	1[g]
	S	1[b]	—	—	—
Brickmaker	R	3[c]	1[d]	1	—
	S	1[b]	—	2	—
Stone mason, Brick mason	R	1	—	2	1[h]
	S	—	—	1	—
Carpenter	R	1	1	5	—
Turner, Cooper	R	2×1	—	—	—
Wagonmaker	R	—	1	1	—
Miller	R	—	—	1	—
Baker	R	1	—	—	—
Other	S	—	2	6	—
All	R	13	10	17	4
	S	2	4	15	2

SOURCE: See Appendix B.
[a] Landowning farmer in U.S. unless otherwise specified.   [b] Laborer in U.S.
[c] One renter, two farmers in U.S.   [d] Carpenter in U.S.
[e] Includes one combined farmer and shoemaker.
[f] *Einlieger* in Germany.   [g] *Kolon* in Germany.   [h] Smallholder in Germany.

some makers of wooden shoes, which were common in northwest Germany and less subject to machine competition. For conventional shoemakers, however, the long-term prospects were not good. John Fuhr, an early immigrant to Augusta, stated in an 1885 biography that he had once "carried on the manufacture of boots and shoes quite extensively, and worked from ten to fifteen men." Since "a few large manufacturing capitalists" and "large factories" now dominated the industry, Fuhr had turned to viniculture for a living. He still made "a few boots and shoes," but "nothing in this line at all to what he formerly did." In the long run, most of those who were shoemakers in the 1860 census probably experienced similar fates. For example, Jacob Diederich was listed as a shoemaker when his son was baptized in Femme Osage in 1855, a rarity since parish records seldom mentioned occupations. He is likewise designated as a shoemaker in the 1860 census, although he also appears in the agricultural schedule. But the 1870, 1880, and 1900 censuses make no further mention of shoemaking, and show all the signs of a full-time farmer.[23]

Blacksmithing also showed considerable continuity from Westfalia to Missouri. But the smith's trade required some business acumen, which was put to other uses by several Tecklenburgers. One smith who remained in St. Louis invested in a bar and boardinghouse, and two of three blacksmiths' sons were engaged in merchandising. Brickmaking, a specialty of Lippe-Detmolders, was usually carried on as seasonal migratory labor, a sideline of the tenant-farmer class. Thus it was often abandoned in rural Missouri where opportunities in full-time agriculture were better. As was noted above, the highly successful brickmaker among the Tecklenburgers had learned his trade in America.

In the building trades, where Germans were noted for high standards of craftsmanship, there were nevertheless few signs of continuity. The two Tecklenburgers who did identify themselves in the census as carpenters—one in St. Louis and one in the country—must have begun on the unskilled level, for both had backgrounds in agricultural labor. The same probably held for most carpenters from Lippe of unknown background. Of five former carpenters, a stonemason, and a cabinetmaker traced from Tecklenburg, all seven had turned to farming, six of them becoming landowners by 1850. With immigrants from Lippe, the low tracing ratio might have masked a good deal of continuity. But a cross-section of about twenty Lippe-Detmolders in county-history biographies included five carpenters and one mason who eventually turned to farming.[24]

For example, Friederich Winter came from Lippe-Detmold to Warren County in 1852 with his parents. His father was a carpenter by trade, and pursued this to some extent in America, but found farming more profitable and gave up carpentry altogether. The craftsmanship

---

[23] *History of St. Charles, Montgomery, and Warren Counties*, p. 245. My grandfather, Walter Diederich, was well acquainted with his grandfather, Jacob, who died when the former was twenty, but told me he was unaware that his grandfather had ever been a shoemaker. For other evidence that declining crafts provided Germans a fast start down a dead-end street, see Griffen and Griffen, *Natives and Newcomers*, pp. 180–184.

[24] Biographical sketches of immigrants from Lippe-Detmold can be found in *History of St. Charles, Montgomery, and Warren Counties*, p. 1034; *Portrait and Biographical Record*, pp. 141, 144, 166, 254, 287, 342, 490, 502, 510, 522, 529, 546; *History of Franklin, Jefferson, Washington, Crawford, and Gasconade Counties*, pp. 723, 757, 834, 1013, 1075, 1077, 1093, 1097, 1100, 1103, 1111, 1113, 1127, 1129.

CHAPTER V

of Henry Meyer, another northwest German from Melle, was proudly related by his son: "His handiwork . . . remain[s] as a monument to his skill as a builder. . . . As a wagon maker he was a skilled mechanic." Nevertheless, he appears in the 1850 census as a farmer, with twenty acres of improved land and another hundred unimproved, real estate worth $350. Often artisanship helped supply the means for obtaining a farm. Conrad Begemann, the son of a carpenter and peasant proprietor in Lippe, had learned his father's trade and "could make nice furniture and almost any kind of dwelling." Emigrating with his bride in 1848, he purchased forty acres and was listed in the 1850 census as a farmer worth $150. As is related, however, "when our subject first came here he experienced very hard times, but during odd seasons on the farm worked industriously at his trade, and thus procured some means." By 1852 he was able to purchase a 160-acre farm in neighboring Lincoln County, and was still there four decades later.[25]

Thus at times the census fails to capture the full complexity of the situation. To take another example, Johann Heinrich Freese went from being a stonemason and *Heuerling* in Tecklenburg to one of the most prosperous farmers among this group in 1850. His brother Steffen, overlooked by the 1850 census, had also been a mason before emigrating. But both practiced their trade at least as a sideline in the early years. In 1840, when the log church at Femme Osage was being replaced with stone, Pastor Garlichs noted that he had been in St. Charles "to arrange the building of the church with the mason Stephen Frese." In mid-May, when they should have been tending their corn fields, Garlichs recorded that "the two Freeses came, in order to begin with the stone laying." Although projects of this size were rather uncommon, even smaller ones must have provided a substantial supplement to agricultural income.[26]

Similarly, wagonmaking was a trade that was often practiced on a seasonal basis in combination with agriculture, both in the Old World and the New. The four wagonmakers who were traced from Tecklenburg had all followed their trade as a sideline to tenant farming before emigrating. By 1850, they or their heirs had all become farmers and substantial landholders (two of the operations were carried on by widows and sons). But there is evidence that at least three of them also carried on their trade to a greater or lesser extent.[27] Of the two from Lippe

[25] *Portrait and Biographical Record*, pp. 546, 380, 510.

[26] For sources of information on Freese brothers, see Chap. 3, n. 38. Diary of Adelheid Garlichs, nee von Borries, 1835–1840 (typescript transcript by W. D. Kamphoefner).

[27] The one with the largest farm identified himself in the census as a wagonmaker and

who became wagonmakers, at least one and perhaps both had followed the same trade back home.

Several other artisan groups were too lightly represented to allow much generalization. Of the two Tecklenburgers who had emigrated as millers, one was a struggling farmer (if indeed this was the same person), the other a highly successful miller also engaged in agriculture, while the only miller from Lippe was of unknown background. The baker from Lippe who turned to farming was probably an exceptional case; the butcher who stayed at his trade in St. Louis was more typical. In general, the trades among Lippe-Detmolders that were restricted to the city were highly specialized, often catering to an affluent clientele. There were two tobacco workers, at least one with European experience, and a cabinetmaker, a finisher, and an engraver of unknown background. But continuity was probably high, as suggested by two piano makers who were father and son. At any rate, no dropouts were discovered among these exclusively urban trades. Specialized, highly skilled trades such as these dominate in the popular image of the German artisan. But it should be clear that they were in fact a rather small minority.

Even among the elite of the craftsmen, rather drastic career shifts come to light on occasion. Moritz Bergfeld, the son of a court musician to the duke of Steinfurt, had been a master goldsmith in Wildeshausen, a town of about 2,000 inhabitants, before he emigrated in the early 1850s. He was still designated as a silversmith in the Augusta parish register when he remarried in 1855. But the 1860 census shows him simply as a farmer, cultivating fifty acres in a hilly, isolated location near the town. Although Bergfeld was past fifty at the time, his only help consisted of two sons, aged seventeen and fourteen, and a single hired hand to handle five horses and a yoke of oxen. Still, he was successful enough at farming that he later took up storekeeping, but there is no further record of goldsmithing in his career.[28]

---

had two apprentices in the household. The head of the second household was listed as a farmer, but also had an apprentice wagonmaker in the house. A third former wagonmaker was also a prospering farmer, but had boarded a greenhorn nephew for one and one-half years, after which the youth worked in St. Louis as a wagonmaker for ten years, so presumably the uncle had taught him the trade (see *Portrait and Biographical Record*, p. 385).

[28] Evangelical parish records of the castle church in Burgsteinfurt, of Wildeshausen, and of Augusta, Mo.; manuscript schedules of population and agricultural census, St. Charles County, Mo. The silversmithing trade was seriously eroded by industrial production, according to Ravenswaay, *Arts and Architecture*, pp. 507–511. An even more drastic shift is the case of Friedrich Stallfort, who emigrated from Westerkappeln to Phil-

CHAPTER V

The immigrants from Westfalia and Lippe were apparently glad to forget they had ever been linen weavers. The daughter of a Westfalian *Heuerling*, working as a domestic in Indianapolis, wrote home in 1867, "I am very contented, I never have to spin or weave, I can go to bed at six at night." Except for the bedtime, most Missouri immigrants would have agreed. The weaving trade never appears once among the occupations of the traced group. If it was practiced at all, it was only for home use. The lack of prospects for weavers could hardly have been a surprise. Nicholas Hesse's guidebook, based on his Missouri experiences, had warned in 1838 that "linen makers would not be able to make a living here. Nearly every American woman can weave wool and linen."[29]

However, immigrants came not to preserve their trades but rather to establish independence and security, which in their minds was rooted in the soil. Despite their recent arrival, a larger proportion of Germans were landowners than was the case with native Americans or any other immigrant group in this part of Missouri. For the most part, this was not the result of imported wealth, as an admiring statement by Friedrich Muench, the elder statesman of the Latin farmers in Duden country, makes clear:

> The great majority of the Germans who came here . . . were of little means, many even completely without means (so called *Heuerlinge* and day laborers). Thus forty-five years ago right in my neighborhood two families in partnership bought a forty-acre piece of "Con-

---

adelphia after the Civil War and worked as a tailor for over twenty years in the city. But in the 1890s, he moved to a hardscrabble farm in Lafayette County, Missouri, an increasingly popular destination for Tecklenburgers as land in eastern Missouri became scarce. After about a decade, he gave up and moved to an urban job in California. The story was related to me by his nonagenarian daughter in Pasadena in 1982, and checks out with information in emigration lists and censuses.

[29] Letter of Margareta and Engel Winkelmeyer, 5 December 1867; in the same letter one of the sisters writes, "If Luise doesn't feel like spinning and weaving, then she should come here." The same concerns are apparent in Margareta's letter of 6 December 1870, where she asks her brother, "Write me a lot about my father and the two girls, whether they already have to spin." Apparently she was referring to her younger nieces. For complete texts of the letters, see Wolfgang Helbich, Walter Kamphoefner, and Ulrike Sommer, eds., *Amerika-Auswanderer im 19. Jahrhundert schreiben nach Deutschland* (tentative title, Munich, forthcoming). On weaving, see Bek, "Nicholas Hesse," 42: 143, 148; Ravenswaay, *Arts and Architecture*, pp. 445–457. It should be noted that Jacquard weaving such as was practiced by John Schneider, a Bavarian in St. Charles County, required much more skill than the linen weaving of the Tecklenburgers. Even Schneider is listed in the 1860 census, no. 1520, as a farmer. However, the presence of a spinning-wheel maker in Warren County as late as 1870 suggests that some hand textile production for home use was still going on.

gress land" on borrowed money. Today the son of one of these buyers is the owner of the valuable farmstead where the famous Daniel Boone settled.[30]

Gert Goebel, another of the early Latin farmers, echoes Muench's testimony, describing a determination bordering on fanaticism with which "people from the working classes ... peasants, cottagers, and ordinary day laborers" went about acquiring land:

> Most of them were very poor, even in debt for their passage money, so poor that in many instances two families had to go in partnership to buy forty acres of government land at the insignificant price of $50. After building a most humble hut, the men usually hired out among their older neighbors, while the women and children cleared away the underbrush.... Some women even made fence rails, though not many. Every spare day and even the moonlit nights were used by the men to build fences.... The first horses, cows, and hogs were bought on credit, and paid for in labor at from fifty cents to a dollar per day.[31]

The German background of these immigrants was a good preparation for such efforts. Those who had been tenant farmers were accustomed to spending much of their time working for their landlords and tilling their own plots at odd times when the opportunity presented itself. Many had also sought seasonal work on the dikes and in the peat bogs of Holland, leaving the farm work at home to wives and children. The difference was, as Goebel pointed out, that in Germany, "in spite of all the hard work and self-denial, they accomplished no more than barely keeping body and soul together, and their children had no better prospects for the future than the parents; as if on a treadmill, they had come no further by the end of the year than they were at the beginning." In America, by contrast, such arduous efforts held the promise of landownership and progress.[32]

If the above statements sound overly optimistic, county-history biographies further demonstrate the extent of mobility that was possible with luck and hard work. One of the woman rail-splitters was Frederick W. Pehle's mother, who shouldered the task when her husband was crippled for life soon after coming to Franklin County around 1840.

---

[30] Friedrich Muench, "Eine deutsche Niederlassung am Missouri," *Der Deutsche Pionier* 11 (1879): 317–318.

[31] Gert Goebel, *Länger als ein Menschenleben in Missouri* (St. Louis, 1877), pp. 47–48.

[32] Ibid., p. 49.

CHAPTER V

The son became a farmer and real estate agent, owned four thousand acres of land, and had at one time owned as much as ten thousand acres, according to an 1888 biography. He had served one term in the state senate and three in the lower house. Henry Schoppenhorst, the American-born son of a Tecklenburger *Heuerling*, managed to acquire a college education and represented Warren County in the Missouri legislature. William Achelpohl's eighty-acre farm was rather small to be featured in a biographical sketch, but it still represented a long, uphill climb. His family was so poor that the father had to work for two years in New Orleans before he could afford to bring them over. He worked three more months in a sawmill, twelve-year-old William helping out with $10 per month hauling sawdust. With "extremely limited means," they rented a farm near St. Charles and bought two horses for $90 in cash. Renting for six years, "years of privation and toil indeed," they managed to save $900 and buy a small farm. William himself was over forty before he bought any land, though his father had given him twenty acres several years before. A second-generation Achelpohl, probably his son, studied at Washington University and had established a dental practice in St. Charles by 1895.[33]

Joseph Giessmann, a tenant farmer's son from near Melle, followed a more tortuous path to farm ownership. Emigrating with a friend at age eighteen in the great wave of 1846, he first worked on several St. Charles County farms, then for one season at a steam mill. Laid low for a year by chills and fever, he resumed working two years for Dr. Krug, probably as a farmhand. After eighteen months driving oxen at Schaaf's mill, he spent another season on a farm, then worked for a New Melle blacksmith for one year. After working on another German farm for one and one-half years, he settled down at age twenty-four, marrying a widow eight years his senior, but with home-town roots. He rented his wife's quarter-section farm for over twenty years before finally buying out his stepchildren. His invocation of the self-made myth seems justified: "Beginning for himself as a poor, friendless boy, by dint of economy and hard work he has accumulated a competence." The goal was always clear though the path was anything but straight.[34]

[33] *History of Franklin, Jefferson, Washington, Crawford, and Gasconade Counties*, pp. 801–802; *History of St. Charles, Montgomery, and Warren Counties*, pp. 1051–1053; *Portrait and Biographical Record*, pp. 202, 393. There are minor discrepancies between the birthdate reported by the elder Achelpohl and that reported by the younger Achelpohl for his father. But the son says he attended school in the city of St. Charles, and the 1880 census shows a son of the right name and age in the household of the elder Achelpohl, who was operating a retail grocery, though this is not mentioned in his biography.

[34] *Portrait and Biographical Record*, p. 308.

Just because most immigrants eventually succeeded in acquiring land does not mean that they were living comfortably, however, particularly in the early years of settlement. When Pastor Joseph Rieger traveled between Pinckney and Marthasville in 1847, he was petitioned by sixty German families, most of them from Tecklenburg, Lippe-Detmold, and neighboring areas, to stay as their pastor. "The people were poor. They were in debt and their crops were not worth much. They said that they had no money, but assured the pastor that he should fare at least as well as they did." Rieger nevertheless accepted the offer, which precipitated another problem. There was no suitable dwelling for him in the settlement at Charette (now Holstein). With one exception, all the members of the parish were living in one-room cabins.[35]

The crude living conditions during the early days of settlement offended the sensibilities of Frederick Gustorf, an urban bourgeois German who visited Duden country in 1836. Traveling between Washington and Union in Franklin County he came upon a settlement of about twenty families from Osnabrück, "the lowest class of German immigrants." Even the chronically pessimistic Gustorf could not deny their agricultural progress, but he was nevertheless appalled. "By constant diligence and hard work they now have large fields of wheat under cultivation, but they are lacking in domestic comforts, and their homes are very dirty. I have never seen such dirt, even in the homes of the poorest squatters.... When the mother came she was so dirty I found it impossible to drink the proffered water."[36]

Though of similar bourgeois origins, Gert Goebel, who lived in the same neighborhood, showed a good deal more sympathy: "It is very understandable that in a household where the woman has to work almost from morning till night in the forest and field, the domestic order and cleanliness cannot be very exemplary; as poor day laborer women they did not have it any better in their old homeland." By and large, Gustorf rather than Goebel was more typical of the attitudes of educated Germans.[37]

---

[35] William G. Bek, "Followers of Duden," *Missouri Historical Review* 18 (1923): 240–242. The majority of Rieger's parishioners were from Tecklenburg and Lippe, to judge by the names of persons he married listed in Mrs. Howard W. Woodruff, comp., *Marriage Records, Warren County, Missouri, 1833–1860* (Independence, Mo., 1969).

[36] Fred Gustorf, ed. and trans., *The Uncorrupted Heart: Journal and Letters of Frederick Julius Gustorf, 1800–1845* (Columbia, Mo., 1969), p. 131. Gustorf thought the peasant children understood neither German nor English, and spoke a mixture of both, citing the sentence, "Mutter is gegangen, water fetschen." They obviously did not speak High German, but rather their local Low German dialect, which Gustorf may have mistaken for English. While the High German word for "water" is *Wasser*, in Low German it is *Water*, just like English except with an initial "v" sound.

[37] Goebel, *Länger als ein Menschenleben*, pp. 48–49.

CHAPTER V

Despite the excellent opportunities for social mobility and the undermining of distinctions between peasant proprietors and their former tenants, the barriers of class so notorious in Europe still persisted to some extent among bourgeois Germans on the Missouri frontier. Rare indeed among persons of such origins was someone like Friedrich Muench, who out of egalitarian principle refused a cabin berth and traveled steerage with the rest of the Giessen Society. A good reflection of the social distinctions persisting in the Duden settlement is found in the diary of Adelheid Garlichs, the Femme Osage pastor's wife, which faithfully records visits made by and to the family. The Tecklenburger peasants who made up the majority of Pastor Garlichs' parishioners are conspicuously absent from the visitors lists. The only times they show up at all are in the context of work or business, as when the Garlichs bought a cow from old Bierbaum or some apple trees from Oberhellmann, tried to collect a debt from Schaberg, or got caught in the rain and had to seek shelter at Knöpker's. Most often mentioned of the peasants was the Brinkmann family, but that was because the wife served as a midwife and a nurse during illnesses.

At the top of the Garlichs' visiting list were Dr. Krug and his wife, members of the Giessen Society. Another frequent guest was Dr. Koch, and in both cases the great majority of the visits were social rather than professional in nature. Another name prominent on the guest list, von Arx, betrays noble ancestry. Higher nobility such as Count Bentinck from Oldenburg and the von Bocks, estate owners from Mecklenburg, each show up several times. In several other cases, bourgeois origins were reinforced by personal ties reaching back to Germany. Even professional rivalry and the theological rationalism of Friedrich Muench did not stand in the way of social ties with the more orthodox Garlichs, nor was their door barred to Gustav Eulenstein, another middle-class freethinker who later fell to the depths of alcoholism and domestic violence before committing suicide.[38]

Though disillusioned Latin farmers were perhaps most susceptible to drink and despair, not every immigrant of peasant stock was equal to the task of hacking a farm out of the wilderness either. The *St. Charles*

---

[38] Adelheid Garlichs diary; a count was made of all persons mentioned during the five-year period, 1836–1840. Among over 400 entries, 28 involved Krug or his wife, and three-fourths of the visits were social. Dr. Koch appeared 18 times, almost always socially. Luise Pöppelmeier was in the same cabin with the Garlichs on their voyage to America in 1835–1836, and her family shows up in 26 entries. Julius Kruse, who was on the same ship with Hermann Garlichs on his first voyage, is mentioned 12 times. Eulenstein was the brother-in-law of Dr. Krug; his fate is related by Friedrich Muench, "Ein Gräslicher Auftritt," *Der Deutsche Pionier* 1 (1869): 310–312.

Demokrat was just in its fourth month of publication in 1852 when it recorded the first suicide: "Caspar Wenke, a capable carpenter from around Femme Osage, cut his throat with a razor.... Neighbors had only noticed that he had spent the whole afternoon ... engrossed in reading the Bible, not at all customary for him." There was another suicide in 1855, this time in Augusta: "Karl Wagner, a saddler by trade, took his own life last Sunday night with a pistol shot, probably in an attack of madness." Christmas of 1856 found the *Demokrat* combating a vicious rumor. Nicholas Heusel, a farmer in the vicinity of St. Charles, died of delirium tremens, not, as had been claimed, from a chest wound that his wife inflicted in self-defense against his brutal violence. About a year later, the editor was again downplaying suspicions of homicide. Stephan Dicks, a German employed as a woodchopper for the railroad, was found the day after payday with empty pockets and a head wound, drowned beneath a railroad trestle. But rather than foul play, it was probably an accident. Dicks had been seen buying rounds in several saloons the day before, and he was known "never to go back to his job without first spending up all his money in drink and revelry."[39]

An additional issue raised by these horror stories is the question of whether such persons were less likely to be identified in a tracing process than more successful immigrants. With these four examples, the evidence is somewhat mixed. Three of the people could be readily identified in the census, and the railroad worker had probably not yet arrived in 1850. Wenke was the only victim reporting any real estate in the census. Two people were boarders, and three were single, which would make them more difficult to trace. But Heusel, at least, appears to have been part of a group of chain migrants from Alsace, and Wenke may have been part of the Melle group, though he lived a few miles away among the Tecklenburgers. Thus the issue of representativeness of the traced groups needs to be explored more systematically.

How typical were the Tecklenburgers and Lippe-Detmolders of German immigrants in their area or in America generally? What influence did their homogeneous settlement patterns or their confession have on their social mobility? One might argue that these two groups present a perfect example of the Protestant ethic and the spirit of capitalism. Lippe-Detmolders, after all, had a strong Calvinist streak that often led them to Methodism in Missouri; in fact, the original immigrant wave

[39] *St. Charles Demokrat*, 17 April 1852; 13 October 1855; 25 December 1856; 17 December 1857. Passenger lists show that Wenke arrived in New Orleans on 29 November 1837 on the bark *Leontine*, along with several families from the Melle area who settled around New Melle, Mo.

CHAPTER V

in 1847 had been a group migration with strong religious overtones. One should not make too much of this, however. Two nineteenth-century accounts by pious observers on opposite sides of the Atlantic stress economic hardship as the dominant motive for emigration. Moreover, in most respects the Lippe-Detmolders strongly resembled their more secular compatriots from Tecklenburg. But even the latter were more pietistic in their religious affiliations than the Lutherans and Catholics that made up the bulk of German immigration.[40]

Upon closer examination, confession appears to be no more important a factor in social mobility than it was as a motive for emigration. The Voelkerding family might appear to be a perfect manifestation of the Protestant ethic. Arnold, a tenant farmer from Oldenburg who emigrated around 1840, owned a farm worth $1,000 as early as 1850. His son Hermann, only a couple of years old when the family came to America, had had little opportunity for education and had started out renting a farm. By 1895, he owned nine hundred acres, mostly prime Missouri River bottomland, which he farmed with his sons. The same family later founded the Bank of Dutzow, one of the few small-town banks in the area to survive the Great Depression. But Max Weber notwithstanding, the Voelkerdings were Catholic. Although perhaps the most prosperous of such immigrants from Oldenburg, they were by no means unique. When the dozen of their compatriots in Warren County in 1860 were compared with the German population as a whole, they proved to be average or slightly above in terms of real estate and other wealth. Several other studies of Germans and Dutch have found a similar lack of correspondence between confession and social mobility.[41]

But like their Protestant counterparts mentioned above, the Oldenburgers formed a compact settlement of chain migrants. Perhaps group

[40] Kate E. Levi, "Geographic Origins of German Immigration to Wisconsin," *Collections of the State Historical Society of Wisconsin* 14 (1898): 366; W. Lohmeier, "Von Lippern in Amerika," *Lippischer Kalendar* (1951): 84–85; W. Lohmeyer, *Die Erweckungsbewegung in Lippe im 19. Jahrhundert*, 2d ed. (Detmold, 1932), pp. 108–110; Jerome C. Arpke, *Das Lippe-Detmolder Settlement in Wisconsin* (Milwaukee, 1895), pp. 1–4.

[41] *Portrait and Biographical Record*, p. 553. Of the fourteen adult males from Oldenburg in Warren County in 1860, Pons and Ulfers were omitted from the comparison because their family names appear neither among persons married by Catholic priests nor in emigrant lists from Catholic parts of Oldenburg. Two others, Renaker and Massman, were uncertain cases; if they were eliminated, the average real estate and wealth of Oldenburgers would be increased by over $100. The Oldenburgers in western St. Charles County, site of the original settlement, were even better off. For emigrant lists sources, see Chap. 3, n. 7. Two other studies that have found a lack of confessional differences in social mobility are Griffen and Griffen, *Natives and Newcomers*, pp. 73–76; Swierenga, "Dutch International Migration," table 10.

solidarity served to promote social mobility. Again there is little evidence to support this, particularly where immigrants from Lippe are concerned. Because of their early arrival, Tecklenburgers were somewhat better off. While exactly half of all Germans aged eighteen and older in St. Charles and Warren counties in 1850 owned real estate, the figure for such people traced from Tecklenburg was over 70 percent. But one-third of the latter were already in the country before 1835, and two-thirds had emigrated by 1840. Moreover, the tracing process may be biased against young, single, and clandestine emigrants—those who had the least resources.

This bias is eliminated with Lippe-Detmolders, who were specifically identified in the 1860 census. Those in Warren County, at least, appear very typical of the immigration as a whole. The mean real estate holdings of a 10 percent systematic sample of adult German males was $918; for immigrants from Lippe it was just 4 percent higher. Their advantage in total wealth was somewhat greater, 17 percent of the overall mean, but hardly what one would call atypical. The proportion of Lippe-Detmolders reporting no real estate was 32 percent, slightly better than the German average of nearly 39 percent; but the proportion from Lippe reporting no wealth whatsoever was only 26 percent, a negligible one point better than their compatriots in general. As in 1850, Germans in Warren County had a 13 percent lead over Americans in the proportion owning real estate, though there was no difference when personal property was also taken into consideration. The mean wealth of Lippe-Detmolders south of the river in Gasconade and Franklin counties was considerably lower, but more evenly distributed; the proportion of landowners was actually slightly higher than in Warren County. Thus it does not appear that chain migrants present an unrealistically optimistic picture of immigrant social mobility. In fact, homogeneous settlements probably produced fewer extremes of great wealth, though perhaps fewer of poverty as well.[42]

The elite of immigrant society, at any rate, included a disproportionate share of outsiders. For example, two Germans were elected mayor of St. Charles before 1860, but neither was from northwest Germany. One was from the Rhineland near Cologne, and the other was a southwest German from Baden, both rather uncommon origins for this area.

---

[42] For instance, immigrants from Brunswick in a homogeneous settlement in Cape Girardeau County showed a lower average wealth than those in St. Louis or the few scattered in the four Missouri River counties studied here. Brunswickers also reported lower mean wealth in St. Louis, where they were overrepresented among the German population, than in Philadelphia, where they were seriously underrepresented (see Table 3.4 for indexes of representation).

CHAPTER V

Likewise, there were in all of Philadelphia in 1860 only four persons who gave their birthplace as Lippe-Detmold. But a young man who emigrated from Lippe around 1870 went on to become the only German mayor of the city. Tecklenburgers and other Westfalians were nearly as scarce there. But a nineteenth-century Tecklenburg chronicle reported that "Sentemeyer in Philadelphia left here as a poor tenant farmer's son. Now he's a millionaire. He also remembered his teacher and sent him a donation of 600 Mark for the education of children. In 1872 he sent a whole barrel of American meat for his former teacher." The typical immigrant success story, it might seem. Emigrant lists confirmed that Sentemeyer was indeed a poor tenant farmer's son when he emigrated in 1842 at age twenty-one. The 1860 census shows him with a grand total of $4,000 in personal property. By 1870, he was worth $16,000, still a long way from being a millionaire, but also a long way from where he started out, or even from 1850 when the census overlooked him and the city directory listed him as a laborer. While this might illustrate what a distorted picture Germans had of immigrant success in America, it could just as well show how even a modest fortune of $16,000 was so far removed from conditions back home that it might as well have been a million. And though not a millionaire, Sentemeyer was doing much better than practically all of the Tecklenburgers in their homogeneous settlement in rural Missouri.[43]

Even the more modest successes must have appeared worth the sacrifices to most immigrants from Germany's rural lower classes. After all, it was their reports that fueled the chain migration in the first place. As long as cheap agricultural land was available, the chances to establish an independent existence were good to excellent.[44] One can con-

[43] Sketch of Fred Gatzweiler in *Illustrated Atlas Map of St. Charles County, Missouri* (Illinois, 1875), p. 31. John Hilbert is no. 850 in the 1860 census. "Ein Lipper als Bürgermeister von Philadelphia," *Lippischer Kalendar* (1915): 64–66. Rudolph Blankenburg was elected mayor in 1911. Friedrich Hunsche, *Westerkappeln: Chronik einer alten Gemeinde im nördlichen Westfalen* (Lengerich, 1975), p. 175. The account mentioned four other men of fortune, one in Chicago, and one in Louisville, both cities where few other Tecklenburgers had settled. My thanks to Lesley Kawaguchi for providing me with additional biographical information on Sentemeyer from her files and those of the Philadelphia Social History Project.

[44] It is clear that the cheap land of the pioneering period was running out by the Civil War. Gert Goebel, who was a county surveyor, stated that the Homestead Act would have been much more effective if it had been passed ten years earlier; by the 1850s there was hardly a free forty-acre tract in the Missouri River German counties halfway suited for cultivation (Goebel, *Länger als ein Menschenleben*, pp. 49, 155–165). For another example of declining rural opportunities as land became scarce, see Kirk, *Promise of American Life*, pp. 34–35, 140–142. The effect was not necessarily that Westfalians remained in St. Louis. Rather, another link was added to the migration chain. Many sec-

clude along with Stephan Thernstrom that a climb from "rags to riches" was highly atypical, but the path to "respectability" was entirely within reach, even for people from the lower ranks of rural German society. Especially for such people, who often made up in determination, talent, and ambition what they lacked in money, the American dream was more than just a dream.

---

ond-generation immigrants from this area moved to Lafayette County and adjacent areas in western Missouri. A tabulation of children resident in nonadjacent counties mentioned by St. Charles and Warren County Germans in *Portrait and Biographical Record* and *History of St. Charles, Montgomery, and Warren Counties* showed that the most popular destination, attracting ten of the twenty-seven residing in outstate Missouri, was Lafayette, while nine other children resided in neighboring counties such as Saline, Jackson, Ray, Pettis, and Cole. Tecklenburgers were more attracted to this destination than others, probably because one of their second generation had located there by 1871 (Fred H. Meinershagen, *The Prosperous and Diligent Blacksmith from Wersen: A Genealogy of Heinrich Adolph Meinershagen* [n.p., 1973], pp. 9–10). Some later Tecklenburg emigrants may have gone there directly.

CHAPTER VI

Westfalians and Other Immigrants: Chain Migration and Acculturation in Comparative Perspective

Through our diligence and through our perseverance we have preserved our German settlement and founded for ourselves a friendly homeland, where we rediscovered in greater beauty the old one, which we did not forsake without some inner pangs.[1]

DESPITE the self-congratulatory tone, one facet of this citation rings true: Immigrants to rural Missouri were able to attain the best of two worlds, to enjoy American economic opportunity and political freedom without being subjected to the wrenching uprootedness in their social and cultural institutions. The first part of this chapter highlights some facets of the assimilation process in this transplanted community, demonstrating that chain migration contributed to a remarkably strong and persistent ethnic identity. The middle section places the transplanted Westfalians in a comparative perspective with other immigrant groups, particularly in the light of several recent studies of other transplanted communities. The concluding section proposes a typology that spells out more clearly the impact of chain migration and the ways it affected the assimilation process.

Carl Schurz visited St. Charles County in the summer of 1867 to reconnoiter the political landscape in Missouri. The region made a very positive impression on him, particularly the area around Augusta, where the immigrants were conserving "the best features of German life," as he related in a letter to his wife. The speeches at his appearance in Augusta were all made in German, for there were no Americans "except the shoemaker's apprentice, who has recently arrived and is learning German, and several Negro families, among whom the children can already speak German." But as pleased as Schurz was with the present situation, he was apprehensive about the future. "The old people have preserved the tradition of the German spirit and German training, but they are unable to bequeath it to their children." The offspring of the Latin farmers, he found, contrasted "strikingly with their elders. The German spirit fades away. If the training remains wholly German and

[1] *Hermanner Wochenblatt*, 19 August 1845.

all contact with Americanism is avoided, a stupid Pennsylvania Germanism results. Where that is not the case, the waves of Americanization soon overwhelm the second and third generations."[2]

No doubt Schurz was partly right. Only an accident of history had brought people of the intellectual caliber of a Friedrich Muench to the Missouri frontier, and the cultural level of his generation could not be maintained, at least not down on the farm. As has been suggested in previous chapters, the children of the educated bourgeoisie were particularly susceptible to assimilationist tendencies. But German culture on a lesser scale, and particularly the German language, did persist among the descendants of the peasant stock, though Schurz may have regarded it with the same deprecation as he did the Pennsylvanians.

The persistence of ethnicity in St. Charles and Warren counties needs to be viewed in the context of population trends in these areas. The period of most rapid growth came before the Civil War, with moderate gains continuing through the 1860s, and the 1870s also showing a slight increase. The decade of the 1880s, however, saw net population losses in both counties. The slight upward trend visible by 1900 was due entirely to the growing city of St. Charles; the rural areas of the two counties had reached their peak in 1880. Already in the 1870s the gains resulted mostly from natural increase, since the number of German immigrants reached its high point with the 1870 census; in fact, their share of the total population had been higher in 1860. After 1870, the nearly 6,500 natives of Germany in St. Charles and Warren counties dwindled at the rate of about one hundred per year, so that by 1910 their numbers had fallen to barely one-third of their all-time high. Of course, their ranks were being largely filled by second-generation immigrants. The published census does not present as detailed information as one might wish. But since Germans made up about three-fourths of the immigrants in this area, the total foreign stock would be largely reflective of German trends. Though no figures are available for 1880, the proportion of foreign (and German) stock in the population probably peaked by then or before, since it was higher in 1870 than in 1890. By 1910, the share of first- and second-generation Germans in the two counties was lower than the proportion of German immigrants alone in 1860. But while natives of Germany were dying out, their descendants were consolidating their hold on the area, particularly in agriculture.[3]

The geographic persistence of Germans in the area is one reflection

[2] Joseph Schafer, ed. and trans., *The Intimate Letters of Carl Schurz, 1841–1869* (Madison, Wis., 1928), pp 379–383.

[3] Based in the 1850 census data set, hand tallies from the 1860 census, and published data from decennial U.S. population census, 1850 through 1910.

CHAPTER VI

of the cohesiveness of these chain migration communities. As early as the 1870s, Gert Goebel observed that Germans had started out in the poor hills of Warren and St. Charles counties, but had since taken over the fertile river bottoms as well. As Friedrich Muench remarked, "The Germans from year to year conquer more ground and extend their settlements. Only in rare cases is German real estate offered for sale—it stays in the family from generation to generation."

This pattern continued well down into the twentieth century. A recent geographic study found that Germans in Gasconade County, where many Lippe-Detmolders settled, had greatly expanded their landholdings at the expense of Anglo-Americans during the century since the Civil War. In one of the county's heavily German townships, three-quarters of the family names of rural landowners in 1870 could still be found in the county a century later, while over half of all names from a heavily native township had disappeared. A similar process can be seen in St. Charles County. In the 1850 census, Anglo-American farmers slightly outnumbered Germans, though the latter may have drawn even by the Civil War. But of the 37 centennial farms—those that had been in the same family for a century—in St. Charles County in 1976, there were at most five owners who did not have German names. In general, Germans had come to dominate agriculture in this area. Over four-fifths of the three hundred-odd members of the county farm boosters club were of German stock. The Lutheran parish in New Melle has shown similar evidence of persistence right down to the 1980s. As part of a 140th anniversary celebration, this historic congregation investigated the whereabouts of everyone thought to be alive who had ever been confirmed in the parish (confirmation taking place at about age fourteen in this denomination). Out of a group of 389, only 30 could not be traced at all, and only 34 others were located outside Missouri. Almost half the group was still in St. Charles County— 188 individuals in all—while the remainder lived elsewhere in Missouri. In part, this reflects the fact that the county is a rapidly growing area on the fringes of the St. Louis metropolitan area. But it also reflects a mentality that has characterized this group since the time of immigration.[4]

[4] Gert Goebel, *Länger als ein Menschenleben in Missouri* (St. Louis, 1877), p. 51; Friedrich Muench, "Eine deutsche Niederlassung am Missouri," *Der Deutsche Pionier* 11 (1879): 317; Russel L. Gerlach, *Immigrants in the Ozarks: A Study in Ethnic Geography* (Columbia, Mo., 1976), pp. 59–65. Gerlach also mentions Warren and Franklin counties as having similar areas of concentrated German landholdings. Stephen D. Livingston, ed., *The Agricultural History of St. Charles County* (St. Charles, Mo., 1976), pp. 169–174. Ethnicity was judged on the basis of family names, considering all doubtful

The extent to which ethnicity persisted beyond 1880 depended on the success with which German culture could be transmitted to the third generation, the grandchildren of immigrants. The degree of language preservation appears to have been much greater in rural areas than in the larger cities. This was true throughout the country, but particularly so in Missouri. The 1940 census showed that third-generation Germans in rural Missouri were nearly five times as likely to claim German as their mother tongue as their counterparts in St. Louis. The city school system had introduced German-language instruction after the Civil War, but had voted it down again in the late 1880s despite a sizable bloc of German voters in the city. Though not provided for in state law, it seems that bilingual public education was quite common in rural German settlements and often went well beyond the hour per day devoted to German in St. Louis schools. As Friedrich Muench testified, "In completely German school districts (like mine) we can use only German teachers, who begin with German instruction and afterward combine English with it."[5]

Nor did a lack of German instruction in public schools necessarily denote eagerness to forsake the language. In 1900, a native-stock public school teacher in Cappeln, Missouri, was fired; the alleged grounds were that he was studying law on the side, but the real reason seems to be his overzealous Americanizing efforts. As he himself admitted, "I came down rather heavily by forcing them to speak English on the playgrounds." In his final report to the school board he noted, "Among the causes of my failures, are poor attendance, obtuseness, and German Language on the part of the children." On the surface there is nothing unusual about this incident. Cultural conflicts of this nature, particu-

---

cases as non-Germans. At the national level as well, there was a tendency for Germans to improve their position in agriculture with the passage of time. Although Germans were somewhat underrepresented in agriculture throughout the nineteenth century, the second generation was overrepresented by 50 percent in 1950. Figures on ethnic identity from the 1980 census show "single ancestry" Germans with an index of 238 among the farm population, higher than any group except Norwegians. Of the nation's 5.6 million farmers, over 1 million were "single ancestry" Germans, a reflection of the insulating effects of the rural cocoon (calculated from *1980 Census of Population: General Social and Economic Conditions, United States Summary* [Washington, 1983], table 76, sec. 1, p. 14; *St. Paul's Lutheran Church, New Melle, Missouri, 140th Anniversary Booklet* [1984]).

[5] Walter D. Kamphoefner, "The German Agricultural Frontier: Crucible or Cocoon?" *Ethnic Forum* 4 (1984): 21–35; Selwyn K. Troen, *The Public and the Schools: Shaping the St. Louis School System, 1838–1920* (Columbia, Mo., 1975), chap. 3; Audrey L. Olson, "St. Louis Germans, 1850–1920" (Ph.D. diss., University of Kansas, 1970), pp. 94–110; F. Muench, "Eine deutsche Niederlassung," p. 318; idem, "Sonst und Jetzt," *Der Deutsche Pionier* 4 (1872): 231.

CHAPTER VI

larly involving public schools, were rife around the turn of the century. This dispute involved language only on the playground, not in the classroom, though it is evident that the children were more comfortable speaking German than English. What is striking, however, is the makeup of the Cappeln school pupils as revealed in the 1900 census. In a class of about forty students, at least three-quarters were third-generation Germans. In fact, there was even one boy of fourth-generation stock. Natives of Germany and British-stock Americans were equally rare among Cappeln school pupils—just one of each. Even the school board that did the firing included no one born in Germany. Two members were farmers and children of immigrants; the other was a young doctor of third-generation German stock.[6]

Around the turn of the century, Germans in this area were just as likely to attend parochial as public schools. Although Lutheran educational efforts are perhaps best known, German Evangelicals showed equal zeal, and Catholics were not far behind. In most cases instruction was entirely in German except for an hour of English daily. An 1896 report showed that all but four of the eighty Evangelical congregations in eastern Missouri maintained parish schools, with an average enrollment of about fifty. Over 70 percent of the confirmands in the church had attended at least one year of parochial school. Practically all the Evangelical congregations in Warren and St. Charles counties maintained schools. The Cappeln school had an enrollment of thirty, not far behind the public school, and the Femme Osage Evangelical school reported forty-five students. It is not clear when these schools converted to English or were phased out. World War I doubtless played a role, but perhaps not so dramatically as in most parts of the country.[7]

[6] Diary of F. L. Audrain in possession of Glenn Luetkemeyer, Lake Sherwood, Mo., as reported by William Schiermeyer, "Cracker Barrel News," *Washington Missourian*, 24 September, 6 October, 10 November 1975; the last article included a reproduction of the 1898/1899 school program with a list of pupils, which was then matched to the 1900 census. Three children from the same family were second generation, while six of the forty-one pupils could not be located in the census. Of these, Carrie Anthony was almost surely of native stock, Schulz and Stiegemeier doubtless German. Three Manger children were of doubtful ethnicity, but were probably German since one was named Otto. Two children named Burgers, native-born of native parentage, were boarders or stepchildren in a household headed by second-generation Germans, and were probably third-generation themselves.

[7] *Protokolle der 11. Jahreskonferenzen der Distrikte der Deutschen Evangelischen Synode von Nordamerika, 1897*, pp. 1–28, includes a statistical breakdown on congregations and schools in the Missouri District, which actually was restricted to the eastern part of the state. About the only parishes without schools were newly founded missions or branch congregations without resident pastors. Summary statistics do show a slight decline in the number of students from 1895 to 1896, but it is impossible to tell if this is

Indeed, one should not mistake cultural loyalty for political loyalty to the German state, as superpatriots during World War I tended to do. There are few indications that Germans in this area—for the most part second or third generation—had any feelings of divided loyalties. During the third Liberty Loan campaign, St. Charles County was second in all Missouri in per capita subscriptions, earning it a place on a propaganda flier that was dropped behind enemy lines. The banner town in Missouri was Treloar in a heavily German part of Warren County, where subscribers pledged nearly $200 each. The survival of the German-language press in eastern Missouri seems to have been little affected by the events of World War I. The *St. Charles Demokrat*, which expired at the close of 1916, might appear to have been a war casualty, but the prime factor in its demise was clearly the age of its editor. John H. Bode had put out the paper for over fifty years, beginning as a twenty-year-old in 1864, and was simply incapable of carrying on. The only German paper in the area done in by the war was the *Warrenton Volksfreund*, which folded in April 1918. Just across the river in Franklin County, the *Washington Post* had already succumbed around 1910. But at Hermann in adjoining Gasconade County, the *Volksblatt* persisted all the way to 1928, by which time its constituency must have included as many fourth- as third-generation Germans.[8]

The place where the German language survived longest was probably in the churches of this locality. At the outbreak of hostilities with Germany, the Lutherans at New Melle felt constrained by patriotic duty to suspend German services for the duration of the war: World War II! World War I appears to have come and gone without making

---

anything more than just the temporary effect of economic depression. The report from the Southern Illinois District, p. 91, included a sample curriculum that provided for only one hour of English instruction daily, and that not even for each class every day of the week. Information is less plentiful on Catholic schools or their language policies, but in 1885 the parishes at both St. Peters and O'Fallon had thriving schools, and the pastor of the latter was publishing the weekly *Katholischer Hausfreund* with a circulation of 2,000. *History of St. Charles, Montgomery, and Warren Counties, Missouri* (1895; facsimile reprint, St. Louis, 1969), pp. 466–470. County history biographies occasionally mention an education in both German and English.

[8] Walter B. Stevens, *Centennial History of Missouri, 1820–1921* (St. Louis, 1921), pp. 873–876. Treloar lies in the southwest corner of Charette Township, not far from Holstein, an area of heavy Tecklenburger settlement. One illustration of the innocence with which some St. Charles County German-Americans approached the language issue: My second-generation great-grandmother wrote the first letter she sent to her son in a World War I training camp in German. Grandpa instructed her to write in English thereafter, lest it arouse the suspicions of his superiors. Carl J. R. Arndt and May E. Olson, *German-American Newspapers and Periodicals, 1732–1955*, 2d ed. (Heidelberg, 1965), pp. 240–246, 250–251, 274–279.

CHAPTER VI

any impact on language use in the parish, though about a dozen of its sons served in the military. The first hesitant steps in the language transition were taken in 1919 when the dedication of a new parochial school was celebrated with a German and an English *Fest*. In 1926, the congregation voted to have four English services per year, for which a guest pastor was required. After a new minister took office in 1928, English services were held once a month on Sunday mornings and once a month in the evenings. From 1933 on, the minutes of the congregation were recorded in English. The year 1935 marked the end of horse-and-buggy days in New Melle: the hitching posts at the church were deemed superfluous and removed. But it was not until 1939 that the English language attained equal status, alternating every other Sunday with German. The balance tipped slightly in 1941, when midweek Lenten services were held only in English. Even after the interruption during the war, worship in German was resumed on every third Sunday in 1945, though it was now compensated for with English services in the evening. Finally in 1950, probably precipitated by a change of pastors, German disappeared entirely as a language of worship.[9]

New Melle was among the last parishes in the area to give up German, but in general the degree of language persistence is impressive. In the nearby Lutheran parish of Augusta, too, the timing of the language transition was influenced more by changes in pastors than by world events. The first English service in the parish came in 1916, before American entry into World War I brought on a wave of anti-German hysteria. English worship was held every other Sunday, but in the evening, in order not to interfere with regular German morning services. It is unclear how long this arrangement persisted, but both the Lutheran and the Evangelical congregations in Augusta switched their parish records to English in the mid-1920s, well after wartime Germanophobia had subsided. In the mid-1930s, Augusta Lutherans were still alternating German and English for their monthly Communion services, though confirmation ceremonies were switched to English in 1936, at which time the church constitution was also translated. An English hymnal was finally adopted in 1944, but German was still preached one Sunday morning every month until 1951. Though theologically less conservative, the local German Evangelical parishes differed little from Lutherans in questions of language. Cappeln, a bit farther back in the hills, changed its parish records to English only in the 1930s. And

[9] Transcript of congregational minutes in *St. Paul's 140th Anniversary Booklet*. There were no signs of any reluctance of church members to serve in World War I; in fact, the church furnished only twice as many soldiers for World War II as for World War I, although the nation had nearly four times as many men in uniform.

the Femme Osage congregation, nucleus of the Tecklenburger settlement and the first Evangelical church west of the Mississippi, did not give up the German language until 1948, 115 years after the first immigrant settlement.¹⁰

In 1937, William Seabrook visited St. Charles County while researching a book on ethnicity. Although he generally took an optimistic view of the melting pot, this area was something different:

> In a village named New Melle, just off a concrete highway and not 30 miles from St. Louis, I walked into a general store, and for a moment passed unnoticed while a group of [American] farm children, some of them barely toddling, were buzzing to each other and to the storekeeper in low German, not one word of English—not even interspersed with English slang.

One of the more progressive farmers related to Seabrook that his children never spoke German at home, nor did he want them to. "They are going to be Americans even though we do live in St. Charles County!" Seabrook assumed that it was just a matter of time, and he was right. In fact, he was witnessing the end of an era. But he thought that immigration had taken place between 1870 and 1890, when in fact it was mostly completed a generation earlier, before the Civil War. It should be noted that it was the local Low German dialect, not the High German taught in schools, that survived the longest—another indicator of the influence of the chain-migration community in cultural persistence.¹¹

Chain migration is only one of a number of features the Westfalian emigration has in common with that from other parts of northwestern Europe. The heavier the emigration rate, the more conducive condi-

---

¹⁰ *Christ Lutheran Church, Augusta, Missouri, 1859–1984, 125th Anniversary*, pp. 6–7; parish records of Evangelical congregations in Augusta, Cappeln, and Femme Osage. As used here, *Evangelical* refers to congregations stemming from the Kirchenverein des Westens, which later became part of the Evangelical and Reformed, and presently the United Church of Christ denominations. For additional sources on denominational backgrounds see above, Chap. 4, n. 15.

¹¹ William Seabrook, "America über Alles," *American Magazine* (October 1937): 48–49, 84–93. The article is reproduced almost verbatim in idem, *These Foreigners* (New York, 1938), pp. 172–182, in which he characterizes the children in the store as "American." He also states in the foreword: "All the characters and places in this book are real ... named by their real names," which certainly proved true for St. Charles County. Thanks to my mother for tracking down some of the persons involved and verifying this story.

For another example of the persistence of local dialect, see Wolfgang Fleischhauer, "German Communities in Northwestern Ohio: Canal Fever and Prosperity," *Report* 34 (1970): 32–34.

CHAPTER VI

tions were to the development of migration chains and homogeneous enclaves. For the greater part of the nineteenth century, push factors appear to have dominated not only in Germany, but in Europe generally. The economist Brinley Thomas has pointed out that up until the Civil War, peaks of immigration preceded rather than followed surges of economic activity, suggesting that immigration stimulated business rather than vice versa. The massive flood of Irish emigration during the potato famine of the 1840s is only the most dramatic example of push emigration. The waves of German emigration peaking in 1846 and 1854, and echoed in the Netherlands as well, were precipitated by harvest failures. Even after the Civil War, the first major wave of Swedish emigration in the late 1860s was set off by successive crop failures in 1867 and 1868. From the Panic of 1873 onward, however, the fluctuations of the American business cycle were echoed ever more closely in the immigration curve.

When one examines regional variations in emigration intensity, moreover, it becomes clear that the impact of rural industry on population pressure extended well beyond Westfalia or Germany. The spread and subsequent demise of potato culture has often been regarded as sufficient cause for Ireland's unequaled emigration rates. But a recent study concluded that "the regional variations in the incidence of emigration over much of the northern half of Ireland were related to the rise and demise of the linen industry." By midcentury, modern industrial growth in Ulster was sufficient to keep emigration low by Irish standards. In the rest of the island, a certain correspondence can be detected even at the province level among protoindustry, population pressure, and proletarianization, particularly in Connaught, the poorest of the four provinces. A quantitative investigation using county-level data from 1841—the eve of the potato famine—has confirmed these suspicions and demonstrated that a high level of employment in the rural textile industry was closely associated with growing population pressure—low age at marriage and high nuptuality leading to high crude birthrates—and with such indicators of pauperization as poor housing and fragmented and infertile landholdings. This did not, however, exert much influence on emigration rates of the famine decade, which were relatively uniform outside Ulster. The throes of de-industrialization were indeed felt most severely in Connaught—a decline of population that was the highest in all of Ireland bears witness to that. However, this was less the result of heavier emigration than of higher death rates during the famine.[12]

[12] Brinley Thomas, *Migration and Economic Growth: A Study of Great Britain and*

A 1982 issue of *Scandinavian Economic History Review* devoted to protoindustry was quite critical of the concept as it is applied to northern Europe. But perhaps this is because these scholars were looking for a "happy ending story," the first stage of modern industrialization. Their efforts might have been more fruitful had they focused their attention on the issue of population pressure. Swedish emigration research, at any rate, has discovered higher emigration rates in districts of rural industry (not always strictly protoindustry) than in purely agricultural areas where a greater proportion of the land was arable. Moreover, the fishing industry and especially its support branches, such as boat building, sail making, and net braiding, have much in common with protoindustry: seasonality and part-time employment, dependence on a distant and uncertain market, and concentration in regions of low agricultural potential.[13]

The Swiss canton of Zurich is another area where a wave of emigration in the 1840s was directly associated with the decline of handloom cotton weaving. The Scottish Lowland district with the most domestic textile production was also the one with the highest emigration rate. Andrew Carnegie's father was only one of many handloom weavers crowded out by technology. A recent study has shown that the great majority of textile workers among British emigrants to the United States were poorly qualified hand workers rather than heralds of the machine age. Protoindustry may also be part of the reason that there were more immigrants from Bohemia than from Austria proper in America in 1870. In rural Flanders, redundant linen weavers were apparently more attracted by industrializing areas of Belgium and northern France than by overseas migration, though adjacent areas of Holland had some of the highest emigration rates in the country. A case study from another area of heavy emigration from the Netherlands concluded that the decline of rural industry was a "more lasting cause" of emigration from North Brabant than potato disease. Taken together, the evidence presented here strongly suggests that the rise and

---

the Atlantic Economy, 2d ed. (London, 1973), pp. 82–122, 155–174; Harald Runblom and Hans Norman, eds., *From Sweden to America: A History of the Migration* (Minneapolis, 1976), pp. 120–121. Brenda Collins, "Proto-Industrialization and Pre-Famine Emigration," *Social History* 7 (1982): 127–146. Eric L. Almquist, "Pre-Famine Ireland and the Theory of European Proto-Industrialization: Evidence from the 1841 Census," *Journal of Economic History* 39 (1979): 699–718; Oliver MacDonagh, "The Irish Famine Emigration to the United States," *Perspectives in American History* 10 (1976): 419–427.

[13] *Scandinavian Economic History Review* 30 (1982), esp. Edgar Hovlund, Helge Nordvik, and Stein Tveite, "Proto-Industrialization in Norway, 1750–1850: Fact or Fiction?" pp. 45–56. Runblom and Norman, *From Sweden to America*, pp. 156–164.

CHAPTER VI

decline of rural industry was a more important factor in European emigration and population dynamics during the first half of the nineteenth century than has been previously realized.[14]

An even more general characteristic of European emigration was that it was disproportionately rural in origin. As was seen in Chapter 1, towns and cities generally exerted a retarding influence on overseas emigration from their hinterlands. One of the reasons for Ireland's massive exodus was that there was so little Irish urbanization or industrialization to offer an alternative. One prime reason for the decline of German emigration after 1890 was that German industry was expanding with enough vigor to absorb the surplus rural population.

Although cities tended to retard overseas emigration from their hinterlands, in some cases the cities themselves experienced higher than average emigration. The city of Copenhagen and Danish provincial towns are good examples of this. In Sweden, overseas migration was highest from rural areas, though when Continental migration is included, cities were more heavily affected than the countryside. Part of the difference is that most of these Scandinavian cities were ports, while the German towns treated here were all inland. But even where cities showed above-average emigration rates, much of the exodus consisted of short-time residents of rural origins. For example, fewer than half of the emigrants from Stockholm toward the end of the nineteenth century had lived in the city as long as five years, and one-fifth had a tenure of less than two years. This phenomenon of migration by stages becomes apparent whenever emigration statistics enumerate both birthplace and last place of residence. In the five years before World War I, Copenhagen was the last residence of 22 percent of Danish emigration but the birthplace of less than 13 percent. Similarly, the towns of Jutland accounted for nearly 22 percent of the emigrants by residence but only three-fourths as much by birth. The same phenomenon is apparent in the urban cantons of Switzerland. The city of Basel ranked fifth among Swiss cantons in emigration, with over 13,000 overseas migrants between 1887 and 1938, but fewer than 5,000 emigrants during

[14] Leo Schelbert, "On Becoming an Emigrant: A Structural View of Eighteenth- and Nineteenth-Century Swiss Data," *Perspectives in American History* 7 (1973): 453–456. Malcolm Gray, "Scottish Emigration: The Social Impact of Agrarian Change in the Rural Lowlands, 1775–1875," *Perspectives in American History* 7 (1973): 102–106, 150–153; David J. Jeremy, *Transatlantic Industrial Revolution: The Diffusion of Textile Technologies between Britain and America, 1790–1830s* (Boston, 1981), pp. 144–149. Yda Saueressig, "Emigration, Settlement, and Assimilation of Dutch Catholic Immigrants in Wisconsin, 1850–1905" (Ph.D. diss., University of Wisconsin, 1982), pp. 24, 42–55.

that period had actually been born there. For Geneva, the contrast was even more dramatic, with only 2,500 of 9,000 emigrants native to the canton, although for Zurich and its rural hinterland the difference amounted to less than 50 percent.

Furthermore, what was statistically recorded as urban emigration includes elements that stretch the definition—for example, merchants intent on returning. The Netherlands provides a good illustration. Two of the "urban provinces," North Holland and Utrecht, sent only 70 and 41 percent of their respective emigrants to the United States, as compared to a national figure near 90 percent. Instead, many "non-emigrants" set out as soldiers or civilian administrators to the colonies of the East Indies or South Africa. Moreover, the Continental migration from Sweden, disproportionately urban in origin, was most likely an "exchange migration" of intelligentsia and specialized skills, a continuation of centuries-old patterns that had little in common with the peasant mass emigration of the nineteenth century.[15]

In terms of class and occupational selectivity of emigration, the Westfalian experience was mirrored in other lands and later time periods. The U.S. Immigration Commission notwithstanding, the occupational makeup of newcomers to America remained relatively constant during the century of mass emigration ending in 1920. During the entire period since the Civil War, the majority of American immigration consisted of unskilled laborers and servants, wherein the distinction between agriculture and other sectors of the economy was undoubtedly blurred in many instances. Nor can a clear-cut decline in status be detected over time. The unskilled categories surpassed 60 percent in the 1880s and 1890s, but fell below 50 percent thereafter. Skilled workers made up only one-fourth to one-fifth of the immigration, and professionals rarely surpassed 2 percent. Agriculture made up nearly one-third of the influx before the Civil War, then fell below 20 percent until the turn of the century, when it again surpassed one-fourth. Only after 1899 did American statistics distinguish between farmers and farm laborers. At that point only one immigrant in 70 was

[15] Runblom and Norman, *From Sweden to America*, pp. 134–137, 158–159; Lynn Lees, *Exiles of Erin: Irish Migrants in Victorian London* (Ithaca, N.Y., 1979), pp. 32–33; Klaus J. Bade, "Massenwanderung und Arbeitsmarkt im deutschen Nordosten von 1880 bis zum Ersten Weltkrieg," *Archiv für Sozialgeschichte* 20 (1980): 265–295, 305–323; Kristian Hvidt, *Flight to America: The Social Background of 300,000 Danish Emigrants* (New York, 1975), pp. 55–61; Leo Schelbert, *Einführung in die schweizerische Auswanderungsgeschichte der Neuzeit* (Zurich, 1976), pp. 28, 32, 191; Robert P. Swierenga and Harry S. Stout, "Dutch Immigration in the Nineteenth Century, 1820–1877: A Quantitative Overview," *Indiana Social Studies Quarterly* 28 (1975): 17, 23.

CHAPTER VI

an independent farmer, and fourteen out of fifteen in the agricultural category were farm laborers. But in all periods and among all nationalities, marginal operators rather than independent, full-time farmers were probably responsible for most of the immigration.[16]

The selectivity of migration from Denmark in the last third of the nineteenth century and from Hungary on the eve of World War I shows striking similarities with that from Westfalia before the Civil War. Three of every seven Danish emigrants stemmed from the class of rural laborers, and many women classified as maids belong in this group as well. Only one emigrant in thirty was an independent farmer, and nine-tenths of these were smallholders. Only about one-fourth of the exodus consisted of skilled artisans or industrial workers.[17]

The Austro-Hungarian Empire might be regarded as the classic source of the "New Immigration," but even there many familiar patterns from earlier eras and other parts of Europe reappear. In emigration from the Hungarian half of the Dual Monarchy in the decade before World War I, agricultural laborers were among the most heavily represented both absolutely and proportionally. They made up half of the emigration but barely one-fifth of the source population. General laborers were even more heavily overrepresented but still constituted only one-tenth of the emigration. While independent farmers made up nearly one-fifth of the exodus, this was less than half their share in the 1910 Hungarian census. Industrial workers fell slightly under their quota, while independent artisans and merchants were underrepresented by a factor of almost three and intelligentsia by a factor of nine.[18]

But official figures from either side of the ocean on the occupations of migrants give a false sense of precision. They particularly fail to convey the extent of seasonal and part-time work, often in other sectors of the economy, carried on by marginal classes of peasants. This becomes very clear when one begins to compare statistics. According to U.S. port-of-entry statistics for the decade after 1899, common laborers outnumbered farm laborers among Polish immigrants by nearly two to

[16] Isaac A. Hourwich, *Immigration and Labor: The Economic Aspects of European Immigration to the United States* (New York, 1912), p. 67. Stephan Thernstrom, ed., *Harvard Encyclopedia of American Ethnic Groups* (Cambridge, Mass., 1980), p. 382.

[17] Hvidt, *Flight to America*, pp. 101–120.

[18] Johann Chmelar, "The Austrian Emigration, 1900–1914," *Perspectives in American History* 7 (1973): 323–325, 342–345. Table 2.11 on p. 340 of the article would appear to contradict my statement, but it seems that some column headings are in error: The column of common laborers is mislabeled as agricultural laborers, and that labeled independent farmers includes the numerically predominant group of agricultural laborers as well.

one, and farm operators were a negligible quantity. But of nearly 33,000 Poles employed in manufacturing and mining investigated by the U.S. Immigration Commission, over two-thirds had been engaged in farming or farm labor in Europe, while only one-eighth professed a background in general labor. Of the Germans employed in the same industries, a scant 30 percent had come off the farm, about the same proportion as had industrial experience. But if one had conducted a similar investigation among St. Louis Germans in 1860, one would have found a much greater similarity to the Poles than to their own countrymen a half-century later. Oscar Handlin was not far wrong in assuming that the bulk of American immigrants were of peasant stock. His error lay rather in imputing to peasant Europe a squalidly splendid isolation and immobility that in fact had broken down well before 1900, if it had ever existed.[19]

A more serious shortcoming of Handlin's interpretation of the immigrant experience is his assumption that it was a movement of isolated individuals or nuclear families. Case studies of Swedish, Dutch, and Norwegian immigration completed within the last decade show remarkable parallels with the transplanted Westfalians. Of the Swedish emigrants from the parish of Rättvik studied by Robert Ostergren, over 45 percent eventually settled in Isanti County, Minnesota. Two-thirds of the county population was of Swedish stock, and one-third of that, in turn, stemmed from Rättvik and the neighboring parish of Orsa. In another study of a neighboring county, Ostergren found an equally homogeneous settlement from another part of Sweden. Jon Gjerde's Norwegian study revealed an even stronger concentration. In the first decade of emigration from Balestrand, a community of about 2,000, roughly two-thirds of the immigrants, over 200 in all, located in Norway Grove, Wisconsin. In two church parishes there, Balestranders made up one-fourth of the membership, and along with immigrants from the rest of the Sogn district, over 70 percent. While the above studies were facilitated by the remarkable system of Scandinavian parish registers, Yda Saueressig's study of Wisconsin Dutch Catholics in

[19] U.S. Congress, Senate, *Reports of the Immigration Commission* (Washington, 1911), vol. 3, "Statistical Review of Immigration, 1819–1910," p. 27; vols. 19–20, "Summary Report on Immigrants in Manufacturing and Mining," p. 95. On European conditions, see for example Josef J. Barton, *Peasants and Strangers: Italians, Rumanians, and Slovaks in an American City, 1890–1950* (Cambridge, Mass., 1975), pp. 40–47; David I. Kertzer and Dennis P. Hogan, "On the Move: Migration in an Italian Community, 1865–1921," *Social Science History* 9 (1985): 1–23; John Bodnar, *The Transplanted: A History of Immigrants in Urban America* (Bloomington, Ind., 1985), pp. 1–56.

CHAPTER VI

the Fox River valley, like my own, had to rely on the more difficult procedure of census linkage. Nevertheless, during the first decade of emigration from three adjacent Dutch towns, over two-fifths of those leaving could be positively linked to this Wisconsin settlement. Of all the Dutch in this two-county area, 28 percent stemmed from these three villages in North Brabant, and over three-fifths from this and other parts of the province.[20]

Not only was chain migration widespread among various nationalities; it also brought with it many of the same cultural patterns. Parallels with the Westfalians begin in the old country. In each of the three northern European cases, there was an initial positive selectivity of migration: landowning farmers rather than tenants in Norway, the more literate in Sweden, those with higher tax assessments among the Dutch. Although it was not mentioned in earlier chapters, this held true for northwest Germans as well. In the long run, though, immigrants were drawn disproportionately from the lower ranks of the social scale, just as were the Westfalians and Osnabrückers. The Norwegian case shows perhaps the greatest structural similarity, since it was also a region of impartible inheritance with a rapidly expanding tenant-farmer class that predominated in the emigration. Still, it was perhaps not the poorest of the poor who emigrated. In the Dutch case, those too poor to be taxed made up the largest share of the emigration in absolute terms, but relative to their share of the total population, those taxpayers in the lowest bracket were most heavily represented in the exodus. Like the Westfalians, the Dutch from North Brabant were largely pushed out by the decline of rural linen weaving. In the Norwegian example, however, Gjerde makes a strong case that agricultural productivity and standard of living was rising in the early nineteenth century, though it

[20] Jon Gjerde, *From Peasants to Farmers: The Migration from Balestrand, Norway, to the Upper Middle West* (Cambridge, 1985), pp. 145–151. Robert C. Ostergren, "Rättvik to Isanti: A Community Transplanted" (Ph.D. diss., University of Minnesota, 1976), pp. 59, 91–92, 106–109; idem, "Cultural Homogeneity and Population Stability among Swedish Immigrants in Chisago County," *Minnesota History* 45 (1973): 255–269. Saueressig, "Dutch Catholic Immigrants," pp. 124–139; some of the figures cited are my calculations from the tables. Robert P. Swierenga is nearing completion of a very ambitious transatlantic tracing study involving the whole of Dutch immigration during the mid-nineteenth century. Results from the tracing part of the study are not yet in print, but the author provides an overview of the project in "Dutch Immigration Patterns in the Nineteenth and Twentieth Centuries," in *The Dutch in America: Immigration, Settlement, and Cultural Change* (New Brunswick, N.J., 1985), pp. 15–42. This volume also includes "Dutch Catholic Immigrant Settlement in Wisconsin," pp. 105–124, a summary of the thesis findings by Saueressig, who used Swierenga's machine-readable emigrant file for her tracing.

is unclear to what extent the tenant class benefited from it. By contrast, real wages in Germany were at best stagnant in the four decades after 1820, and experienced at least temporary declines in the harvest crises of the 1840s and 1850s. Moreover, the emigration-prone regions of northwest and southwest Germany were doubtless worse off than the national trend.[21]

Like the Westfalians, most of the Dutch and Scandinavians had a farm as their ultimate destination, though the path they took was not always direct. The Dutch often worked on the Fox River canal to earn money to buy land. Swedes commonly spent the first winter or two in the lumber camps, though Norwegians, the most agricultural of all immigrant groups in America, were more likely to get a start as farmhands for Yankees. It seems there were very few full-time artisans among Norwegian or Swedish emigrants, but the Dutch study repeats the familiar pattern of craftsmen turning to agriculture. Of emigrants traced to the 1860 census, over three-fourths were reported as farmers, whereas only two-fifths had been so in Holland. However, the 1870 census showed a stability in occupation among those who had arrived within the last decade, a sign that most of the cheap land had been taken up. Gains made by Scandinavians were if anything more striking. With partible inheritance customs in Rättvik, only 16 percent of its emigrants were landless, but the average family had only eleven acres in crops and meadows, though another ninety in forest. The majority of emigrants from Balestrand were tenant farmers and their children, and even the largest farm had only eight acres under the plow. Already in 1860, the average immigrant in the Norway Grove settlement owned sixty improved acres, and ten years later it was over a hundred. Likewise, the average Swede in Isanti County had more land than his father, and considerably more arable land. Only 14 percent of the households were landless in 1890, and the value of farms in America depended much more on how long one had been there than on what one had been

---

[21] During the first three decades of emigration from Osnabrück, the average amount of money per emigrant was 80 taler, but during 1832 and 1833, the first two years of emigration, it was 143, and through 1839 there was only one year when the average fell below 90 taler (Karl Kiel, "Gründe und Folgen der Auswanderung aus dem Osnabrücker Regierungsbezirk [1832–1866]," *Mitteilungen des Vereins für Geschichte und Landeskunde von Osnabrück* 61 [1941]: 176). Gjerde, *From Peasants to Farmers*, pp. 63–84, 120–124; Ostergren, "Rättvik to Isanti," pp. 50–55; Saueressig, "Dutch Catholic Immigrants," pp. 80–84. On German real wages, see Rainer Gömmel, "Realeinkommen in Deutschland: Ein internationaler Vergleich (1810–1914)," *Vorträge zur Wirtschaftsgeschichte* 4 (1979): 1–29. On southwest Germany, see Wolfgang von Hippel, *Auswanderung aus Südwestdeutschland: Studien zur württembergischen Auswanderung und Auswanderungspolitik im 18. und 19. Jahrhundert* (Stuttgart, 1984), pp. 113–280.

worth in Sweden. Thus the opportunities that northwest Germans found in American agriculture were by no means unique.[22]

As with the Germans, the achievements of the Scandinavians were facilitated by their quick adaptation to American farm methods. There were some subtle differences to be seen in Norway Grove. Immigrants initially grew more oats and barley, which they knew from the homeland, than did their neighbors. But Norwegians also sowed considerable wheat, which had been a negligible quantity back home, and in later decades specialized even more heavily in this cash grain than did other farmers in their neighborhoods. Further abandonment of cultural baggage could be seen in the changing sexual division of labor, with women largely restricted to household and gardening instead of participating in dairying and haying as they had in Norway. The Swedish case presents much the same picture, showing "little evidence that there ever was much resistance to the dictates of the new environment and the local market economy." Nearly half the acreage was devoted to wheat, which was unknown in Rättvik, while barley, the main crop back home, was never of any importance in Isanti.[23]

Ostergren sees the immigrants participating in two societies: a folk society, or *Gemeinschaft*, centered around the church parish and based on the old socioeconomic order; and a competitive, individualistic *Gesellschaft*, the larger economic community, with its center in the county seat of Cambridge. The same characterization would apply in large part to the Westfalian and Norwegian cases. Still, one should not overstate the degree of harmony in European peasant societies, especially where impartible inheritance had led to a polarization between the landowning class and propertyless tenants. Moreover, as Gjerde makes clear in the case of religious and sexual mores, transplantation almost always involved considerable adaptation as well.[24]

Nevertheless, to an impressive degree, ties based on locality channeled the migration and helped shape the immigrant communities of transplanted Westfalians, Scandinavians, and Dutch. In all three cases, migration chains extended beyond a core village to adjacent areas, but on the other hand, neighborhood and family ties below the village level

---

[22] Saueressig, "Dutch Catholic Immigrants," pp. 101–108, 164–171; Gjerde, *From Peasants to Farmers*, pp. 122, 169–171, 180; Ostergren, "Rättvik to Isanti," pp. 124–125, 141–149.

[23] Gjerde, *From Peasants to Farmers*, pp. 168–201; Ostergren, "Rättvik to Isanti," pp. 140–141.

[24] Ostergren, "Rättvik to Isanti," p. 152; Gjerde, *From Peasants to Farmers*, pp. 202–222.

could also influence the migration decision and location on the American side. There, ties based on chain migration were reflected and reinforced by marriage patterns. Over three-fourths of the immigrants from Rättvik married someone of the same origins. The endogamy rate from the smaller geographic unit of Balestrand was lower, only about three-fifths, but barely 10 percent took mates from beyond their home district of Sogn. Chain migration communities also showed greater residential stability. A comparison of a number of Swedish settlements showed that the more homogeneous the population origins, the less out-migration a community was likely to experience. Church parishes formed the nucleus of this community life, and in the Norwegian example, the poorest quartile of church members was more residentially stable than the richest quartile of nonmembers. But within the church group, "insiders" from Balestrand and the surrounding district were more likely to persist than Norwegians generally.[25]

In both Scandinavian cases, as with the Germans, theological proclivities—low church versus high church, pietist versus orthodox Lutheran—were often carried over from the old country. The Dutch group not only carried over its Catholicism, but established national parishes that were largely served by Dutch priests throughout the nineteenth century. As late as 1905, less than one-fifth of first-generation and about one-third of second-generation Dutch in the area had intermarried with other groups. Even that figure is deceptively high, for partners were drawn almost exclusively from the Belgians or more often from Germans, who may well have originated from the lower Rhine area and spoken a Low German dialect similar to Dutch. Those who were higher on the occupational scale—skilled workers and particularly white collar—were more likely to intermarry than farmers or laborers. As with Lippe-Detmolders and Westfalians, the Dutch residing in urban centers were more prone to intermarriage than their rural counterparts. And like those Germans, urban Dutch in towns such as Green Bay were very diverse in terms of employment, residence, and place of origin, and included a disproportionate number of single immigrants.[26]

---

[25] Ostergren, "Rättvik to Isanti," pp. 55–58, 91–93, 131–136; idem, "Cultural Homogeneity and Population Stability," pp. 268–269; Gjerde, *From Peasants to Farmers*, pp. 138, 150–157, 161–167, 236–238; idem, "The Effects of Community on Migration: Three Minnesota Townships, 1885–1905," *Journal of Historical Geography* 5 (1979): 403–422; Saueressig, "Dutch Catholic Immigrants," pp. 131–144.

[26] Calculated from Saueressig, "Dutch Catholic Immigrants," pp. 218–229, 189–190, assuming that married households were divided between first and second generation in

CHAPTER VI

Thus neither the chain migration and homogeneous settlements of the transplanted Westfalians nor the social patterns of their communities were in any way unique among American immigrants. Nor was this phenomenon restricted only to northern Europeans, as other studies of Italians and Slovaks have demonstrated.[27] In fact, chain migration in its narrower sense was a nearly universal trait of American immigration, at least in the early twentieth century when official statistics on the subject were first compiled. On the eve of World War I, only 6.1 percent of all immigrants arrived in American ports without intending to join family or friends. Almost four-fifths already had relatives in America, while about 15 percent were joining friends. The only groups for which the figure was appreciably lower were from Asia or the Western Hemisphere. Nearly 30 percent of the small contingent from Spain had no one awaiting them when they arrived, but the English had the next highest rate among Europeans, almost 18 percent. Thus it was not a distinction between old and new immigrants.

A considerable proportion of the newcomers not only had someone waiting for their arrival, but had their fare advanced from America as well. On average across all nationalities, 31 percent of all immigrants were traveling prepaid from 1908 to 1910, the great bulk of them financed by relatives. Although one might have expected this figure to increase with time (and it was considerably lower from some parts of southern and eastern Europe where the onset of emigration was relatively recent), Scandinavians fell right at the national average and probably experienced a slight decline in prepaids since the 1880s. Germans, with a 37 percent rate, were slightly more likely than the average immigrant to travel prepaid on the eve of World War I.[28]

It should be apparent by now that chain migration and local, per-

---

the same proportions as all households. Kate E. Levi, "Geographical Origins of German Immigrants to Wisconsin," *Collections of the State Historical Society of Wisconsin* 14 (1898): 372. Neither of the Scandinavian studies mentions any intermarriage with natives or other immigrant groups. Since their investigations were based on Scandinavian parish records, they may obtain an exaggerated view of endogamy if out-marrying individuals availed themselves of a justice of the peace or non-Scandinavian pastor.

[27] One of the first scholars to criticize the Handlin thesis on this basis was Rudolph J. Vecoli, "Contadini in Chicago: A Critique of *The Uprooted*," *Journal of American History* 51 (1964): 404–417; see also idem, "The Formation of Chicago's Little Italies," *Journal of American Ethnic History* 2 (1983): 1–20. June G. Alexander, "Staying Together: Chain Migration and Patterns of Slovak Settlement in Pittsburgh Prior to World War I," *Journal of American Ethnic History* 1 (1981): 56–83. Barton, *Peasants and Strangers*, pp. 54–58.

[28] *Reports of the Immigration Commission*, vol. 3, "Statistical Review of Immigration," pp. 360–365.

sonal ties played an important role not only with Germans, but for American immigration in general. But we now need to examine more closely just how this affected the process of acculturation and assimilation. People who arrived in the New World without knowing a soul were only a small minority of the total immigration. Still, it also made a difference whether just one relative or friend was waiting upon arrival, or if the majority of the settlers in the community were of the same local origins and dialect. The "transplanted village" was one end on a continuum, but as the above instances have demonstrated, it was fairly common, especially in rural America.

An important related question is how large a group must be in order to perform effectively the functions of *landsmannschaftliche* solidarity. What is the "critical mass" necessary to sustain the internal functioning of this sort of ethnic community? First of all, it must be large enough to make widespread outmarriage unnecessary. Secondly, since a church parish usually formed the nucleus of an ethnic community, the group must be able to support a viable congregation. One Midwestern study found that where clusters of German settlement lacked a church, they tended to shrink and disappear over time; otherwise, they usually expanded. In the mid-nineteenth century, this was not so severe an obstacle as it might appear at first glance. Catholic missionaries in frontier Missouri allowed the formation of a new congregation wherever fifteen families could be organized without depleting an existing parish of its requisite fifteen. Assuming five children per nuclear family, this would come to about one hundred individuals. It is probably not just coincidence that this is exactly the size considered optimal by Hutterite communities; when a population of roughly 130 is obtained, it is time to "hive off" into two halves. This was about the size of the transplanted village of Oldenburgers discussed in Chapter 3 above: thirteen households in 1850, and about one hundred persons of the first generation in 1860. The number of Tecklenburgers was larger, but was divided into three subsettlements, each about this size.[29]

What difference did it make for immigrant acculturation whether one settled in such a homogeneous community? Were the effects more negative or positive? To explore further the effects of chain migration it is perhaps useful to construct a typology contrasting chain migrants with individualistic ones:

[29] Hildegard Binder Johnson, "The Location of German Immigrants in the Middle West," *Annals of the Association of American Geographers* 41 (1951): 1–41; John Rothensteiner, *History of the Archdiocese of St. Louis*, 2 vols. (St. Louis, 1927), 1: 689–699; John Hostetler, *Hutterite Society* (Baltimore, 1975), pp. 185–186.

CHAPTER VI

Individualistic	*Chain Migrants*
pull	push
high proportion single	high proportion families
young adults	broader age distribution
male predominance	more balanced sex ratio
more urban	more rural
more in areas and times of light emigration	more in areas and times of heavy emigration
higher wealth, education, occupational status	lower wealth, education, occupational status
Anglo-conformity, assimilation	cultural pluralism, acculturation

It should be kept in mind that these represent *tendencies* and not absolutes, and that not every migrant can be unambiguously classified as an individualistic or chain migrant. The distinction is similar but not identical to that made by German scholar Peter Marschalck in "economic-speculative" and "socioeconomic" emigrants.[30] To the extent that "push" and "pull" represent responses to short-term economic fluctuations on respective sides of the ocean, individualistic emigrants were more influenced by pull, chain migrants by push. Since the former were not emigrating out of absolute material want, they were less affected by economic trends in Europe, and thus made up a greater proportion of the total in times and places where emigration was light. In fact, the intensity of emigration is perhaps the most important factor influencing the potential for chain migration. Where there is only a scattered or irregular exodus, a large proportion of the migrants will of necessity be pathfinders and risk takers. Because of the low volume of overseas migration from German cities, people of such origins would usually be found outside major chains, and might also be better equipped in terms of education, financial resources, and job experience to make their way up in America. On the other hand, areas of heavy emigration would also be those where more families were driven to migration, hence the broader age and sex distribution of chain migrants as opposed to the predominance of males in the mobile age groups among individualistic migrants.

To some extent, then, individualistic immigrants represent a self-selected population that was more amenable to assimilation in the first place than chain migrants. But whether by choice or chance, individu-

---

[30] Peter Marschalck, *Deutsche Überseewanderung im 19. Jahrhundert* (Stuttgart, 1973), p. 71; he imputes to "economic-speculative" migrants the goal of return, which probably holds true for only a minority of individualistic migrants, but certainly more often than was the case with chain migrants.

alistic immigrants found themselves in a situation with strong incentives, whether of the carrot or stick variety, toward assimilation. Chain migrants would usually be content with the moderate degree of acculturation necessary in an ethnic "decompression chamber." This would then be reflected in such areas as intermarriage rates and social mobility. While urban residence does not preclude chain migration among German or other northern European immigrants, cities would contain a higher proportion of individualistic migrants of such origins than would rural areas. Groups such as Irish or Italians with a higher degree of urbanization would include a greater share of chain migrants in the cities. Here the difference between chain and individualistic migrants would be between cities where the group was heavily or lightly represented.

While the positive characteristics of individualistic immigration are initially most apparent and have been emphasized above, there was probably a trade-off operating. Heterogeneity certainly helped break down provinciality in all areas of life. It helped, for example, to promote High German as a common medium of understanding, replacing various regional dialects that persisted in more homogeneous settlements. But a homogeneous community certainly helped ease both the material-economic and the personal-psychological strains for new arrivals. However, this was somewhat of a mixed blessing. A certain amount of stress can be invigorating. There certainly was a contingent of individualistic loners who clawed their way to the top of the social ladder, but there may have been another, probably smaller contingent at the bottom as well, with chain migrants clustering in the middle ranges. The quickest way to learn to swim is to be thrown into cold water, though a certain percentage will drown in the process. Or to use another aquatic image, one's chances of drowning are greatly reduced when wearing a life jacket, but so are one's chances of winning the 200-meter crawl.

It would be impossible to test this typology on German immigrants without resorting to individual-level data from the manuscript census. The only published American data broken down by German state of origin are the locational data discussed in Chapter 3. However, the three Scandinavian countries of Denmark, Sweden, and Norway present a good alternative. Culturally similar to Germans in many respects, Scandinavians settled in similar regions and time periods. Moreover, they differ so little from one another that contrasts in assimilation rates could hardly be explained by cultural factors such as religion, education, and literacy, or affinity of the mother tongue with English. On the other hand, there was considerable variation in the intensity of em-

CHAPTER VI

igration and the homogeneity of settlement patterns in the New World. Norway was a land of extremely heavy emigration, surpassed only by Ireland in this respect. Sweden fell into the middle range, while Denmark experienced a relatively light exodus. It is remarkable how consistently this ranking of the three countries holds up across a number of social indicators.

As can be seen from Table 6.1, the Danish emigration rate was just half that of Sweden and not much more than one-third that of Norway.[31] Heavier migration also led to heavier local concentrations. Even though Norwegians and especially Swedes greatly outnumbered Danes in America, only 20 percent of all Danish-Americans could be found in the two states where they were most numerous, as compared to over one-third of all Swedes and nearly 45 percent of all Norwegians. Loyalty to ethnic religious denominations corresponded closely to the intensity of emigration and the degree of dispersion, with Danes showing the strongest tendency to forsake ethnic institutions and Norwegians being the most reluctant. While it is difficult to obtain a single summary measure of social mobility, a look at the three largest white-collar job categories shows the Danes leading in all three. Although the Norwegians were the earliest arrivals among Scandinavians, they were outperformed by Swedish latecomers in two of the three categories. One indicator that these differences were indeed related to chain migration is the proportion of immigrants traveling on prepaid tickets, which was lowest by far in Denmark, though perhaps not much higher from Norway than from Sweden.[32]

---

[31] Hvidt, *Flight to America*, pp. 14, 167–169, 191–193. E. P. Hutchinson, *Immigrants and Their Children, 1850–1950* (New York, 1956), pp. 19, 172–175. U.S. Bureau of the Census, *Twelfth Census of the United States, 1900, Vol. 1: Population*, pp. 732–735, 806–862. U.S. Bureau of the Census, *Thirteenth Census of the United States, 1910, Abstract*, p. 191; *Thirteenth Census, Vol. 1: Population*, p. 879. Intermarriage figures for Wisconsin were calculated directly from marriage records by Richard M. Bernard, *The Melting Pot and the Altar: Marital Assimilation in Early Twentieth-Century Wisconsin* (Minneapolis, 1980), p. 66. U.S. Bureau of the Census, *Sixteenth Census of the United States, 1940*, Series P 15, No. 10: *Mother Tongues of the White Population*, pp. 5–7.

[32] The contrasts in ethnic clustering at the state level were reflected at the local level as well. In Minnesota in 1905, there were 33 townships dominated to 75 percent or more by people of Norwegian stock, and 26 townships similarly dominated by Swedes. But there were no townships where Danish stock reached the 75 percent level, only 6 where it constituted a majority, and only 16 other townships where Danes fell between the 25 and 50 percent level. Nor was this simply reflective of the size of the groups: Finns, no more numerous than Danes, dominated 17 townships at the 75 percent level or above. See June Holmquist, ed., *They Chose Minnesota: A Survey of the State's Ethnic Groups* (Minneapolis, 1981), pp. 229, 259, 279–280, 300–301. According to figures of the 1906 census of religious denominations in America, it appears that the contrasts between Nor-

TABLE 6.1. SOCIAL CHARACTERISTICS OF SCANDINAVIAN IMMIGRANTS IN AMERICA

	Danish	Swedish	Norwegian
Migration Intensity per 1,000 Population, 1860–1900	23.2	39.4	61.7
Population Concentration			
in one state	10.4%	19.6%	28.6%
in two states	20.0%	36.5%	44.7%
Proportion in Ethnic Denominations, 1900	25%	40%	75%
Index of Employment in Nonmanual Occupations, 1900			
Clerks	42	39	34
Merchants	86	55	70
Salesmen	56	50	48
Proportion with Prepaid Tickets, 1883–1886	27.5%	46.2%	
Sex Ratio: Men/100 Women			
1910	150.5	125.3	132.5
1920	151.9	122.9	125.9
American-born Children, 1900, with Fathers of Specified Nationality and Mothers of			
same group	63.6%	80.6%	78.1%
other Scandinavians	9.6	5.2	4.4
other foreigners	9.9	3.6	2.1
native-born	16.9	10.6	15.4
American-born Children, 1900, with Mothers of Specified Nationality and Fathers of			
same group	77.4%	85.1%	81.1%
other Scandinavians	6.0	5.1	7.0
other foreigners	8.4	3.7	2.7
native-born	8.2	6.1	8.5
Intermarriage, Wisconsin, 1910			
1st generation	46.5%	39.2%	30.4%
2d generation	76.7	67.9	45.7
Proportion of Foreign Stock			
2d generation, 1900	50.5%	46.2%	57.4%
Proportion of 2d generation with Foreign Mother Tongue, 1940	30.1%	41.3%	50.2%
Proportion of 3d generation with Foreign Mother Tongue, 1940, as Percentage of 2d generation, 1910	4.2%	4.8%	14.1%

SOURCE: See note 31.

CHAPTER VI

The interpretation of intermarriage rates is complicated somewhat by differing sex ratios of the three groups, but one thing is clear—the Danish had the highest outmarriage rates for both sexes, however one measures it. The differences between Swedes and Norwegians are less striking, if only because the latter had been subjected to the forces of assimilation for a longer period of time. While it appears that Norwegians were more attracted to native-born Americans, other studies have shown that many of these intermarriages, especially by men, were in fact with the second generation of the same ethnic group; indeed, the proportion of the foreign stock that was American-born was highest among Norwegians. In the one category that unquestionably involved outgroup marriage—that with non-Scandinavian foreigners—there was a regular upward progression from Norwegians to Swedes to Danes among both sexes. This was also true with both first- and second-generation Scandinavians in Wisconsin before World War I.[33]

Retention of the mother tongue is perhaps the least ambiguous indicator of the degree of assimilation. Here there are consistent contrasts among the three groups persisting into the second and third generations. Norwegians held most tenaciously to the language of their forefathers, while Danes abandoned it most quickly. According to the 1940 census, over half of all second-generation Norwegians but less than one-third of such Danes still claimed the old mother tongue; as in so many other cases, Swedes fell right in between. The 1940 census was the first to record the mother tongue also of the third and subsequent generations, that is, the native-born of native parentage. One problem in using these figures is the difficulty in determining the "population at risk," the total size of the third-generation contingent. However, the size of the second generation thirty years earlier should provide a reasonable approximation. On that basis, third-generation Norwegians were more than three times as likely as Danes to retain their mother tongue, though by this point, retention rates for the more urban Swedes were not much higher than for the Danes.[34]

The Danish historian Kristian Hvidt, who first called attention to

---

wegians and Danes were if anything more dramatic than they appear in the table. On prepaids, see also Gjerde, *From Peasants to Farmers*, p. 131.

[33] The U.S. Census statistics do not actually record intermarriage, but rather persons of foreign or mixed parentage. It was assumed that all foreign-born would also have both parents born in the country of origin, so the number of foreign-born from a given country was subtracted from the number with foreign parentage to obtain the number of American-born of foreign or mixed parentage. Fathers and mothers were then percentaged separately according to the nativity of their partners.

[34] Both second- and third-generation Germans fell about midway between Swedes and Norwegians in language retention according to the measures used here.

some of these differences, attempts to explain them by the timing of immigration. Norwegians were the first Scandinavians to immigrate in substantial numbers, and according to Hvidt, Danes were the last, their late arrival preventing the development of ethnic enclaves typical of the other two groups. I would argue that the timing of emigration was influenced by the degree of economic and demographic pressure in each of the three countries. The same factors that led to heavy chain migration in Norway also caused it to begin earlier. Moreover, the ratios between first- and second-generation immigrants showed that on the average, Danes had been in the country longer than Swedes.[35]

The differences observed in cross-sectional comparisons among the three Scandinavian nationalities are further confirmed by the patterns of longitudinal trends in migration. Econometric analyses using very similar sets of variables have been conducted for all three countries for the period between the Civil War and World War I. While the Danish study concluded that economic conditions in the United States had a considerably greater influence than those at home, both the Swedish and the Norwegian study stressed that push was every bit as important as pull. Moreover, the Norwegian study showed that teen-agers and young adults were more responsive to American conditions, whereas those above age thirty were more affected by unemployment at home. Likewise, the Danish study showed women more influenced by European conditions than men. This provides further evidence that chain migration was more influenced by personal ties than by short-term economic fluctuations in America, and that family and chain migration tended to be "push" emigration.[36]

The heterogeneity of Germany and its emigration have been sufficiently stressed in recent historical literature. The German Reich was in

---

[35] Hvidt, *Flight to America*, pp. 166–175. In 1860, the Danish contingent was over half as large as the Swedish, although by World War I nearly four times as many Swedes as Danes would have emigrated.

[36] Thorvald Moe, *Demographic Developments and Economic Growth in Norway, 1740–1940* (New York, 1977), pp. 153–218; John M. Quigley, "An Economic Model of Swedish Emigration," *Quarterly Journal of Economics* 86 (1972): 111–127; Ulla Margrethe Larsen, "A Quantitative Study of Emigration from Denmark to the United States, 1870–1913," *Scandinavian Economic History Review* 30 (1982): 101–128. In general, Danes appeared to be most responsive to economic conditions, Norwegians least so. The Danish study was able to explain a greater proportion of the variance (95 percent) than did the Swedish (84 percent). Both of these studies treated total emigration, while the Norwegian model, though simplifying its task by considering only the most mobile group, those aged fourteen to forty-four, showed little better predictive power (87 percent) than the Swedish. In fact, using an identical set of variables, the Danish study was able to explain total emigration as well as the Norwegian study could account for the more restricted age group.

CHAPTER VI

TABLE 6.2. RATE OF EMIGRATION FROM SELECTED GERMAN STATES AND DEGREE OF CONCENTRATION IN AMERICA
(Through 1870)

	Index of Emigration Intensity to 1870	Concentration, 1870 in:		
		1 State	2 States	N
Brunwsick	17	19%	34%	4,876
Oldenburg	42	31	45	10,285
Mecklenburg	67	26	44	39,670
Saxony	21	14	27	45,254

SOURCE: Calculated from U.S. and German census figures; see Appendix C for details.

many respects more diverse than the whole of Scandinavia. There were regions that resembled Norway and those more like Denmark in their emigration patterns. Some of the same contrasts that were observed between immigrants from different Scandinavian countries can be seen between those from various German regions as well.

A comparison of several of the smaller German states shows the effects of emigration intensity on the degree of concentration in America (see Table 6.2). Immigrants from Brunswick were few in number, but because their emigration rate was too low to support many chains, they were much more widely scattered than the larger contingents from Oldenburg and Mecklenburg. The mass emigration from the latter two states was very heavily concentrated in the United States. With the lighter emigration from the Kingdom of Saxony a more dispersed pattern is again apparent.[37]

The limited evidence available on Germans suggests that more-dispersed immigrants were also better off. Taking advantage of the fact that natives of Brunswick are easily identified in the manuscript census, my latest research has begun to examine them in various environments, rural and urban, concentrated and dispersed. Clear contrasts can be seen in wealth, occupation, and intermarriage, reflecting the differences between chain and individualistic migrants. Nearly one-tenth of all immigrants from Brunswick nationwide were concentrated in Cape Girardeau County, Missouri, but they showed the lowest average wealth and the strongest propensity for in-group marriage of the four sites investigated. The few of their compatriots scattered among the Westfa-

[37] Calculated from 1870 U.S. Census figures and 1871 German census figures. For more detail, see Appendix C.

lians and Lippe-Detmolders in the four Missouri River counties were considerably better off and more likely to marry outside the group. Likewise, there were distinct contrasts between immigrants from Brunswick in Philadelphia, where they were greatly underrepresented, and in St. Louis, where they were overrepresented. Those in Philadelphia showed a higher average wealth, a more favorable occupational profile, and a greater propensity to marry non-Germans or Germans from outside their region of origin than did St. Louisans. Moreover, in each of the four areas, those men marrying American women were better off than average, while those who married within their local group were generally below average, those marrying Germans from other regions falling somewhere in the middle.[38]

The work of other scholars points in the same direction. A 1983 dissertation investigated the German community of Philadelphia, where southwest Germans were heavily overrepresented and Prussians relatively rare. The latter were also more likely to be found in white-collar occupations and the higher ranks of wealth, and more often married Americans or Germans of different origins, while southwest Germans fell below average in all these categories. One might be tempted to write this off as a contrast between progressive, modern, Protestant north Germans and the backward, conservative, Catholic south, but in fact the confessional and social geography of Germany is much more complicated than that. Moreover, a study of Bloomington, Illinois, where the population proportions were reversed, found that in this case the Prussians, and particularly a core group of chain migrants, brought up the rear, while south and central Germans were overrepresented among the local elite. Thus it appears that in general, outsiders rather than insiders were disproportionately clustered in the top ranks of immigrant society.[39]

---

[38] Some results from my parallel study of immigrants from Brunswick are presented in Kamphoefner, "Predisposing Factors in German-American Urbanization," paper presented to the Organization of American Historians, Philadelphia, April 1982; idem, "Chain Migration and Local Homogeneity of Immigration: Cape Girardeau County Germans in Comparative Perspective," in *French and German Folk Landscape in the Mississippi Valley*, ed. Michael Roark (Cape Girardeau, Mo., 1986). Of immigrant men from Brunswick, less than 10 percent in Philadelphia were unskilled laborers, compared to over 30 percent in St. Louis. Only 4 percent of the latter married non-Germans, compared to 10 percent of the former. In Philadelphia, only 37 percent married women from Brunswick or neighboring Hannover; in St. Louis it was 63 percent.

[39] Lesley Ann Kawaguchi, "The Making of Philadelphia's German-America: Ethnic Group and Community Development, 1830–1883" (Ph.D. diss., University of California, 1983), pp. 150–239; Robert W. Frizzell, "Prussian Protestant *Kirchendeutsche* in a

CHAPTER VI

Similar contrasts between chain and individualistic migrants can be observed in Josef Barton's comparison of New Immigration groups in Cleveland. A large proportion of the Italian migration consisted of major village chains, while the origins of the Rumanians were much more scattered. As a result, Italian ethnic organizations had a much more localistic character than those of the Rumanians. The latter also showed much higher rates of educational attainment and social mobility than did the Italians, and were also much more prone to outgroup marriage.[40]

The patterns of Dutch immigration would seem at first glance to contradict the association between heavy emigration rates and clustered chain migration, for despite a relatively light exodus from the Netherlands, the Dutch stuck together very tightly in America. The great majority of them—72 percent in 1850 and 56 percent in 1870—were concentrated in less than 1 percent of America's counties. In fact, at midcentury, over half of all Dutch were squeezed into just fifteen minor civil divisions (townships or city wards). But on the European side, what looks in the aggregate like light emigration was in fact either mass emigration or virtually none at all. One-third of the Dutch exodus stemmed from just 22 of the Netherlands' 1,156 municipalities, and 12 percent of these local jurisdictions provided nearly three-fourths of all emigrants. The Dutch experience thus fits very well into the framework of chain migration.[41]

A reviewer perhaps went too far in characterizing the subjects of Stephan Thernstrom's mobility study as "most uncommon Bostonians." But Thernstrom may well have obtained an exaggerated picture of the disadvantages of Irish immigrants by studying Boston, a city where they were strongly overrepresented, and comparing them with the highly atypical minority, probably in a positive sense, of Germans or Scandinavians who found their way to New England. Another study by Jo Ellen Vinyard compared the occupational profile of Irish and Germans in various cities and found that Boston was one of the places where the Irish were at the greatest relative disadvantage, while Milwaukee, the most German city in the United States and the site of another important New Urban History case study, was one of the places where the gap between Germans and Irish was narrowest. Charlotte Erickson, in her book on British immigrants, includes a chapter entitled

---

Small Midwestern City," paper presented to the Society for German-American Studies, Lincoln, Nebr., 26 April 1985.

[40] Barton, *Peasants and Strangers*, pp. 48–63 and passim.
[41] Swierenga, "Dutch Immigration Patterns," pp. 32–36.

"The Uprooted," but it deals not with the industrial proletariat, as one might expect, but with immigrants in white-collar occupations.[42]

Miami's Cubans are often regarded as an immigrant success story, and compared to most ethnic groups, they are. But where in this country are Cubans doing best? Not in Florida, where their mean household income falls right at the state average for all races, but below that of whites. Certainly not in New York or New Jersey—the two states with the next highest concentrations—where Cubans fell 13 percent below the mean, although in absolute terms their incomes were just as high as in Florida. No, the most successful Cuban immigrants, both in absolute terms and relative to the rest of the population, were the remaining 22 percent of Cuban-Americans scattered across the other forty-seven states, whose mean family income surpassed the average for those states by 9 percent. An ethnic enclave does offer some compensations, but they are mostly nonpecuniary.[43]

So in the end, Oscar Handlin's thesis can be practically turned on its head. There were indeed some individuals who were uprooted in the migration process. But it was the uprooted who most quickly entered into the mainstream of American life. Whether condemned to freedom or choosing it of their own free will, they tended to make the most of it. But the peasant immigrant masses were anything but uprooted. Like the transplanted Westfalians, they were deeply rooted in an ethnic community, acculturated to some extent to be sure, but insulated from the most direct and drastic confrontations with the dominant society.

---

[42] Stephan Thernstrom, *The Other Bostonians: Poverty and Progress in the American Metropolis, 1880–1970* (Cambridge, Mass., 1973), pp. 130–175. Jo Ellen Vinyard, *The Irish on the Urban Frontier: Nineteenth Century Detroit, 1850–1880* (New York, 1976), pp. 312–317. My own calculations from the 1870 census for the fifty largest cities confirm Vinyard's conclusions. The higher the German proportion in a city's population, the less favorable the German occupational profile compared to the rest of the immigrant or native population. Milwaukee was the city where Germans came off worst (except for one mill town with only a few dozen Germans), while in Boston they were well above average. See Charlotte Erickson, *Invisible Immigrants: The Adaptation of British and Scottish Immigrants in Nineteenth-Century America* (Coral Gables, Fla., 1972), pp. 393–407. She states in her introduction to the chapter titled "The Uprooted: Immigrants in Professions" that these writers were "not very different in social origins" from the farmers and workers treated in the book. "They are distinguishable from the migrants in other groups by the occupations they chose to enter in America, and also by the fact that they broke more ties in emigration than did most of the farmers and industrial workers." Moreover, she notes the "relative absence of any references to economic pressure" as motives for emigration of these "uprooted."

[43] "Cubans Gain Economically, but Many Are Left Behind," *Miami Herald*, 18 December 1983; see also Thomas D. Boswell and James R. Curtis, *The Cuban-American Experience: Culture Images and Perspectives* (Totowa, N.J., 1983), pp. 108–113.

CHAPTER VI

The price they paid for this greater security was to be largely denied access to the more spectacular (and risky) heights of the social scale. But it was security more than mobility that transplanted villagers such as the Westfalians had sought in America in the first place. Those of their children or grandchildren who felt differently could emerge from the ethnic cocoon at their own pace and without any great handicap, and it is clear that some erosion did take place at the edges of the ethnic community. For the most part, however, it was the community itself, though still tightly knit and homogeneous, that gradually, almost imperceptibly, lost its distinctively ethnic character. But even as of this writing, there are back roads and small towns in Missouri where traces of a transplanted culture remain.[44]

[44] See for example Gerlach, *Immigrants in the Ozarks*, pp. 130–131; Berton Roueché, "Profiles: Schönheit muss leiden (Hermann, Missouri)," *New Yorker*, 28 February 1977, pp. 37–50; also reprinted in *Special Places: In Search of Small Town America* (Boston, 1982), pp. 59–86. For a German perspective on the area of study, see Ingeborg Meyer-Sickendieck, "Noch immer ein Hauch vom frühen Amerika: Wie die Amerikaner in einst 'deutschen' Dörfern am Missouri leben," *Frankfurter Allgemeine Zeitung*, 21 April 1976.

APPENDIX A

Sources and Coding Procedures for Emigrant List Data

THE INFORMATION in Table 2.1 on emigration from the Münster District was obtained from Friedrich Müller, "Westfälische Auswanderer im 19. Jahrhundert: Auswanderung aus dem Regierungsbezirk Münster," *Beiträge zur Westfälischen Familienforschung* 22–24 (1964–1966): 57–389, a transcription of rather complete lists forwarded to the District level by the *Landrat* of a given *Kreis*. Included are all legally registered emigrants and all clandestine ones who came to the attention of authorities. It appears that the majority of the clandestine emigrants from the District were included in these lists. In his introduction (p. 12, n. 28) Müller refers to a large number of unrecorded emigrants from *Kreis* Lüdinghausen in 1832. However, a look at the original document cited shows that it recorded not international migration, but the aggregate volume of all in- and out-migration that crossed village boundaries. Though nowhere indicated in the publication, the original documents upon which Müller's transcriptions were based also recorded the amount of money possessed by legally registered emigrants from 1846 through 1850. This material was added to the data set in order to produce the breakdowns of emigrant wealth by occupation, and is described in more detail below.

For the Minden District, only scattered lists have survived for the period before 1880. Those which have were also transcribed by Friedrich Müller, who generously allowed me to use the manuscript that was subsequently published as "Westfälische Auswanderer im 19. Jahrhundert: Auswanderung aus dem Regierungsbezirk Minden," *Beiträge zur Westfälischen Familienforschung* 38–39 (1980–1981). The information presented is based on emigration from *Amt* Versmold in *Kreis* Halle and *Amt* Rietberg in *Kreis* Wiedenbrück, the only areas from which lists were available over longer periods of time. In terms of economic structure, Versmold, bordering on the Münster and Osnabrück Districts, had a heavy concentration of weaving, while the inhabitants of Rietberg were moderately involved in spinning.

Data from the Osnabrück district are based on material from the *Amtsvogtei* Osnabrück (Rep. 360 Osn. A3 Nr. 6) and Buer (Rep. 360 Buer Nr. 66) in the Niedersächsisches Staatsarchiv Osnabrück. The lists from *Amtsvogtei* Osnabrück, the rural hinterlands of the city, covered the years 1832 through 1858, and were arranged in neat columns listing name, occupation, age, amount of money, and number of dependents. Those from Buer were in such neat order only for 1842; for the years 1843 to 1849 the information had to be dug out of applications and permits, resulting in more missing data. The areas from which the lists came have about average emigration rates for the region. A project is

APPENDIX A

currently under way at Staatsarchiv Osnabrück to publish these and other emigrant lists from the District.

Emigrant lists for the Duchy of Brunswick were obtained from Fritz Gruhne, *Auswandererlisten des ehemaligen Herzogtums Braunschweig, ohne Stadt Braunschweig and Landkreis Holzminden, 1846–1871* (Brunswick, 1971). As the title indicates, these lists do not cover the entire duchy, and appear to include only legally registered emigrants. They were assembled from announcements emigrants were required to make in the official government newspaper, supplemented by Gruhne with information from parish registers. Despite the title, they extend through 1875. For the years from 1853 to 1872, the totals run closely parallel, though about 20 percent lower than the official statistics on legal and clandestine emigration from the parts of Brunswick covered.

In these emigrant lists, occupations were normally listed only for heads of families and single males emigrating alone. Since there was and still is no standard coding scheme for dealing with preindustrial German occupations, I had to develop my own. For the most part I kept each occupational designation discrete, but grouped them so they could be easily collapsed into categories reflecting sectors and strata.

In the agricultural sector, the rural lower classes consisted primarily of farmhands, day laborers, and *Heuerleute*; smallholders of those who owned some land, but probably required supplementary income from other sources; full peasants of those who appeared to own enough land to live from agriculture alone. In retrospect, the distinctions between smallholders and peasants are somewhat ambiguous, and rural society was primarily divided into landowners and landless, or groups such as *Neubauer* with next to nothing. In fact, such a bipartate rather than tripartate division of agricultural occupations was used in Chapter 5 above. Persons designated as *Arbeiter* (laborer) or *Handarbeiter* were relegated to the rural lower class. They appeared to be casual laborers in an area where most of the employment opportunities were in agriculture. In part, the designation depended on the whim of the recording bureaucrat. The term *Arbeiter* appeared only among clandestine emigrants, *Handarbeiter* primarily during the years 1845 to 1847, and both terms were applied to persons who appeared in other sources as *Heuerleute* or even sons of landowners.

With artisan occupations, the rather arbitrary distinction was made between apprentices and journeymen, masters, and those who were designated simply by the name of the trade, either because they worked independently but without assistants, or because they worked in trades like weaving, which had never had a strong guild system and was practiced at will. Although the distribution across these categories varied somewhat from Brunswick to Münster, the average age and proportion married in each strata is very uniform across the two regions (see table in Walter D. Kamphoefner, "Transplanted Westfalians: Persistence and Transformation of Socioeconomic and Cultural Patterns in the Northwest German Migration to Missouri" [Ph.D. diss., University of Missouri, 1978], p. 216). An attempt was made to distinguish between artisan and industrial laborers, though in retrospect it appears that iron and coal production was still being carried on by rather traditional methods. Since the numbers were so small, they were relegated to a residual category along with people in the tertiary sector for all the analyses in the text.

It is clear that a certain level of ambiguity will remain in any occupational classification based on nominal designations. But the great majority of occupations pose no questions. With those which do, errors were probably random or tended to overestimate the status of emigrants, as the relative youth of several high status groups suggests.

The information on amount of money taken along by emigrants from the Münster District, presented in Table 2.3, was not included in the transcriptions published by Friedrich Müller, but had to be added to the data set from the original archival sources in Staatsarchiv Münster for cases numbered 2140 through 3992, officially registered emigration from early 1846 through the end of 1850. The cases did not always match the sequence numbers in the published lists exactly because of extended families, siblings recorded together, etc. The preprinted forms normally used by Prussian officials explicitly stated "inclusive of travel costs." A test showed that approximately 10 percent of the cases not recorded on such forms were above average in wealth, suggesting that these, too, were inclusive figures. Similarly, those who qualified their information with "circa" or "*etwa*" were very close to the mean. In cases where a range of values was given for a person, the average was taken, and this was also well above the average for emigrants as a whole.

Excluded from the analysis were about 200 persons with faulty or missing information: 86 with no information on funds; 50 who explicitly stated "none," thus ignoring the instructions to include travel costs; 37 who stated that they possessed only travel costs but gave no amount; 20 whose passage was paid by a third party or the village; and 13 whose stated that the amount given excluded travel costs, thus underestimating their wealth. About two-fifths of the above listed no occupation, but the rest differed little from the group as a whole in their occupational profile. Also excluded were family groups headed by single men (often with a widowed mother and several siblings), since such a person's wealth would be less reflective of his own occupation than that of his father, especially if the family owned land. Emigrants from the *Stadtkreis* or city of Münster, about forty in number, were excluded so that the Münster and Osnabrück data sets would be more comparable. Of the roughly 1,800 cases initially in the data set, 1,535 remained to form the basis of the analysis; a few scattered occupations are left out of the table.

APPENDIX B

Use of Census Data and Procedures of Matching with Emigrant Lists

THE 1850 DATA set consists of the complete enumeration for St. Charles and Warren counties. The transcriptions published by Elizabeth Prather Elsberry (*1850 Federal Census for Warren County, Mo.*; *1850 Federal Census for St. Charles County, Mo.*) were used as an aid in data entry, but any questionable entries were rechecked with the original. Also, entries in the agricultural census were consulted to arrive at the most plausible spelling of family names. German family names were particularly subject to mutilation. The Warren County census taker, for example, rendered the typical Westfalian name of Meyer in all its permutations and compounds simply as "Mire." The St. Charles County official, though also an Anglo-American, claimed that "having done the duties of Sheriff during four years and possessing a knowledge of the German language I have enjoyed faculties for collecting the information required by the census act possessed by few." He also followed the same route when completing the agricultural and slave schedules as with the population census, making it easier to match the respective entries and resulting in fewer that were unmatched than was the case in Warren County.

While most data entry involved straightforward transcription, several value judgments were made. The Old French, most of them Missouri natives, were assigned to a separate category, mostly on the basis of family and given names. The census numbers of people so assigned is given in Kamphoefner, "Transplanted Westfalians," p. 220. A similar distinction was made on the basis of family names between Alsatians of German tongue and "genuine" Frenchmen, which likewise involved little ambiguity. Census dwelling and family numbers were in all cases identical in Warren County. In St. Charles County, I took the dwelling rather than the family as the unit of aggregation, since shared dwellings often contained subfamilies. I devised my own household code in order to be able to identify married couples besides those who were heads of households. Individuals were coded as being either a head (male or female), a spouse, or a child within a conjugal unit, or a boarder. The following conjugal units besides that of the head of household were identified: parents of head, married children or siblings of head, or conjugal units unrelated to the head. Marriage records from the area of study were used to determine the maiden names of wives, and confirmed the widespread presence of relatives who might otherwise be considered as unrelated on the basis of family names. Lippe-Detmolders in the 1860 census were coded according to the same principles, and in this case the household and family units in the census were always identical.

Occupations were for the most part treated nominally in this study, but where they are aggregated into vertical strata, the Philadelphia Social History Project code was used. A few additions and substitutions had to be made, and one outright change: a "Tobacconist" was obviously a tobacco worker, not a cigar shop owner, in these rural areas. Persons of this and a few other occupations in the primary sector, such as Drover, Overseer, and Dairyman, were assigned to the three categories of Farm Owner, Renter, and Farm Laborer by whether they owned land and whether they were listed in the agricultural schedule of the census.

Emigrant lists from *Kreis* Tecklenburg were among those from the Münster District published by Müller, described in Appendix A above. The procedures of matching between entries in the census and in the lists are outlined in Appendix B of "Transplanted Westfalians," which also gives a list of matched immigrants, examples of "sure" and "doubtful" matches, and a comparative profile of sure and doubtful matches (pp. 201, 224–232). Since then I have drawn upon unpublished village-level lists from the town archives of Westerkappeln and Lienen, where the bulk of emigrants originated. These were in some cases more complete, expanding the data set by about 10 percent, and more detailed, confirming matches otherwise doubtful, but revealed no errors more serious than confusing an emigrant with his brother, which would not affect the crucial variable of social origin.

Emigrant lists from Lippe-Detmold were transcribed and published by Fritz Verdenhalven, *Die Auswanderer aus dem Fürstentum Lippe (bis 1877)* (Detmold, 1980). While Prussian emigrant lists usually gave names and birthdates or ages of the spouse and all accompanying children, those from Lippe-Detmold were much more deficient, sometimes not even giving the first name or age of the principal emigrant, not indicating whether he was alone or with family, or simply stating "with family" or "with wife and children," but not giving any particulars. However, the approximate time of emigration could often be established from the ages and birthplaces of children, or entries in American marriage registers. But there were more doubtful matches from Lippe, though they resulted less from discrepancies between the sources than from simple lack of information. Clandestine emigrants were also more likely to escape notice of officials in Lippe-Detmold than in Prussian Westfalia. As a result, only about three-fifths of the Lippe-Detmolders in the rural area and three-eighths of those in St. Louis could be matched to emigrant lists. The lower matching ratio in the city was probably the result of a higher proportion of young and single migrants. A comparison of real estate and wealth holdings showed that there was no tendency for poorer persons to be among the unmatched or doubtful matches, however, so the traced individuals are probably representative of the whole. There was no way of knowing what proportion of all Tecklenburgers were matched, since they were indistinguishable in the census from other Prussians (or in 1850, other Germans, since the census did not give state of origin).

The occupational categories used in examining transatlantic social mobility differ slightly from those used in Chapter 2 and explained in Appendix A, the main difference being that unmarried farmhands were further distinguished be-

APPENDIX B

tween those from poor families and those from propertied ones. I have attempted to construct similar occupational categories for Tecklenburg and Lippe-Detmold, aided by the fact that the rural social structure, and the form of the emigrant lists, are very similar for both areas. For Tecklenburg, the District level emigrant lists could be supplemented by tax lists (published by Wolfgang Leesch, *Schatzungs- und sonstige Höferegister der Grafschaft Tecklenburg, 1494 bis 1831* [Münster, 1974], pp. 270–323), and by the more detailed local emigrant lists from Westerkappeln and Lienen. In Tecklenburg, tax lists confirm that persons designated as a *Kolon* or *Kötter* all had holdings large enough to live from full-time agriculture. In Lippe, a considerable number of more marginal smallholders were subsumed under the term *Kolon*. These could be identified because in northwest German villages, farmsteads were numbered consecutively from the largest down to the smallest, the largest being number 1, the next largest, 2, etc. A somewhat arbitrary cutoff point of 25 was selected, roughly splitting the *Kolon* category in half. While the varying number of farmsteads per village makes this boundary somewhat imprecise, the results in the table suggest that the distinction is justified. Unmarried farmhands in Lippe usually had no occupational designation at all, and those in Tecklenburg were not distinguished between sons of propertied and propertyless families. I made this distinction for Tecklenburgers on the basis of tax lists, supplemented by local emigrants lists that often gave farmstead numbers, or in the case of tenant farmers, gave the landlord's number followed by *a, b*, or *c* depending on the number of tenants. In Lippe, the distinction was made as with propertied peasants and smallholders; those from farmsteads numbered 25 or lower were assumed to be from propertied families; those with numbers above 25 or none at all were assumed to be from the rural poor. The same distinctions were applied to persons who had emigrated as dependent children and had since reached adulthood.

APPENDIX C

Data and Calculation Procedures for Figure 1.1

IN ORDER to compare rates of emigration from different parts of Germany without the distorting effects of the varying accuracy of record keeping in individual German states, emigration rates were calculated backward from the United States Census of 1870 by the following method: The German states of Thuringia, Anhalt, Lippe, Schaumburg-Lippe, and Bremen, not separately enumerated in the U.S. Census, were assumed to comprise the same proportions of the immigration as they did of the German population in 1871: 3.9 percent. This amount was subtracted from the number of "Germans, not specified" in the census, the remainder of which was allocated proportionally to the other states, increasing the total for each by about one-eighth. For smaller states—Mecklenburg, Brunswick, Hamburg, and Lübeck—this figure was simply divided by the population in 1871 to obtain an index of the emigration rate. For larger states a two-step process was used. Immigration from each state was first "allocated" to individual Districts proportional to that District's share of the total emigration from that state, as shown by state-level statistics for as much of the period prior to 1871 as were available. See Table C.1 for exact index figures, sources of German state statistics, and the years they cover. For Germany as a whole, the index was 43.

One might object that the more recent emigration from East Elbian Prussia would have been reduced less by death than that from the western provinces, where emigration began much earlier, but this is compensated in that emigration before 1844, almost entirely from the west, is not included in the calculations. A slight distortion may have taken place in Baden, where the allocation was made on the basis of the years 1850–1855, a period of especially heavy emigration. At such times, Districts with the heaviest emigration provided a greater share of the total than during times of light emigration.

In general, internal evidence inspires confidence in these American data. From 1860 to 1870, the number of Badenese, Bavarians, and Hessians in the United States increased by nearly identical proportions: 36, 36, and 38 percent respectively. For Württemberg the increase was somewhat greater, 57 percent. With the onset of mass emigration from the eastern provinces, Prussia not surprisingly showed the largest gains, 162 percent. But emigration from Nassau was definitely undercounted in 1870, showing an absolute decrease to 88 percent of the 1860 total. The 1860 figure must be relatively accurate since the ratio between immigrants from Hesse and Nassau in the U.S. Census was practically identical to the ratio of the volume of emigration from the respective states from 1852 to 1858 (see Wolf Heino Struck, *Die Auswanderung aus dem Herzogtum Nassau, 1806–1866* [Wiesbaden, 1966], p. 132). Even if the same ratio with Hesse were applied in 1870, the index for Nassau (Wiesbaden District minus the city of Frankfurt on the Main) would still only be 29.

TABLE C.1. DATA FOR FIGURE 1.1
(Immigrants in the United States per 1,000 Inhabitants in the District of Origin, 1870/1871)

ID and District	Index	ID and District	Index
PRUSSIA[a]		BAVARIA[d]	
01 Ostpreussen	3	35 Oberbayern	6
02 Danzig	23	36 Niederbayern	13
03 Marienwerder	30	37 Pfalz	152
04 Berlin	8	38 Oberpfalz	29
05 Potsdam	31	39 Oberfranken	60
06 Frankfort on the Oder	26	40 Mittelfranken	34
07 Stettin-Stralsund	98	41 Unterfranken	69
08 Koslin	49	42 Schwaben	22
09 Posen	17		
10 Bromberg	64	SAXONY[e]	
11 Breslau	11	43 Dresden	17
12 Liegnitz	15	44 Leipzig	24
13 Oppeln	15	45 Zwickau	20
14 Magdeburg	23		
15 Merseburg	27	WURTTEMBERG[f]	
16 Erfurt	58	46 Neckarkreis	86
24 Munster	66	47 Schwarzwaldkries	110
25 Minden	113	48 Jagstkreis	63
26 Arnsberg	17	49 Donaukreis	49
29 Koblenz	85		
30 Düsseldorf	16	BADEN[g]	
32 Trier	105	50 Konstanz	85
33 Aachen	23	51 Freiburg	104
34 Sigmaringen	137	52 Karlsruhe	147
		53 Mannheim	133
HANNOVER[b]			
18 Hannover	45	57 MECKLENBURG	67
19 Hildesheim	31		
20 Lüneberg	37	OLDENBURG[h]	
21 Stade	82	59 Hzt. Oldenburg	42
22 Osnabrück	104	60 Fst. Lübeck	20
23 Aurich	93	61 Birkenfeld	84
28 NASSAU	26	62 BRUNSWICK	17
HESSIAN STATES[c]		66 LUBECK	6
27 Kassel	87		
54 Starkenburg	93	68 HAMBURG	26
55 Oberhessen	100		
56 Rheinhessen	65		

[a] Basis years: 1844–1871. SOURCE: T. Bödicker, "Die Einwanderung und Auswanderung des preussischen Staates," *Preussische Statistik* 26 (1874): iv–viii.

DATA FOR FIGURE I.I

One possible source of distortion is that with the Prussian annexation of Hannover and Hesse-Nassau in 1866, some emigrants from these states were enumerated in the U.S. Census as Prussians. This may account for the decrease in number of immigrants from Nassau in the 1870 census, and might also explain why Minden shows a heavier emigration rate than Osnabrück from these calculations, when the opposite would have been expected. Given the strength of Hannoverian particularism, however, the distortion was probably minimal in its case. At any rate, the impact would be greatest with a small state, and would be negligible when spread over the whole of Prussia, statistically speaking. Thus a comparison of emigration rates from Prussia on the one hand and the larger south German states of Baden, Württemberg, and Bavaria on the other can be made with a considerable degree of confidence, especially since all these states were mentioned by name in the official instructions for census takers in 1870 and 1880 (see E. P. Hutchinson, *Immigrants and their Children, 1850–1950* [New York, 1956], pp. 179–280). In fact, this is probably the most accurate estimation of regional emigration intensity in Germany before 1871 that has been made to date.

NOTES TO TABLE C.1 *(continued)*

[b] Basis years: 1858–1864, 1867–1871. SOURCE: *Zur Statistik des Königreichs Hannover* (Hannover, 1863–1865), 9: 156–158, 11: 90–91; Bödicker, "Einwanderung und Auswanderung," pp. iv–viii.

[c] Basis years: allocating between Hesse-Kassel and Hesse-Darmstadt, 1852–1858; allocating within Hesse-Darmstadt, 1841–1847, 1853. SOURCE: Wilhelm Mönckmeier, *Die deutsche uberseeische Auswanderung* (Jena, 1912), pp. 75, 160; Hans Richter, "Hessen und die Auswanderung," *Mitteilungen des oberhessischen Geschichtsvereins* 32 (1934): 107, 137.

[d] Basis years: 1844–1871. SOURCE: Georg Krieg, "Entwicklung und gegenwartiger Zustand des Auswanderungswesens im Königreich Bayern," in *Auswanderung und Auswanderungspolitik in Deutschland*, ed. Eugen von Philippovich (Leipzig, 1892), pp. 90–93.

[e] Basis years: 1853–1861. SOURCE: L. Pohle, "Auswanderungswesen und Auswanderungspolitik im Königreich Sachsen," in *Auswanderung*, ed. Philippovich, p. 386.

[f] Basis years: 1843–1852. SOURCE: *Wurttembergisches Jahrbuch* (1853), pt. 2, pp. 118–119.

[g] Basis years: 1850–1855. SOURCE: *Beiträge zur Statistik der inneren Verwaltung des Grossherzogtums Baden* 5 (1857): 34–35. Slightly different figures in Kamphoefner, *Westfalen in der Neuen Welt*, resulted from the false assumption that District boundaries did not change between 1855 and 1871.

[h] Basis years: 1855–1864. SOURCE: *Statistische Nachrichten uber das Grossherzogtum Oldenburg* 9 (1867): 164–177. It was assumed that only immigrants from the *Herzogtum* were enumerated as Oldenburgers in the U.S. Census. The index figures for the exclaves of Birkenfeld and *Fürstentum* Lübeck were set according to the ratio of their per capita emigration rates with that of the duchy.

INDEX

NOTE: Geographic names can also refer to migrants from or to that place.

Adelsverein, 73
Africa, 56, 58, 181
agents, emigration, 5, 57–58
agriculture: in Germany, 10, 18–22, 25–28, 36, 41, 44–45, 50–52, 81; in Missouri, 118, 122–23, 125–34, 139–47, 152–54, 157, 172. *See also* livestock, peasant, wine production
Ahaus, Westfalia, 33, 49
Alsace, 60, 75, 87, 111, 165
Anglo-Americans, 108–14, 117–34, 172
Arnsberg District, 17n, 19–20
artisans: in Germany, 41–46, 50–51, 61, 81; in Missouri, 119–21, 124, 137–42, 144, 147–48, 150, 152–59
Asia, 56, 58, 181
Augusta, MO, 88–89, 132–33, 165, 170, 176

Baden, 13–15, 28–29, 60, 74–76, 80–82, 86t, 167, 207–209
Baltimore, 77–79, 81, 84, 95, 98–100
Bavaria, 13–14, 66, 74t, 80–82, 84–86, 103, 207–209
Belgium, 17, 31, 179, 187
Belleville, IL, 88, 150
Bentheim, Hannover, 37, 64
Berlin, 32–33, 38, 68, 91, 208
Berlin emigration society, 96, 99, 101, 116–17
Bersenbruck, Hannover, 15, 25
Bielefeld, Westfalia, 19n, 33, 40, 61
biographical sketches, 67–68, 79, 83, 90, 114, 142–46, 161–62
blacks, 111, 125, 170. *See also* slaveholding
Bochum, Westfalia, 33–34
Boone, Daniel, 111, 161
Boston, 78, 81, 198
Braun, Rudolf, 17
Bremen, 7n, 72, 78–79, 100, 104
Britain: industry, 19, 31; immigrants from, 111–14, 117–20, 123–24, 179, 188, 198
Brunswick, 16, 32–33, 43–44, 56, 62–65, 72–74, 77, 82t, 84–87, 101–102, 149–50, 167n, 196–97, 207–209

Calvinists, 37–38, 165
Canada, 111, 112n
Cape Girardeau Co., MO, 150n, 167n, 196–97
Cappeln, MO, 89, 144, 173–74
Catholics, 37, 62, 88–89, 99, 104, 111, 115, 117, 166, 174, 183, 187, 189, 197
chain migration: Dutch, 183–87, 198; European, 188–90, 198–200; German, 3–10, 57, 71, 73, 74–75, 87, 103–105, 149, 170, 172, 177, 195–97; Scandinavian, 11, 183–87, 190–95
Chicago, 77, 81–85
Cincinnati, 81–82, 84–85, 151
Civil War, U.S., 55–56, 134
commons, division of, 36, 62–63
Conzen, Kathleen, 83, 134n
cultural rebound, 132–33

Damme, Oldenburg, 15, 35, 45n, 51, 88–89
demography, 17–18, 20, 25, 38, 47, 113–14, 149
Denmark, 11n, 32, 66, 70, 180, 182, 191–96
Duden, Gottfried, 5–7, 75, 77, 93–97, 99, 117
Dutzow, MO, 88, 166

East Elbian Prussia, 27, 38, 77, 91, 114
Eifel, Rhineprovince, 30–31
Einlieger, 52, 137–39, 141–42, 153t, 156t
emigration, German: clandestine, 42–43, 47, 66; motives for, 40–41, 57–61, 64–69, 71; occupation of, 27, 40–46; prepaid, 188; publicity, guidebooks, 5–7, 50, 75, 77, 150; regional rates, 13–15,

211

INDEX

emigration, German (cont.)
36, 38, 43–44, 196, 207–209; time trends, 52–57, 178; wealth of, 46–52, 66, 81n, 185

emigration, non-German, 8–11, 31–32, 70, 113, 177–87, 190–95, 198–200

emigration societies, 6, 94–96, 99–101. *See also* Berlin, Giessen, and Solingen societies

Erickson, Charlotte, 198

Erie Canal, 75, 81

ethnicity: and agricultural practices, 125–34; intermarriage, 112–13, 117; and occupation, 118–24; segregation by, 117–18; and slaveholding, 115–17; stereotypes, 106–10

Evangelical church, 101, 115, 174, 176–77

Eversmann, Louis, 93, 116–17

Femme Osage, MO, 88, 93, 99, 102, 108, 118, 158, 164–65, 174, 177

Follenius, Paul, 95–96, 100; Wilhelm, 133

Franklin Co., MO, 86–89, 91, 95, 97, 99, 110, 136, 146, 161–63, 167, 172n

Freiburg, Baden, 32–33

Frontier thesis, 136

Garlichs, Adelheid, 108, 110, 164; Rev. Hermann, 110, 164

Gasconade Co., MO, 86–88, 97, 132, 136, 146, 167

German immigrants: agriculture in Missouri, 125–34; assimilation in Missouri, 112–18, 170–77; occupation in Missouri, 118–24; settlement patterns in U.S., 70–79; urbanization, 79–85. *See also* specific places of origin

German language: dialect, 16, 89, 103–104, 163n, 177, 187, 191; preservation, 163, 170–71, 173–77

Germany: regional emigration rates, 13–17, 37–39, 107–109. *See also* specific localities

Giessen emigration society, 94–97, 100, 116, 133, 164

Gjerde, Jon, 11, 183–84, 186

Goebel, Gert, 94–95, 97, 110, 117, 131, 161, 163, 168n, 172

grain prices, German, 27n, 29–30, 52–55, 59, 64, 66

Hamburg, 72, 74–77, 79–80, 82t, 84–86, 90

Hamerow, Theodore, 63

Handlin, Oscar, 5, 11, 183, 199

Hannover, 14–16, 21, 24–26, 32–33, 35–38, 41, 56, 74–78, 82t, 84–87, 89, 91, 101–103, 115, 133, 207–209. *See also* Osnabrück, Luneburg, Hildesheim

Häusling, 59, 62, 63

Havre, 72, 75, 78

Hermann, MO, 87, 109–10, 132, 175

Hesse, 13–14, 28, 46, 61, 74–75, 81, 82t, 84–86, 100, 133, 207–209

Hesse, Nicholas, 99, 150, 160

Heuerling, 4, 18, 23, 26, 36, 40–42, 47, 50, 59, 62–64, 68–69, 100, 126, 137–39, 141–42, 158, 160, 162, 202, 206

Hildesheim, Hannover, 91, 101–102

Holland, *see* Netherlands

Holstein, MO, 89, 163

Hungary, 182

Hvidt, Christian, 11n, 194–95

Illinois, 74t, 77–79, 82, 84–85, 151, 197

Indiana, 75, 78, 160

inheritance, 12–13, 16, 27–28, 30, 124, 145, 186

intermarriage, 112–13, 149, 167n, 196–97; of Scandinavians, 193–94

internal migration, German, 33–34, 37–38, 52

Iowa, 76–78, 103

Ireland, emigrants from, 107, 111–14, 117–20, 123–24, 127, 191–92, 198; linen industry, 19, 178, 180

iron industry, German, 20, 30–31

Italy, 188, 191, 198

Karlsruhe, Baden, 32–33

Kentucky, 97, 111

Koerner, Gustave, 107

Kolon, 18, 42n, 47–48, 51, 59, 138–39, 141–43, 153t, 156t, 202, 206

Kossuth, Louis, 67

INDEX

Krekel, Arnold, 68, 117

Ladbergen, Westfalia, 73, 92
Lafayette Co., MO, 160n, 169n
landownership, 124, 126–28, 135, 137–43, 146, 160–61
Latin America, 56, 58
Latin farmers, 94, 96, 116, 135, 160–61, 170
Lengerich, Westfalia, 92, 98
Lienen, Westfalia, 3n, 92–93, 98–99
life cycle, 83, 123–24, 142–43, 145–46, 148, 150, 154–55
linen industry: Germany, 4, 9, 16–27, 29, 35–37, 52–55, 64, 131, 137, 160; Europe, 178–80
Lippe-Detmold, 8, 10, 16, 35–36, 51–52, 62, 78, 86–87, 89–91, 101, 103, 114–15, 136–43, 146–49, 151–59, 163, 165–68, 187, 197
Lippstadt, MO, 89, 101
livestock, 25–26, 30, 36, 50, 127–28
Lüneburg, 26, 56–57, 67
Lutherans, 37–38, 89, 99, 114–15, 166, 172, 174–76, 197

Marschalck, Peter, 41, 55, 58–59, 190
Martels, Heinrich von, 94n, 99n, 107
material culture, 124–25
Mecklenburg, 74–78, 81–86, 91, 103, 196
Melle, Hannover, 46, 87, 89–91, 133, 158, 162, 165
Mendels, Franklin, 17
Menslage, Hannover, 89–91, 101
Methodists, 114–15, 165
Michigan, 74–75, 77
military service, 61–63, 66
Milwaukee, WI, 60, 75, 77, 81–85, 134, 198
Minden District, 13–16, 19–23, 33, 35–38, 42–44, 61–62, 89–91
Minnesota, 76–77, 183–87, 192n
Missouri, 3, 6, 74t, 76–78, 82–87; state legislature, 6, 96, 162
mobility, social: in Germany, 44–45; German-American, 135–47, 152–69
Muench, Friedrich, 94–95, 100, 115–16, 129, 133, 144, 160, 164, 171–73

Meunch, Georg, 116, 133
Munster District, 12–16, 20–24, 32–33, 35, 37–38, 41–43, 46, 49, 55–56, 58–59, 66, 77, 100. *See also* Tecklenburg

Nassau, 73–74, 82t, 84–86
nativism, 109
Nebraska, 76–77
Netherlands, emigrants from, 32, 166, 178–79, 181, 183–86, 198; migratory labor in, 4, 35–36, 52, 161
Neubauer, 47, 50, 202
New England, 76t, 84, 198
New Immigration, 181–82, 188, 198
New Jersey, 76t, 199
New Knoxville, OH, 73, 92
New Melle, MO, 87–89, 99, 118, 162, 172, 175–77
New Orleans, LA, 76–79, 95, 99
New York, 74t, 76–79, 81, 83–85, 155, 199
newspapers, German-American, 175. *See also St. Charles Demokrat*
Norway, 11, 183–86, 191–95

occupation: in Europe, 181–83; in Germany, 27, 40–42, 46, 51, 60, 73–74; in Missouri, 118–24, 152–60
Ohio, 74–79, 81–86, 103
Oldenburg, 14–16, 35, 37, 41, 47, 51, 60, 73–74, 76–77, 82, 84–86, 88, 91, 97, 103, 115, 164, 166, 189, 196, 207–209
Old French, 106–107, 111–14, 117–20, 123–34
Osage Co., MO, 86, 97, 102–103
Osnabrück District, 7n, 13–16, 21, 26, 29, 32–33, 35–37, 42–43, 46, 53–56, 59–62, 64–65, 88–91, 99, 102, 104, 115, 163
Ostergren, Robert, 183, 186

Paderborn, Westfalia, 12–13, 33
Palatinate, 13–14, 75, 81n
peasant, 60, 63–64, 97, 117, 134, 164, 183, 186. *See also Einlieger, Heuerling, Kolon*
Pennsylvania, 74t, 76t, 79, 84–86
persistence, geographic, 171–72

213

INDEX

Philadelphia, PA, 78, 80–82, 84–86, 168, 197
place names, 73, 89–90, 102–105
Poland, 182–83
population density, 22, 24–25, 30
Portage, MO, 106, 118
Presbyterians, 114–15, 117
Protestant ethic, 37, 165–66
Protestants, 62, 92, 104, 113–15, 166
protoindustry, *see* iron industry, linen industry
Prussia, 13–14, 37–38, 73–74, 77, 82t, 84–87, 89–91, 103, 114, 133, 197, 207–209. *See also* specific locations

railroad: in Germany, 33; in U.S., 77, 165
Ravensberg, *see* Minden District
Ravenswaay, Charles van, 152
religion, 37, 62, 103, 114–15, 187. *See also* specific confessions
Republican party, 116
Revolution: of 1830, 59–60, 68, 95; of 1848, 58–68
Rhine Province, 13–14, 30–31, 60, 91, 102–103, 114–15
Ruhr district, 12, 20–21, 31–35, 65

St. Charles, MO, 67, 89, 132, 143–45, 162, 167, 171, 175
St. Charles Co., MO, 8, 85–88, 91, 93, 97, 100, 102, 106–109, 111–33, 136–49, 152–61, 167, 170–77
St. Charles Demokrat, 106–108, 117, 164–65, 175
St. Louis, MO, 4–5, 79, 81–86, 95, 102, 104, 137, 144, 147–48, 150–51, 153–55, 157, 172, 197
Saueressig, Yda, 183
Saxony, 14, 32, 38, 74t, 80–82, 84–86, 91, 114, 196, 207–209
Scandinavia, 8–10, 34, 70, 179–80, 183–87, 190–95. *See also* specific countries
Schleswig-Holstein, 90–91, 104
Schmoller, Gustav, 28
schools, 134, 173–74
Schurz, Carl, 68, 170–71
segregation, ethnic, 117–18
sex ratio: in Germany, 25; in Missouri, 113–14, 148–49

shipping: ocean, 3–4, 40, 46, 72, 75, 77–79, 99; inland, 77, 81
Silesia, 14, 32, 38, 91
slaveholding, 108, 115–17, 125–28, 130–31, 134
Solingen emigration society, 95, 100–101
Stallo, Franz Joseph, 60n, 73, 77, 103
Steines, Hermann and Friedrich, 95, 100–101
Stuttgart, Wurttemberg, 32–33
Sweden, 32–33, 34, 70, 113, 178–81, 183–86, 191–95
Switzerland, 87, 111, 133, 179–81

taxes, in Germany, 59–63
Tecklenburg, Westfalia, 8, 12, 15, 21–24, 33, 36, 42–44, 49–50, 60, 62, 68–69, 73, 89–92, 97–98, 110, 114–15, 125, 133, 136–48, 150–53, 155, 157–59, 163–68, 189
Teutoburger Wald, 21, 89
Texas, 73–74, 76t, 78, 124n, 125n
Thernstrom, Stephan, 169, 198
Thistlethwaite, Frank, 7
Thomas, Brinley, 178
Thuringia, 87, 94n
Trier, Rhineprovince, 30–33

urbanization: in Germany, 21, 31–35; German-Americans, 80–86, 147–51

Virginia, 108, 111

wages: in Germany, 50; in the United States, 150
Walker, Mack, 13n, 41, 45, 65–66
Warren Co., MO, 3, 8, 85–89, 91, 93, 97, 102, 111–29, 132–33, 136–49, 152–61, 163, 166, 171–72, 175
Washington, MO, 89, 104, 163, 175
Westerkappeln, Westfalia, 5–6, 58, 89–93, 97–98, 100
Westfalia, 4–7, 10, 14–16, 19, 29, 34, 58, 65, 71, 77, 86–87, 89–91, 102–104, 115, 136, 183–84, 185–87, 197, 199–200. *See also* Minden, Munster, and Arnsberg districts
Westphalia, MI, 102–103
Westphalia, MO, 99, 102–103, 125, 160

wine production: in Germany, 29; in Missouri, 125, 132–33
Wisconsin, 74t, 76t, 78–79, 81–85, 115n, 183–86
women, as emigrants, 42–43, 48–49, 112–13, 161–63

World War I, 175–76
World War II, 175–76
Württemberg, 8, 13–15, 28–29, 46, 55, 74–76, 80–82, 84–86, 207–209

Zollverein, 37–38

LIBRARY OF CONGRESS CATALOGING-IN-PUBLICATION DATA

Kamphoefner, Walter D.
The Westfalians.

Includes index.
1. German Americans—Missouri—History—19th century. 2. Immigrants—Missouri—History—19th century. 3. Missouri—Emigration and immigration—History—19th century. 4. Westphalia (Germany)—Emigration and immigration—History—19th century. I. Title.

F475.G3K354   1987   977.8'00431   87-3365
ISBN 0-691-04746-4

GPSR Authorized Representative: Easy Access System Europe - Mustamäe tee 50, 10621 Tallinn, Estonia, gpsr.requests@easproject.com

www.ingramcontent.com/pod-product-compliance
Lightning Source LLC
Chambersburg PA
CBHW060511300426
44112CB00017B/2624